AA
Essen

explo

THAILAND

AA Publishing

Essential

Written by Martin Clutterbuck, Tim Locke and Dick Wilson
Series Adviser: Ingrid Morgan
Series Editor: Nia Williams
Copy Editor: Diana Payne
Designer: Design Directions Ltd

Edited, designed, produced and distributed by AA Publishing, Fanum House, Basingstoke, Hampshire RG21 2EA.
© The Automobile Association 1993.
Maps © The Automobile Association 1993.

A catalogue record for this book is available from the British Library.

ISBN 0 7495 0568 0

This book was produced using QuarkXPress ™ , Aldus Freehand ™ and Microsoft Word ™ on Apple Macintosh ™ computers.

Colour origination by L C Repro & Sons Ltd, Aldermaston
Printed and bound in Italy by LEGO SpA, Vicenza

The contents of this publication are believed correct at the time of printing. Nevertheless, the Publishers cannot accept responsibility for errors or omissions, or for changes in details given. Assessments of attractions, hotels, restaurants and so forth are based upon the author's own experience and, therefore, descriptions given in this guide necessarily contain an element of subjective opinion which may not reflect the Publisher's opinion or dictate a reader's own experience on another occasion. The views expressed in this book are not necessarily those of the Publisher. Every effort has been made to ensure accuracy in this guide. However, things do change and we would welcome any information to help keep the book up to date.

Published by AA Publishing.

Fishing boat, Southern Thailand

Martin Clutterbuck has lived and worked in Thailand for six years. He speaks fluent Thai and has written two editions of The Traveller's Guide to Thailand, as well as producing a regular newspaper column on Thai literature. Tim Locke is the author of several walking and touring guides published by the Consumers' Association and editor of *Southeast Asia on Business*, published by Economist Publications; he has travelled widely in the Far East. Dick Wilson is a current affairs and modern history specialist and the author of 16 books. He has been editor of the China Quarterly and editorial adviser to The Straits Times, and has recently completed a book about Thailand for St Martin's Press/Macmillan.

About this book

This book is divided into three principal sections.

The first part of the book discusses aspects of life today and in the past. Places to visit are then covered region by region, along with Focus on... and Close-up features, which highlight areas and subjects in more detail. Drives and walks are also suggested in this section of the book. Finally, day-to-day practical information for the visitor is given in the Travel Facts chapter, along with a selected Directory of hotels and restaurants.

Lo Dalam beach, on the main island of the Ko Phi Phi archipelago, Southern Thailand

Some of the places described in this book have been given a special rating:

 Do not miss

 Highly recommended

 See if you can

General Contents

CONTENTS

CONTENTS

*An evening view from the resort of
Mae Hong Son, Northern Thailand*

My Thailand

Mechai Viravaidya is an energetic and original campaigner for family planning and AIDS awareness. The son of two doctors, he gained a degree in Commerce and Economics at Melbourne University in 1964. He has gone on to hold an impressive list of national and international appointments, most recently as Minister of the Prime Minister's office. He has published widely and his work has been acknowledged with numerous honorary doctorates and awards in Thailand, Australia and the US. In 1981 his achievements were recognised with the United Nations Gold Peace Medal. He is the Founder and Secretary-General of the Population and Community Development Association in Bangkok.

by Mechai Viravaidya

I should like to take this opportunity to welcome you to Thailand. I hope you will find the Thai people to be among the most hospitable on earth, the countryside some of the most enchanting and the beaches some of the most spectacular. I also hope you will forgive our short-sightedness in neglecting some of the obvious and serious issues facing Thai society today. We are now doing our best to improve our country.

Thailand is a kingdom of integrity. We have a long cultural tradition and a rich natural heritage, both of which attract visitors. I hope that you can join us in preserving and strengthening these features of our country. You, as a visitor, can help tremendously through example, by not supporting the prostitution industry, not leaving litter, not purchasing products made from endangered species, and by writing to our newspapers with any observations and suggestions you might have.

Thailand is a great place to visit, with something to offer everybody. The important Thai cultural principle *sanuk*, or fun, is guaranteed to make a lasting impression. Ten years ago, Thailand drew a little over two million tourists to her shores. In the ensuing years, however, the secret got out, and now we see five million visitors per year.

Although Bangkok has enjoyed some of the fastest economic growth of the past decade, much of the rest of Thailand remains unchanged. Poverty persists in rural Thailand despite rather different appearances in Bangkok.

While you are here, I urge you to venture out to seldom-visited ancient ruins, to enjoy natural splendour in our national parks, to explore Thai culture by staying in a village...see Thailand! Our road system is generally good and most people are friendly. Learn a few key Thai words and expressions and you will find yourself in a new world – a world of *sanuk*. Most of all, enjoy Thailand.

My Thailand

Angkhana Petbun graduated in Computer Studies from Phuket Teachers' College. She now teaches at the small Phuket Computer School.

9

by Angkhana Petbun

Thailand is a good place to live. Foreigners have come to know it as 'Siam, the Land of Smiles', and it really is true. Every province has its own attractions and identity; Phuket and its beaches, Chiang Mai with its flower festivals – and so on.

I am originally from Songkhla, where my parents have a long-established wholesale ice-cream business. I came to Phuket after finishing high school, because no colleges in Songkhla had Computer Studies on the curriculum. My parents were happy for me to learn this subject, because they figured I would have no problems finding work in the future. The introduction of computers to Thailand means that we can work faster and develop the country's economy. A good economy is essential for earning the trust of foreigners, so that we can turn to them for financial help if we need to. It is a great pity that political events have lost our economy a great deal. I believe in democracy, and in government which is both representative of the people and efficient at its administrative duties.

Thailand's culture and ancient monuments are important to us, and are carefully preserved. They also attract tourists, and thus assist our economic progress. We all appreciate the country's beauty, its trees and waterfalls; they reduce the stress of our daily lives. But too many visitors, Thai and foreign, have spoiled many of these features. I would ask all visitors to try and preserve this country's special beauty.

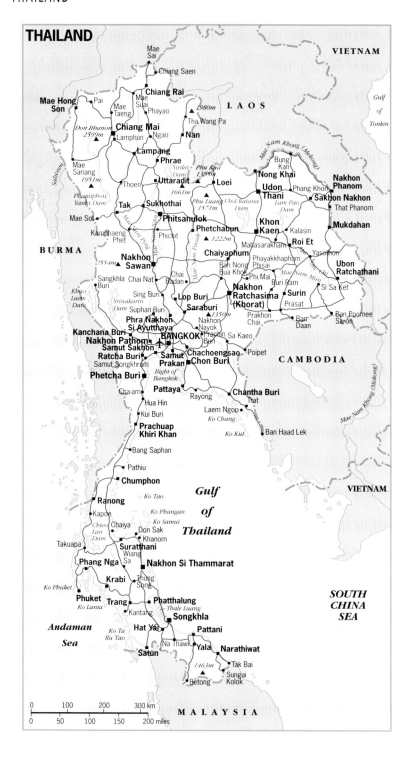

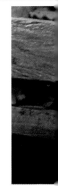

■ Thailand is a country of rich tropical abundance, inhabited by gentle and courteous people mostly professing Buddhism. 'Land of the free': this is the literal meaning of Thailand and the Thais consider themselves, with justification, to be one of the more free societies in Asia. They have borrowed in the past from both Chinese and Indian civilisations, and the resultant mix is most distinctive and interesting. The Thais themselves are happy-go-lucky, spontaneous and carefree....■

Something for everyone To the Western visitor, Thailand is not just another land; it's another way of life. Tradition and development rub shoulders here as nowhere else. In Bangkok, wooden houses built on stilts over the water stand in the shadows of gleaming condominium blocks. The air is filled with different smells: stir-fry cookery, *tuktuk* fumes, dried coconuts, incense, canal water...Exotic *wats* glimmer in the sunlight, their cool interiors a welcome refuge from the city din. A bus-ride into the country brings a vivid glimpse of Thai variety. Buses equipped with hi-fi and videos also have their mirrors draped with garlands of everlasting flowers for good luck. Instead of pin-ups there are photos of venerable monks above the driving seat. The driver tears along the road, blaring his horn, passing the occasional ox-drawn cart. Women mount the buses to sell Coke from plastic bags and sticky rice concoctions wrapped in banana leaves to the passengers – who include immaculate schoolchildren, saffron-robed monks and hill tribe women in dazzling home-embroidered clothes and grubby, Western-style trainers.

Economic leap Since the later 1980s Thai economy, traditionally agricultural, has been dependent more on manufacturing and services. For a while this was the fastest-growing economy in the world, and it is about to follow the 'four Asian tigers' (Korea, Taiwan, Hong Kong and Singapore) into the newly industrialising category. Government policies favouring free enterprise and market forces and foreign investment from Japan and other Eastern Asian countries havel played their part. Thailand now exports electronic and textile products as well as foodstuffs all over the world.

Sex industry There is another side to modern Thailand: it has acquired a reputation as a sex capital (a situation which some Western visitors help to perpetuate). However, this aspect of life may recede now that the enormity of the AIDS threat has been revealed.

Special style Behind everything lies a richly complex society which has kept its ancient traditions. Thailand is quite as modern as other Asian countries, but totally in its own style. For anyone with time to spare, this unique quality is worth seeking out.

A Thai classical dancer

■ Thailand has a distinctive shape on the map, tailing away in the south into a long, narrow strip of land. Some people have likened the outline of the country to an elephant's head, with the trunk curling down towards Malaysia. With a land area of 514,000 sq km, Thailand is no small state – it is, in fact, roughly the same size as France or Texas, and it has a population of 58 million. .....■

How the land lies Thailand has Malaysia as its neighbour in the south, Burma in the west and Laos and Cambodia in the northeast and east.

<< In the 19th century, French and British cartographers decided to leave a narrow stretch of Burmese and Laotian territory in order to cordon off Thailand from China. >>

The north of the country is mountainous and hilly, with outriders of the Himalayas separated by narrow valleys, notably formed by the Nan, Yom, Wang and Ping rivers. The high ground gradually rises towards the west and north, where Doi Inthanon (2,595m), Thailand's highest mountain, is to be found. The rivers flowing down these north – south valleys come together to form the Chao Phraya, Thailand's principal river, the floodplain of which constitutes the central plateau of the country. The **central plain** is Thailand's rice bowl, and the area where population is most dense. Most of the political, economic and intellectual life of Thailand goes on in this central area.
The east is dominated by the Khorat plateau, shut off from the central plain by the Phetchabun range. The Khorat plateau is drained by the Mun and Chi rivers, and by the Mekong into which they ultimately flow, and which forms Thailand's border with Laos. A large shallow basin, the Khorat plateau is 200m above the sea, encircled by hills; its rolling

terrain gives way to swampland at the approach to the Mekong.
A long cordillera, the Tennasserim range, runs from northern Thailand down the **western border** to connect with peninsular ranges that continue down the centre of the Thai isthmus into Malaysia. This **southern peninsula** is rich in rubber, tin and tropical vegetation.
The main coastline is round the Gulf of Thailand, which merges into the South China Sea and thus gives Thailand a window on to the Pacific. There is also a shorter coastline on the Andaman Sea, on the other side of the peninsula, which makes Thailand an Indian-Ocean state as well.

Weather and natural resources
Tropical forest used to cover much of Thailand, supporting a variety of animals and plant life, but over the past 40 years forests have disappeared at an alarming rate, with a consequential decline in the natural resources to be found in those areas. In 1945, over 90 per cent of Thailand was forested, now estimates are nearer 18 per cent.
Until recently, farmers made use of the natural nutrients brought down by annual floods of streams and rivers in order to grow rice. On the hill farms of **northern Thailand** elaborate systems of irrigation – ditches, dykes and terraces – can still be seen.

Population The rapid increase in population, especially between 1950 and 1970, unnaturally swelled the size of the capital city in Bangkok, which is now about 40 times bigger than Chiang Mai, Thailand's second largest city.

Population growth has now been brought down to about 1.5 per cent a year, largely as a result of a successful campaign by the government to popularise family planning, especially through the use of condoms. But today the population faces a bigger threat in AIDS, which some Thai experts believe may reach disastrous proportions in another 10 or 15 years.

Three-quarters of the inhabitants are ethnic Thais, with the Chinese providing about 15 per cent and the remaining 10 per cent including Malays, Khmers, Laotians, Mons, Shans and numerous hill tribes.

>> Thailand is in the tropical belt, and stands in the path of the monsoon storms which boil up from the South China Sea. There is heavy rainfall from July to October, cool dry weather from November to February and dry heat from March to June. >>

The image presented to the world: two girls in formal Thai dress

>> The Chinese population in Thailand is said to be the largest outside China itself. Some go so far as to dub Thailand China's number one colony. >>

■ Thailand is a constitutional monarchy with a democratic government under a Prime Minister elected by the National Assembly, which in turn is elected by universal suffrage. However, military dictatorships seem to occur roughly every decade. The military junta which staged a *coup d'état* in February 1991 introduced an interim constitution under which elections were held in March 1992, leading to a democratic civilian government (see also pages 68–71). .....■

Working with change During the greater part of 1991, there was a caretaker government whose Prime Minister, Anand Panyarachun, was appointed by the military junta. Anand, himself a former diplomat and businessman, chose a largely technocratic cabinet of former bureaucrats and businessmen, which was praised for resolving a number of problems inherited from the previous government.

Normally the Thai Prime Minister operates very much like counterparts in Western democracies, though responsible ultimately to the King in matters of grave importance involving national interest and morality. But the army has frequently intervened if dissatisfied with the government's behaviour, always appealing for the King's approval or acquiescence in order to gain popular legitimacy. There is then pressure from liberal quarters for the army to return power to civilians, and to reinstate democracy. Unlike the army in some other Asian countries, the

<< The main issues between the army and civilian politicians are excessive corruption in big infrastructure projects requiring ministerial approval; the handling of senior army appointments; the army's right to be represented in the cabinet and the former system of holding elections, which involved money changing hands. >>

Thai army has always done this, though it sometimes takes a while.

The main parties Chart Thai ('Thai Nation Party') was the party with most seats in the national assembly before the *coup* of 1991. Its then leader, General Chatichai Choonhavan (a former cavalry officer and wealthy businessman), became Prime Minister from 1988 to 1991. After the *coup* the Chart Thai party reoriented itself to align with the very military leaders who had deposed it.

By the end of 1991 there were two new parties reflecting the ambitions of senior generals: the New Aspiration Party (NAP) of General Chaovalit Yongchaiyudh and the Samakki Tham. (In 1992 General Chatichai Choonhavan formed a new party, the Chat Pattana, or National Development Party.)

In a typically Thai compromise, therefore, the generals were competing with each other on democratic lines to become 'civilian' prime ministers. Samakki Tham, Chart Thai (which later merged with eachother) and NAP dominated the new 1992 parliament.

The Thai system of elections makes it easy for candidates to bribe voters, but actually makes it hard for any politician to succeed without having large sums of money to pay out to supporters, godfathers and the like.

The 1992 elections The constitution drawn up after the last *coup* gave the military the right to name a prime minister. This they duly did in the person of General Suchinda Krapayoon. That a prime minister who had not been elected should be imposed in this way caused immediate unrest and dissatisfaction.

Bangkokians favoured local hero Chamlong Srimuang, who stormed home on a reform ticket. The resulting demonstrations underlined how people felt cheated, not only by this but also to see that old-style politicians can come back to power after a purge on their allegedly corrupt wealth. Tens of thousands of demonstrators took to the streets to voice their protest in May 1992; the militia responded with water cannons at first, hastily resorting to live ammunition. in an action claiming possibly hundreds of lives.

Rural politics Local political institutions and systems have lagged behind national developments. The villages used to be uninvolved in politics, receiving decisions rather than making them.

Then Phibul (see pages 60–1)set up *sapha tambol*, or village commune councils, which provide a means for rural inhabitants to engage in the political system. These are much under the influence of the village headman, who normally has the respect of the villagers and can bring them together to work with local authorities in socio-economic and political developments.

The 1991 junta wanted the headman to be appointed by the local officials instead of being elected by the villagers. The villagers are insufficiently experienced, for example in financial, managerial or administrative matters, to go against a determined district officer who represents the forces of bureaucracy in the area and who may well be a political science graduate.

The *sapha tambol* are under the control of the Ministry of Interior, and this at once brings in both a bureaucratic and, ultimately, a political party intervention.

Democracy is easy to legislate through the national assembly, but not so easy to establish effectively and healthily on the ground.

Government House, Bangkok

15

■ **King Bhumiphol Adulyadej was born on 5th December 1927 in Cambridge, Massachusetts, where his father was a hospital doctor. He came to the throne unexpectedly in 1946 when he was only 18, after his elder brother, King Ananda Mahidol, was found dead with a bullet in his head. The mystery of that death has never been explained. ......■**

King Bhumiphol has now become the longest-reigning king in Thai history, and one of the most respected. The Thai royal family is one of the very few remaining in Asia, succeeding in increasing the *de facto* authority of the monarchy within the political system of Thailand.

In his earlier years on the throne he cultivated a dilettante image, gaining fame as the King who played the saxophone well enough to accompany Benny Goodman and Louis Armstrong in Dixieland

> << King Bhumiphol won a gold medal for Thailand in the Southeast Asian Peninsular Games in 1967. His musical compositions include *Blue Day* (revue song of the 1950s), the Thai national anthem and the ballet *Manohra* . >>

numbers.

The King was an enthusiastic sailor, building his own boats and winning many trophies. He painted in oils, published translations from English and exhibited much-admired photographs.

When he got married it wastoSirikit, one of the great Thai beauties of her day, who became his queen.

Gradually the King's interests shifted to the more serious concerns of rural, social and political reform. In a country where the pace of economic growth swamped the interests of traditional farmers and tribespeople who found it hard to adapt, Bhumiphol used his mystique as king to good effect.

Practical involvement The King took the lead in putting rural development programmes firmly on the Thai agenda, jogging the government into giving them higher priority. He regularly tours rural areas to see the problems for himself, and has become something of an expert on small irrigation projects and introducing better farming practices as well as reafforestation.

In the political arena, the King found a place as a focus of national unity, mediator and source of stability. While generals, prime ministers and dictators rose and fell from power, he supplied the balancing role. No *coup d'état* has sought to overthrow him: on the contrary the prospective *coup* leaders have always sought to gain his approval, if necessary by moderating their programme.

The immense popularity and adoration which he has built up with the ordinary people of the kingdom during his 46 years on the throne enable him to play this role to the utmost, sometimes tipping the balance in a power struggle or actually

Celebrating the King's birthday

preventing a *coup* in the making. The King lives with his family in the Chitralada Palace close to central Bangkok. Queen Sirikit also carries

> **<<** Bhumiphol once calculated 14 chemical formulae for seeding clouds with rain, paying for the research himself and sending up specially equipped light aircraft to test the formulations. **>>**

out a wide range of social duties including the leadership of the Girl Guides and the very successful promotion of peasant handicrafts.

The succession Bhumiphol's health is not of the best, and there may be a controversy over the succession when that occurs. His eldest daughter, Ubol Rattana, abdicated her title to live in the United States where she married an American engineer. The only son and heir to the throne, Crown Prince Vajiralongkorn, does not share his father's popularity. Trained as an air force pilot, he has a reputation for bad-temperedness and has not shown any interest in politics.

The ceremonial Royal Barges

Some Thais would like to see Princess Sirindhorn succeed instead. As the princess royal she is the king's second daughter, but a woman has never taken the throne in Thailand, and the prevalent male chauvinism would probably stand in the way despite her great popularity and capability.

Bhumiphol is a very wealthy man, with properties including a controlling share of the Siam Cement Corporation as well as many banks and other companies. These are managed by the Crown Property Bureau, which is the second largest asset holder and the fourth largest investor in Thailand. Dividends from these investments supplement the king's government budget allocation and help him play a larger part in the political arena.

The King has a strong scientific bent, having studied science in Lausanne in Switzerland. His quick reaction to the arrival of artificial rain-making in Western science has led to a regular scheme and programme within the Ministry of Agriculture.

Undoubtedly, King Bhumiphol has built up goodwill for the monarchy which should last for some time afterwards. Without a monarch in the middle, Thai politics would be much more unstable.

17

■ Thai society is built on the family, though there is also scope for individualism; group discipline is not one of the strong points. Nowadays modern middle-class children usually choose their own marriage partners and parents usually approve but rural fathers expect deference to their wishes, and rural society teaches loyalty to parents. Even in the towns family solidarity is the norm. ....■

Housing In Bangkok the relatively affluent middle class lives increasingly in a style similar to its counterparts worldwide. Some of the wealthier élite prefer to live in traditional spacious wooden houses, with high roofs and lots of garden, including a fish-pond. Such houses are cool and breezy and can also be moved to another place if necessary. Now, however, new estates of Western-style white-walled houses with stone balconies and red tiles are springing up.

A modern Thai wedding

<< Many Thai men have two or more wives. The first wife of General Sunthorn, the leader of the 1991 *coup*, took his second wife to court to prevent her using his surname. In response the general invited the press round to meet his lover. >>

The fashion for the rich Thais is to buy, say, two traditional houses-on-stilts (the stilts protect from wildlife and floods) from the countryside, dismantle them, take them by lorry to a quiet suburb of Bangkok and reassemble them as old-fashioned bedroom wings of a modern concrete house – thus gaining the advantages of both styles.

Life is considerably more basic and simple in the countryside, but a TV, refrigerator and other modern appliances are commonplace.

Marriage, customs, equality
A wedding is usually celebrated in stages, the couple being ceremonially blessed in the morning at the bride's house, and having holy water poured into their hands (a Brahmin ritual in origin) in the afternoon. That is usually followed by an informal party. In rural areas ceremonies can last for two or three days, during which time the groom is not supposed to touch the bride. Women rank below men in the traditional order of things, and do not get equal treatment in the legal aspects of marriage and divorce. In practice, however, they can pursue successful careers. Thailand was the

18

first Asian country to give women the vote (in 1933), and several big corporations have women at their head. There is one woman priest, who was ordained outside Thailand.

Education Six years of primary school are compulsory, but only a small proportion of children go beyond to secondary or higher education, something which will place Thailand at a disadvantage in the long run compared with some other Southeast Asian countries. In the schools there is a morning ritual of flying the national flag and singing the national anthem.

Buddhist groups are opposing the new government curriculum, cutting down the hours devoted to Buddhism in favour of the sciences. The two best-known universities are Chulalongkorn, the oldest, and Thammasat, which is traditionally the more radical. Both are in Bangkok. There are many others, in the capital as well as in the provinces.

Health and family planning Health facilities in Bangkok are generally good, but those in the more distant provinces are very poor. One area of public health where Thailand excels is family planning: children in many primary schools sing a family planning song, promising not to have more than two children when they grow up, and not to marry before 25 (girls) or 30 (boys). Buddhist monks will even bless contraceptives.

The rate of increase of the population is only about 1.5 per cent, lower than most Third-World countries. The man most

<< When the first consignments of American condoms to arrive in Thailand proved to be too big, Mechai Viravaidya hired five 'massage-parlour girls' to measure more than 500 of their customers to produce a Thai national size for manufacturers to meet. >>

responsible, Mechai Viravaidya, is tough, imaginative, bold and determined. He is a remarkable publicist who has championed the controversial issues of population growth and AIDS with great enthusiasm and some success (see page 8).

Mechai's plain speaking about the need for condoms, vasectomies and sterilisation has made him so much a part of the health education scene that condoms in Thailand are often referred to as 'Mechais'.

In publicising their use he has employed unorthodox but effective methods such as making them into balloons, filling them with water and introducing them at festivals. He also invented catchy slogans to put on T-shirts.

<< Meatball vendor Tek Kop lives in a house with seven wives and 22 children. Mechai Viravaidya offered to pay for the children's education if Tek had a vasectomy. He refused, and Mechai acknowledged his worst failure. >>

■ Thailand's economy has become such a success that it will probably soon join the ranks of the Asian NIEs (Newly Industrialised Economies) presently composed of Korea, Taiwan, Hong Kong and Singapore. It has been growing very fast in the past few years, although its standard of living is still low – about US$1,300 in national income per head, much below the NIEs.. ....■

Agriculture Thailand has always been a rich agricultural producer, especially of rice. More than 20 million tons are normally harvested every year – and of better quality than that of other countries. Not only rice, but also rubber (about a million tons a year), maize, cassava, sugar, soyabean, coconut, fish and shrimps are also produced in large quantities. Spectacular increases in crop yields have been won in recent years through the use of chemical fertilizers and pesticides, and irrigation canals. Unfortunately some of the new strains of high-yielding rice which were introduced have proved vulnerable to insects and other pests. This has resulted in a new trend towards what some Thais call 'Buddhist farming', where natural organic fertilizer and herbal sprays are used to deter rather than kill pests. On some farms the natural balance has been restored under this regime, so that birds have returned to prey on the insects which eat the crops. This is praised as being consistent with Buddhism and with the Thai tradition, although it is still only a minority system.

Some Thai **exports** are restricted. The European Community made Thailand cut its exports of tapioca although it gave funds for the development of alternative crops. Thai textiles and garments are restricted in most Western markets, and British manufacturers once demanded restrictions on Thai TV sets.

One in every two cans of pineapple opened in America comes from Thailand, while a Thai company now stands as Asia's largest exporter of

<< Textiles are currently the biggest export, followed by rice, rubber, precious stones and jewellery, tapioca, sugar, integrated circuits and canned fish. **>>**

tuna fish, commanding one fifth of the world market and having absorbed one of the largest American companies.

Today traditional farming is beginning to give way to agribusiness, in particular the production of broiler chickens and shrimps. This is symbolised by Charoen Pokphand, the Chinese-founded agribusiness conglomerate.

Manufacturing industry A more recent development, this now accounts for over a third of the Gross Domestic Product, while service industries account for almost half. Tourism alone supplies a tenth. The manufacturing industry benefits from the pool of cheap unskilled labour (newly landless poor farmers) which can be supplied from the Thai rural areas. Two out of three Thai workers are in agriculture, yet they account for only one-sixth of the national production. Many multinationals and manufacturers from Japan, northeast Asia, Europe and America are attracted by this, and electronics and textiles in particular are flourishing as a result. These developments are pursued by private enterprise, the government taking a back seat in the economy. This results in some problems, such as the inadequacy of infrastructure

<< Charoen Pokphand is the world's largest prawnfeed producer, fifth largest feedmill producer and the largest Southeast Asian investor in China. It has the tallest skyscraper on Bangkok's Silom Road and a turnover of more than US$ 2.5 billion a year. >>

(especially transport and communications) and the inferiority of higher education, technology and technical training. There is a severe shortage of engineers.

Steel and petrochemical industries are in evidence, and exports to markets as far afield as Africa have been established. Several companies are assembling cars, notably Mitsubishi Motors, and some of these have been exported with almost 60 per cent made of locally produced parts.

The country is blessed with mineral deposits, notably tin, lead, zinc and lignite. The relatively recent discovery and exploitation of natural gas offshore has rendered Thailand less dependent on oil imports.

Thai silk is one of the best dollar-earners from the traditional textiles, a business developed initially by Jim Thompson, an American who stayed in Thailand after World War II. He built a major industry of Thai silk by introducing modern dyes and designs to the hand-loom workers.

<< Jim Thompson started by selling silk in the foyer of the Oriental Hotel, and later introduced it to Hollywood costume designers with great success. Jim Thompson silk is still considered the best in this billion-dollar export industry. >>

Working conditions These are appalling in many of the smaller Thai factories. Safety records are poor and several cases of illegal child

workers have been exposed.

Only one worker in ten is organised in a trade union, although that is mainly because Thais prefer to retain their individual freedom. The unions are relatively strong in public enterprises. There is a minimum wage, which has been raised more than once in the past three or four years. It is now about $4 per day.

Finance There is an active finance centre, with 15 commercial banks and 14 foreign banks in the Bangkok market, and almost 100 finance and securities firms. The stock exchange is volatile but still attracts a good deal of Western custom; the baht is one of the stronger currencies in Asia. At the end of 1992 exchange rates gave approximately 25 baht to the US dollar and 45 to the pound sterling.

One of the most popular vocations now for school leavers and graduates in Bangkok is banking. The

biggest local bank is the Bangkok Bank, still controlled and largely owned by the Sophonpanich family, now second-generation Chinese immigrants. Thousands of young men and women in almost identical navy-blue and white outfits flock into the headquarters in Silom Road and the myriad branches around the country every morning — and at lunchtime you will see them tumbling out to head for their favourite cafés and street stalls. The Bangkok Bank is now the biggest commercial bank in Southeast Asia. There are many other successful local Thai banks, and the foreign banks are still kept out to some extent in order to protect these. Buddhism does not favour the collapse of bankrupt companies since that causes hardship for employees and shareholders.

Individuals are taxed on a sliding scale from 5 to 55 per cent, while corporations pay 35 per cent on profits (less for those publicly traded on the Securities Exchange).

Pepsi plant at Bangkok

Significant tax holidays and reductions are available for approved new investments. A 7 per cent value-added tax was implemented in 1992.

Looking to the future Financial liberalisation is progressing, with exchange control already ended. The government intends to loosen regulations and controls on many more aspects of Thailand's financial activities.

The economy In the early 1990s the Thai economy began to slow down a little, in response to the world recession, Gulf War, oil price increase and domestic overheating. It was predicted to expand and to resume rapid growth in the next few years, but many Thais believe the price is too high. Growth at that pace widens the gap between rich and poor, making for social unrest. The World Bank estimates there are about 14 million Thais below the poverty line.

Among many worries for the future are the decline in rice exports, and the likelihood of Vietnam taking away some of Thailand's old markets at

the cheaper end. In the 1980s Thailand was the world's top rice exporter, supplying one-third of world exports, but that may prove difficult to sustain.

Western managers in Thai factories have often carped about their workforce. But the degree of hard graft put in by Thais is evident: for proof, look at the many building sites in Bangkok, mostly manned by relatively new labour from the northeast.

Neither does the lazy image square with the US$1 billion which some 300,000 Thais have sent home while under long-term contract in construction projects in the Middle East and other Asian locations. None of the recent economic achievements of Thailand could have been attained if every Thai was shirking work.

The tourist industry now brings more than 5 million foreigners to Thailand every year. They arrive at

A ruby mine in the southeast: gems are still a major export

the rate of 600 an hour, and the average tourist spends about US$ 1,000, which adds up to US$ 5 billion a year, about half of total Thai exports. One factor in this is sheer quality.

The natural attractions of Thailand, in climate, scenery, historical sites, colourful festivals and exotic experiences add up to a powerful draw. Half of Thailand's tourists come from Western countries, the remainder from Asia – especially Japan, Taiwan, Korea, Malaysia and Singapore.

<< The Oriental Hotel, beloved of Somerset Maugham, has been consistently voted 'best in the world' in international travellers' polls every year for the past decade. >>

■ The Thai mentality is shaped in part by the country itself. Its hot, tropical climate receives periods of intense heavy rain; it is a land of plenty, where food is bountiful. The Buddhist philosophy has a strong hold on the Thai people, teaching them to put self-cultivation above social works. It does not offer a universal ethic, but rather accepts the inequalities among men in their spiritual progress. .....■

24

Social attitudes Thailand is a society of vertical hierarchy, where people respect the authority of those above them (fathers, the King, prime ministers, schoolteachers) but this is not quite the same system as is found in Japan. Even family ties are looser in Thailand than in Northeast Asia.

This also means that Thais are more receptive to foreign influences, something reinforced by their history of resisting colonialism in the 19th century. The inferiority complex which can be noted amongst former colonised states (such as India and Indonesia) is missing with the Thais, whose authority structure has been unbroken for centuries.

It is almost a taboo to oppose another person to their face. Maybe national politics is an exception, where slanging matches during election time are acceptable and enjoyed.

The self-respect of other people is normally considered so important that it must never be infringed. One story tells of the Thai who was hired to teach the Thai language to a foreigner, but never corrected the foreigner because he would not embarrass a person by drawing attention to his mistakes.

A Thai will make a big effort not to inconvenience or upset another person, and on that basis he expects to get the same treatment in return. There is heavy reliance on the smile, but if that suggests an underlying gentleness of character it has to reconciled with the extraordinary violence which does occasionally break out. A servant may endure the rude treatment of his employer for many years without complaint, but then his patience might suddenly break, and he might even kill his persecutor. There are many *crimes passionnels*, and Thailand is said to have one of the highest murder rates in the world.

Becoming absorbed in self-cultivation, and dealing with the intricate problems of social relationships in such variety has another consequence. Thais avoid

People at prayer

<< The ideal man would have '...the moral principles of a *farang*, the diligence of a Chinese and the heart of a Thai.' Heart is: 'Love of peace, contentment with little, concern for others and a sense of moderation.' – From Botan's novel Letters from Thailand. >>

Bangkok's Brahmin Erawan shrine

<< During World War II villagers in Thailand brought food to British POWs in a Japanese camp . When the Japanese surrendered in 1945, they brought food for the Japanese prisoners with the same solicitude. >>

<< 'The Thai way of life is an elegant sort of life, surrounded by benevolent and exuberantly plentiful nature, with adaptable morals and a serene detachment to the more difficult problems of life... To a Thai, life itself is one long relaxation.' – Kukrit Pramoj, Thailand's ex-prime minister and most famous novelist. >>

becoming involved in other people's problems. They are not 'good Samaritans'. They normally avoid conflict, and keep contacts with other people down to a minimum. There is a legitimate outlet for relaxation in *sanuk* (fun). *Sanuk* is a very old feature in Thai life. It means getting pleasure from carefree amusement with congenial friends or companions. No one is criticised for doing this, it has a positive value in the code of behaviour.
Spontaneity is valued. Thais dislike planning, and interviews are often much better without an appointment because the impromptu encounter is more enjoyed.

It sounds idyllic, but for Westerners the Thai mentality can be difficult to work with.
Objectivity is an elusive quality in Thai life, even at the university level. If a professor gives an opinion on a matter under discussion, junior lecturers or students will rarely argue with him or put a different point of view. If they think it important enough they might beard him privately afterwards. It is not timidity, or fear, but a concern for the professor's self-respect that prevents what Westerners would regard as a normal productive discussion opening up.

■ **Thais have a strong sense of hierarchy, and take immense care in their behaviour towards other people. Different gradations of respect or treatment need to be given and this is reflected in the language. Learning Thai involves a system of 'honorifics', where different pronouns are used according to social status. Speaking to a bus conductor, a teacher, a student or to royalty all call for different words. To a Thai, these distinctions in social status are very important indeed, and even a foreigner is expected to show some awareness of them. .....■**

Putting a foot in it Never touch a Thai, even a child, on the head. The Thais consider that the head is the most important part of the body, deserving the most honour – while the foot is the least honoured. The head is the seat of the *khwan,* or vital spirit, which lives in the body. Students who have to pass in front of a seated teacher will instinctively lower their heads as they pass. A servant will do the same in a house.

<< Traditionally, Thais should not stand higher than their royal family. A prince was unable to inspect the first printing press because there were residences over it whose occupants might walk over his head. When President Lyndon B Johnson visited in 1966, police cleared the second and higher storeys of buildings lining the route. >>

Forms of greeting The traditional Thai form of greeting is the *wai,* in which both hands are raised slowly and gracefully, palm to palm and close to the body. More than a greeting, it is a way of paying one's respects. The higher the hands are raised the greater the respect signalled.
The *wai* is the normal form of greeting between Thai people but some more Westernised Thais are just as likely to shake hands with foreigners.

<< It is still said that men are comparable to the front legs of an elephant, and women to the hind legs. Male chauvinists in Thailand like to say that the elephant seems to be walking backwards these days. >>

Women's rights and wrongs Women have traditionally deferred to men in society, and are thought to have adverse *khwan.* Thai men will still refuse to walk underneath a clothesline where female clothing is hanging, in case their heads are touched by them. For this reason women's clothes are usually hung out to dry on a very low clothesline which has to be walked around.

Dos and don'ts No one would ever enter a house or a temple without taking off the shoes first. Nowadays, although it is impractical to have everybody leaving shoes at the door

<< 'If you want to be somebody in this country you have to dress like a European', complained Sulak Sivaraksa, the well-known critic and writer, after an incident when, wearing his usual traditional Thai dress, he was refused admittance to the Oriental Hotel in Bangkok to see the then German Foreign Minister Herr Genscher. >>

>> 'Never sleep with your head facing to the west. That is where the sun sets, and the setting sun symbolises death'. – Thai superstition. >>

of a very large building, like a bank or department store, in temples, or private houses belonging to Thais, foreigners would be expected to take off their shoes and walk about inside in socks or in slippers provided by the host. Never give a Thai friend or colleague a red pen with which to write a signature. Names are written in red at the side of coffins awaiting cremation.

Thai people do not touch each other and rarely hold hands or have physical contact in the same easy-going manner that Westerners do. In the northeast such behaviour can even result in a fine. The traditional dance, the *Ramwong*, demonstrates how this avoidance of bodily contact does not inhibit a graceful dance movement in which neither partner touches the other.

You bet! The Thais are inveterate gamblers. They bet on horses, with cards, and on all kinds of contest – Thai boxing, cockfights, fish fights, bullfights...if there is scent of a competition they will be there with a wager. Poker, mahjong, checkers and chess are all played with rising excitement for sums of money. The national lottery is a huge business; the generals who managed it became rich men. Thais will devote enormous time and energy to accumulating enough merit by their actions to get a lucky lottery number.

Thai boxing: a chance to lay bets

■ **Thailand is a predominantly Buddhist country. More than 90 per cent of the population believe in some form or other of Buddhism, even though they may not perform the ceremonies or visit the temples frequently. The picturesque temples in every village and dotted about in each city are tranquil oases to which almost all Thais are drawn at some time in their lives. ....■**

28

Buddhist traditions Thai Buddhism follows the Theravada tradition, which is based on the oldest Buddhist writings recorded in Pali, the ancient Indian language. **Theravada Buddhism** aims to preserve the way of life described in those early writings. The other important Buddhist tradition is the **Mahayana**, which spread to China, Korea, Japan and Vietnam, and developed Buddhist philosophy while also trying to make the early teachings more accessible to lay followers. Buddhism was founded in the 6th century BC by Siddhartha Gautama, an Indian prince who turned ascetic. After years of fasting and meditation he arrived at a unique vision of the world, centred around the Four Noble Truths. The Thais became converted in the 7th century, and can now boast the largest unbroken ordination chain in any of the Theravada countries. The millions of Buddha images which can be seen in Thailand in every house and temple, though not

always approved of by Thai intellectuals, are deeply respected by ordinary men and women. Visitors must be very careful not to give offence by behaving disrespectfully towards Buddha statues which are felt to represent the Buddha in person. Some tourists who were photographed sitting on the head of a big Buddha statue aroused a furore of criticism. It is forbidden to take Buddha statues out of Thailand without special permission from the Fine Arts department. Shops will advise you and can sometimes get an export licence.

Buddhist beliefs Buddhism does not involve a belief in any god or gods. The central feature of Buddhism is the concept of *karma*, which literally means action. Every action, word or thought has a consequence which becomes manifest sometime in the future. Evil acts produce evil consequences or suffering. Inequalities between people in the present world are rationalised by the idea that *karma* can be carried over from previous lives.

The effort to achieve a high degree of spirituality is left on the whole to the monks in their monasteries or *wats* (temples). The central building of the *wat* is the most sacred and is known as the *bot*. It is here that the ceremonies of ordination, the daily morning and evening chanting of monks and services on days of fasting (on the first, eighth, 15th and 23rd days of the lunar month) take place. Lesser buildings called *wiharn* are often used for religious services for lay people and as living

<< The Four Noble Truths:
- dukkha or suffering is life's central problem
- the cause of suffering is desire
- the way to eliminate suffering is to eliminate its cause, desire
- the way to achieve this is to follow the Eightfold Way which describes standards of morality and qualities to be encouraged in meditation to this end. >>

accommodation for the monks. Lay Buddhists gain merit by giving alms to the monks, as well as by following basic moral guidelines – not to kill or tell lies, and to be moderate in physical indulgence. Every morning at dawn the saffron-robed monks go out with their begging bowls to ask for alms in the form of food, and traditionally every house will spare a little for them.

Religious hierarchy All monks are members of the *sangha* or the Buddhist order of monks. The *sangha* is supervised by an executive council headed by a supreme patriarch who is appointed by the King. There are two main sects in the Thai *sangha*: the **Mahanikai**, by far the larger of the two, and the **Thammayut**, which was formed in the last century and follows rather stricter rules – for example, taking only one meal a day.
The tradition survives of laymen

The central mosque in Pattani, where Muslims have a strong presence (see page 31)

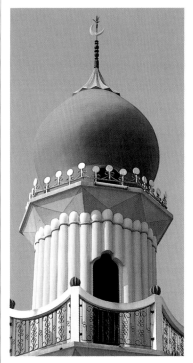

<< The Buddhist teachings (*dhamma*) are taught to every child in primary school: that is how Buddhist morality is diffused. >>

spending a week or so as monks in a monastery subject to the same discipline and routine as the monks. Even King Bhumiphol took alms from the people on the streets of Bangkok when he performed this traditional act early in his reign.
Monks are greatly respected by the public. They get free food in the morning, and travel free or half-price on the buses and trains. Some are involved in local development projects, helping to plan and build bridges, dams and schools, and to modernise farming methods.

Buddhist temples Bangkok has the greatest concentration of important temples. The most renowned is the **Wat Phra Keo**, which is also called the Temple of the Emerald Buddha, containing the mysterious Emerald Buddha statue, a Thai national symbol. Established in 1782, adjoining the Grand Palace, it is the ceremonial temple of the Thai Kings. **Wat Mahathat** is the chief temple of Thailand's largest monastic sect, the Mahanikai. The national headquarters of the Thammayut sect is **Wat Bowonniwet** (Bowornives) which is where King Bhumiphol was ordained as a monk. **Wat Pho** (Wat Phra Chetuphon) is the oldest and largest *wat* in Bangkok, containing the largest collection of Buddha images in Thailand.

Buddhist sects There is a general consensus that the *sangha* is becoming remote from everyday problems and for this reason, new

<< Thai intellectuals were furious when a 13th–century carved stone lintel from the Khmer sanctuary of Phanom Rung turned up in a museum in Chicago. The lintel has now been returned. >>

Religion

Muslim people in Narathiwat

sects have been founded. These frown on old-fashioned fortune-telling, and the traffic in amulets and charms which are supposed to carry good luck. They try to teach a combination of Buddhist philosophy and meditation techniques suitable for the urban lifestyle. The best known of these is **Santi Asoke** (Peace and No Sorrow), founded by Phra Bodhirak. He is half Chinese and was a TV producer and singer before his ordination. His followers, strict vegetarians who wear white robes, were excommunicated from the *sangha* in 1989. A major theme of theirs is that monks have to be involved with the people, and cannot therefore remain distant from politics.

Dhammakaya (Body of Truth) is the other influential new sect. It is highly practical in its financial ideas, being founded by a Thai Chinese, Phra Dhammachayo, who graduated in economics. This sect holds many industrial investments, and its leaders will drive out in a Rolls Royce or Mercedes to collect their morning alms. In a neat dovetailing of *karma*

and property management, Dhammachayo persuades his lay supporters to donate land to his monks with the promise that the merit acquired will ensure that they enjoy more land in their next life. There is also a sect called **Suan Mokh** (Garden of Liberation), which preaches 'dhammic socialism', a decentralised and non-competitive form of social co-operation among farmers which is free from greed.

<< Phra Bodhirak once claimed that he had personally attained the same level of enlightenment as the Buddha himself, something which no Thai had ever dared to claim before. Although it led to his excommunication he still has a popular following. >>

Other religions There is an undertow of Indian Brahminism that the Thais acquired from the Indian-influenced societies which they conquered and absorbed as they settled into the present territory of Thailand. Some of the shrines with figures of deities to be seen in

Bangkok are Brahmin rather than Buddhist. One of these is the *naga*, a semi-divine god and fertility symbol which often takes the form of a dragon-headed serpent.

Buddhism is a tolerant religion, and there are small minorities of other faiths, notably the two million **Muslims** in the southern provinces, adjoining Malaysia. They are mostly Sunni Muslims although there has recently been some concern about the growth of fundamentalist Shiite adherents. Three provinces, Yala, Pattani and Narathiwat, are dominated by Muslims, especially in the countryside. There is a smaller minority of **Christians**. The Roman Catholic cemetery in Silom Road and the Protestant one on the river bank are two of the historical sites of Bangkok. A few Thais have become Catholic or Protestant, and some of the refugees from Vietnam are Catholic, but they are all able to co-exist in Thai society without difficulty. The Buddhist ideas of the 'Middle Way', compassion and *karma*, still operate for them, too, having become, as it were, part of the Thai national character.

Buddhist monks receive their alms

>> Women are not allowed to attend Buddhist schools, but they enter *bots* in large numbers. They can take eight or 10 precepts and wear the white robes of a nun, or *mae chi.* >>

>> Buddhism injects an element of fatalism into the Thai mentality. This accounts for the passiveness, acceptance and social calm which the outsider observes in Thai society. >>

The Chinese Connection

■ It is believed that that the Thais first migrated into their country from China many centuries ago. That ancient connection has been reinforced by further large-scale immigration of Chinese into Thailand; an estimated nine million-odd Chinese may have crossed during the past hundred years, making the Chinese the largest minority group in Thailand. .....■

32

Roots Archaeological evidence in the past 30 years has raised the interesting possibility that prehistoric sites such as Ban Chiang, Mae Hong Son and Kanchana Buri could have predated the Chinese by several thousand years. If these theories are verified, it will call into question the ideas of who came from where originally.

The Chinese coming into Thailand in the early days of commerce were merchants, who travelled widely in Asia. The Thais were tolerant towards the Chinese immigrants, allowing them to settle and gradually to become Thai. There was a time in the 1930s when Thai nationalism made things difficult for the Chinese. Further immigration was stopped – and halted completely in 1950, but in the period following World War II the Chinese completed their assimilation into Thai society. They could be said to be responsible for much of Thailand's economic success.

The borders are blurred Most of those coming into Thailand were single males who married Thai women, starting a process of intermarriage which has gone on over many generations. It is almost impossible now to disentangle the ethnic origins of the mainly Chinese, the mainly Thai and the full Thai. Almost everyone in the ruling élite, from the royal family to the politicians, civil servants and army officers – and especially business leaders – admits to some degree of Chinese ancestry.

Many Chinese in Thailand no longer speak or read Chinese, but still perform some occasional Chinese rituals. Thailand is their home, and inspires their loyalty and patriotism, but many feel curious about China rather as many Australians take a special interest in Britain.

Trading places Coming in from outside, the Chinese immigrants had to slot into whatever niche there was available to make a living. Many turned towards trade and industry and other forms of business. From fairly humble merchants and shopkeepers to major bankers and industrialists the Chinese are well represented. Indeed, some very big names on the present scene are Chinese.

Virtually all of Thailand's industrialists and entrepreneurs are either recent Chinese immigrants or 'Sino-Thais', as the mixed lineage people are sometimes called. Dhanin Chearavanont is the most successful Chinese businessman, running the

> << The best way to understand the motivation and early experiences of the migrant Chinese is to read the heart-warming novel *Letters From Thailand* by Botan (a pseudonym). >>

Charoen Pokphand agribusiness group. Other famous Chinese business families are Sarasin, Sophonpanich (owning the Bangkok Bank) and Techapaibul.

Patpong Road, which many foreigners visit because of its red-light notoriety, was originally built by a typical Chinese immigrant, Poon Pat. He came to Bangkok from Hainan (a large island off the south

A glimpse of life in Bangkok's Chinatown

China coast) at the age of 12 and became a skilful buyer of rice who made his fortune supplying limestone for the king's new cement factory.

Integration The Chinese resemble the Thais physically in many respects – although there are no distinctly typical Thai features – and the two can easily be confused. By now most of them have taken Thai names, and the fact that they were not made to adopt an alien religion, as the Chinese immigrants did in Malaysia and Indonesia, was a great help.

Nevertheless, there are differences, some of which are cherished by the Chinese. With typical Thai tolerance, these are accepted and respected. One of the few traits which mark out the Chinese from the Thai is the Chinese respect for the family tree. Another is the practice of burying their dead, whereas Thais have traditionally practised cremation. There tends to be a greater prevalence of Christianity among the Chinese than there is among the Thais, who believe in reincarnation.

Dual identity Some of the Sino-Thais lead, in effect, a double life, being Thai in public but reverting to Chinese among their family. There are still some Chinese-language newspapers published, and there are several Chinese Christian churches. As time goes by, however, and certainly in recent years, the tendency is for more and more Chinese children to become completely integrated into the Thai way of life.

>> All children, whether they be Thai, Chinese or another race, are expected to learn the Thai language from an early age in school. Until relatively recently, Chinese languages were not available for study at university level. >>

A Chinese Taoist shrine in Bangkok

■ **Thais are natural and spontaneous about sex in private, though they can be somewhat reserved in public, especially where women are concerned. It is an open and tolerant society and people tend to accept most things, as long as a degree of discretion is employed. .....■**

Dictator Field Marshall Sarit's 100 or so mistresses did not shock the Thais. Older men hark back to the days of their youth when a man could have as many wives and/or mistresses as he could afford. The public health ministry in Thailand estimates there are around 600 brothels in Bangkok but until recently their existence was officially denied. Countless women and boys earn their living from sex. Girls as young as 13 are pressurised into prostitution in provincial towns. Recent moves to decriminalise prostitution have had the support of Mechai Viravaidya, who has campaigned hard for AIDS awareness. Making prostitutes carry health cards and legalising brothels would make it easier to enforce health standards in a country where commercial sex is part of everyday life for Thai men.

The woman's point of view Within a marriage a women overtly takes second place, but in practice she is often the keeper of the purse.

<< Virtually every town in Thailand has a brothel. Usually it will be 'Thai only' clientele. Most 'service girls' have never had sex with a *farang*. >>

Attitudes are changing slowly. Women are becoming more assertive and vocal. There are scores of capable women heading large corporations, trade unions and public offices.

The gay scene There are many gay bars and clubs in Thailand and a number of specialised magazines.

Although the Thais do not frown on homosexuality, AIDS is making everyone think hard. There is now anxious debate about the economic consequences of sexual permissiveness and who will pay the medical expenses of employees who contract AIDS.

<< A Thai doctor describes AIDS as '...worse than any war. It will destroy every fibre of our social and economic life. We need a movement so intense that it can uproot men's sexual habits...' >>

An AIDS awareness poster

■ **The army has been an extremely important group in Thai society and politics, ever since the 1932 revolution when it forced King Prajadhipok to abandon his absolute powers. Periods of civilian rule have often been interrupted by military coup attempts – 17 in all since 1932. ....■**

The military profile was kept high from the 1950s by the perception that Thailand was the 'next domino' likely to fall to Communism in Southeast Asia, and by the continual threat of Communist insurgency. The army runs its own bank, radio and television stations, and regional economic development programmes. It is firmly part of the Thai establishment; the army Chief of Staff is Chairman of the Telephone

<< Thai military leaders commonly control private business concerns, sometimes through their wives, children or friends, a trend which reached its peak in the early 1970s when the military dictators Thanom and Praphas held 150 company directorships. >>

Organisation of Thailand. The Air Force Commander has in the past doubled as the Chairman of Thai Airways International, but the political and economic role of the army is now under serious review.

The 1973 student revolution produced a sea change in Thai politics which permanently weakened the legitimacy of military rule in Thailand. The military, however, retained enormous influence and have made comebacks – first in the late 1970s as part of a rightist reaction to the weak and unstable civilian coalition governments of the mid-1970s, and most recently in the 1991 coup as a result of corruption and personality clashes with members of Chatichai Choonhavan's administration.

<< The Thai armed forces are well equipped. A few years ago they purchased cheap Chinese arms, but on finding the reliability and quality poor they placed orders again with the Americans for M60A1 and M48A5 tanks, Kaman SH2 anti-submarine helicopters and torpedoes. Some of these new arms are to be installed on the four Chinese frigates bought earlier by Thailand. >>

Armed guard at Bangkok's National Assembly

In recent years With the ending of the Vietnam war, the subsiding of domestic Communist insurgency, and the withdrawal of Vietnamese troops from Cambodia, the Thai army has sensed a loss of purpose. The air force wants more F16 fighters and the navy is lobbying for more powerful vessels, but these are hardly necessary for Thailand's current defence needs and civilian bureaucrats have resisted their demands.

■ With very fast economic growth in recent years and a culturally permissive attitude to life, Thailand now presents a very bad case indeed of pollution of the natural environment. .....■

Forests This can be seen most dramatically with the forests, which covered more than three-quarters of the land area 50 years ago but now covers less than 20 per cent. Thailand used to be a famed exporter of teak, but today it is actually a net importer of wood. Reafforestation campaigns did not begin until as recently as the mid-1980s. Tough measures against illegal logging were introduced only in 1986, when sawmills were shut down and concessions revoked. Yet still it continues.

The military has been used to protect reserve forests threatened by villagers. The hilltribes used to practice 'slash-and-burn' agriculture, staying on a given plot of ground for only a short time and burning the trees to make fertilizer. That is now illegal.

After the disastrous 1987–8 floods commercial logging was banned. The loss of trees from watershed areas

A coconut-picking monkey, trained to work for men in the forests which men are destroying

36

in upland districts shifted the pattern of rainfall and actually reduced the water supply to farmers below.
In that bad flood, hundreds of people were drowned in the south and whole villages washed away. The removal of the trees resulted in disastrous soil erosion; whole communities were buried in mudslides.

Legislation Unfortunately legislation is hard to implement. Many logging companies, including army enterprises, negotiated alternative contracts across the border in the Burmese, Laotian or Cambodian forests, thus exporting Thailand's environmental problem.
The logging companies are powerful politically and do not find it hard to continue logging in remote areas of Thailand by bribing officials. In Laos Thai logging companies are building hotels in return for access to the local forest stands.

Positive progress Some constructive measures were started in the 1980s. One interesting conservation project is at Ban Sup Tai village on the edge of one of Thailand's last virgin forests. This forms a national park, sheltering 180 elephants and 50 tigers.
The villagers had been poaching and encroaching on the national park. In response to this, voluntary groups from Bangkok organised German finance and set up a number of measures including a credit co-operative, a co-operative store, animal husbandry activities, tree planting and conservation awareness sessions.
Now these villagers have stopped farming inside the park boundary and the barking deer and elephants have returned to the fringes of the village for the first time in over a decade. In

<< Bangkok was an idyllic 'village of wild olive groves' when the Chakri kings founded their capital there 200 years ago. There were only 12,750 registered motor vehicles in the city when King Bhumiphol was born. >>

fact, wild pigs are now feeding freely on the villagers' rich corn and soybean crops and are not being killed as they were in the past – because villagers have caught the new conservation bug and do not like to shoot them!

Air pollution By the 1980s the number of cars on Thailand's roads was increasing by their original total figure every month. Today there are nearly two million on the roads. More than five tons of lead, not to mention quantities of other toxic matter, are released into Bangkok's air every day. The problem has been aggravated by the proliferation of factories in Bangkok since the 1960s. The number has increased more than a hundredfold.

Boom! In the 1960s and '70s the urban area in the capital doubled and then doubled again during the first half of the 1980s. This rapid sprawling development swamped any ideas of planning for transport or other infrastructure. More than half of the country's manufacturing takes place in Bangkok. Together with Bangkok's governmental and administrative functions this has created a nightmarish problem of traffic congestion. The average speed of traffic in the central area is only 5 mph. During the school term time, or in the rainy season floods, it is even worse. Some 70 per cent of

Thailand's energy consumption is used in transportation.

That sinking feeling Bangkok is slowly sinking, at the rate of about an inch a year. It has been suggested by a city official that it might just collapse under its own weight one day. Little can be done about it; the city grew up over a riverine delta with what used to be a network of khlongs or canals, reminiscent of Venice, but which are now mostly built over. Bangkokians await their doom with customary fatalism, and will no doubt go and build a new city somewhere else when it happens.

Rivers The rivers are in a disastrous state. At the mouth of Bangkok's Chao Phraya River the mercury contamination is between seven and 40 times the accepted safe level, and accumulated heavy metal in fish and shellfish is 10 to 20 times above safety standards.
Bangkok uses so much water that there is now talk of diverting a major northeastern river into the Chao Phraya. The booming tiger-prawn fishery business has caused the destruction of many of Thailand's ancient mangrove swamps. Things

A traffic policeman equipped with respirator in Bangkok

<< 'The purpose of development is to create a liveable environment.'
– King Bhumiphol. >>

are no better in the countryside, where farmers have for decades been applying too much chemical fertilizer and insecticide. The malignant residue remains in canals, rivers and reservoirs. Once in the soil it gets into the food chain and builds up to fatally toxic levels in animals. This will inevitably affect humans too. Only when the enormity of this has sunk in will effective action for change take place as has been the case in other parts of the world.

Alternatives There are some signs that the process has begun. An Eastern form of 'green' response has been 'Buddhist Farming', a form of organic farming influenced by the Japanese pioneer Masanobu Fukuoka (author of *The One Straw Revolution*). Its main features include the abandonment of chemical pesticides and herbicides in favour of natural herbal sprays and the encouragement of natural predators such as birds. Soil fertility is maintained by natural leaf-based fertilisers and intercropping (the practice of growing a variety of crops in the same field). The growth of interest in organic farming in the West is giving Thai pioneers in this field, such as Prawase Wasi and Wibul Khemchalerm, renewed confidence.

Fighting back Some local lobbies have succeeded in protecting their environment against development damage. Popular opposition buried the important Nam Choan dam scheme in 1988, despite determined efforts of successive governments to launch it. The $44 million tantalum plant at Phuket, constructed against intense local objections, was burnt to the ground in 1985 after 50,000 people had demonstrated outside it. The Phuket environmentalists maintained their militant reputation in 1990 with forceful protests against

*Choking the city to death?
Bangkok's traffic*

the encroachment of a new Yacht
Club development on to public land,
as well as demanding that a massive
planned development involving the
construction of seven new hotels be
abandoned. The Swiss consortium's
offer to include an ecological
research institute in the
development did not impress them:
many beaches are now severely
polluted, with raw sewage pumped
straight into the sea, and
unfortunately not much is being
done to remedy it.

Meanwhile, in the northeastern
province of Maha Sarakham, 1,500
villagers recently clashed with police
in a violent demonstration against
pollution of their local river by rock-
salt mining. The salination of the
Siew river was killing fish and turning
sparkling green riceland into a
moonscape. According to the
National Environmental Board 15 per
cent of Isan (northeast Thailand) soil
is already badly salinated.

Changing attitudes The climate of
opinion is thus moving in favour of
environmentalism. Those leaders
with influential opinions are not just
talking: they are taking action. The
Thai Environmental and Community
Development Association, led by
Chodchoy Sophonpanich, wealthy
daughter of the founder of the
Bangkok Bank, launched a
programme to clean up Bangkok's
river and *khlongs*.

Future development There is a
debate in Thailand over the pace of
economic growth, and whether
Thailand should aspire to become
the fifth of Asia's 'Newly
Industrialised Economies'. Some
argue that Thailand's future does not
lie in industrialisation and all its
associated environmental problems,
but rather in an agricultural, food
processing and service economy.

■ **Thailand provides a very pleasant surprise when it comes to food. Eating is a great social event and Thai food is one of the major Asian cuisines, quite distinct from Chinese, Indian or Indonesian cookery. And now Thai food, with its low meat and fat content and profusion of skilfully prepared vegetable dishes, is becoming increasingly popular in the West (see also pages 102–3). .....■**

Fifty years ago the dictator, Field Marshal Phibul, made the use of spoons and forks compulsory, in his naïve attempt to Westernise the country. Before this the Thais used to eat with their hands.

As Buddhists, Thais avoid eating too much red meat, so the main dish could be shellfish, game or fish, perhaps cooked with a sauce of galingale (mild ginger), tamarind, lemon grass and chilli. The dishes are often washed down with chilled beer – Singha is a favourite local brand.

The introduction of spices into Thai cooking dates roughly from the time of King Mongkut, whose encouragement of openness to Western ideas and technology also extended to the import of spices from China, India and Java. Once introduced, they became subjected to the distinctive application, mixtures and measures of Thai taste.

Quintessentially Thai That taste begins with the five flavours which also lie at the root of Chinese cookery, namely bitter, salt, sour, hot and sweet; but the Thais use them in quite a different way from the Chinese.

<< The staple food is rice, usually eaten with a spoon. One type, a fine long grain called *khao hom mali*, is so delicious that some Thais see it as a meal in itself. Thais grow many varieties of rice, and its pearly white rice grain is in particular demand for export. >>

<< At least six different types of *phrik* (chilli pepper) are used. The smaller the chilli, the stronger it is. The smallest variety, known as 'mouse droppings' (*phrik kee noo*), should be handled with particular care. >>

Some ingredients used in Thai cuisine are not found in either Chinese or Indian cooking. Lemon grass is a tall grass (totally unrelated to the lemon), the leaf and root of which are used to flavour soups and salads, as well as curries and stews. The makrud leaf comes from a large type of lime tree native to Thailand. Its juice and rough green skin add a strong, tart flavour to soups, sauces and curries.

There is almost a national obsession with sauces. *Nam phrik* is an extremely spicy sauce which often proves too fiery for the Western palate, but the Thais adore it. *Nam plah* (literally 'fish water')is a pungent fish sauce made from fermenting anchovies. It is as common a condiment on the Thai dining table as salt is in the West.

Tom yam, a spicy soup containing shrimp flavoured with lemon grass, kaffir lime leaves, fish sauce and lemon juice, is extremely popular. *Khao tom* is a clear rice soup flavoured with vinegar or chillies with scraps of meat or poultry. It is regarded as a cure-all for fevers, colds and especially hangovers.

A typical dinner might include boiled rice; two soups; a bland

Chinese-style stir-fry vegetable; a pungent Indian-style curry; and boned chicken wings, stuffed with minced pork and spices and then steamed and subsequently fried, served with a sweet-sour plum sauce.

Thai curries (*kaeng*) are cooked with coconut milk or cream to thicken the stock at the end, thus softening the fierceness common in Indian curries. Red curries (*kaeng dang*) are made with Indian chilli, garlic, and onion laced with Thai lemon grass, *makrud* leaf and galanga root. Green curries are made with green chilli, usually with chicken and beef. Sour curry is made with shrimp paste, used with seafood.

Coconut cream ranges beyond the curry pot to find uses in soups and desserts as well – eg spicy coconut

An evening meal, Thai style

cream and chicken soup (*tom kha gai*) or bananas in coconut cream with mango and sticky rice.

Chinese influence Thai chefs use the wok to stir-fry crispy green vegetables, sauté seasoned slivers of pork, beef and chicken, and to prepare fried rice and fried noodles. Steaming fish (*plah neung*) is another technique which the Thais have adopted from China. Thai cooking

<< The harvest of many fruits is marked by annual pageants featuring beauty competitions to find 'Miss Pineapple' or 'Miss Mango'. >>

also mirrors in some ways the regional division of staple grains found in China. Rice predominates in the south, while dumplings and Chiang Mai noodles are a speciality of the north.

The Thais are extremely fond of fresh vegetables and salads (known as *yum* in Thai). Freshly cut cabbage and lettuce leaves, scallion stalks, coriander sprigs, chilli pods and mint leaves are served with lightly poached seafoods, eggplants, roast chicken or duck.

Fruit is by no means the least of Thailand's culinary pleasures. Thailand's tropical climate is ideal for the growing of a wide variety of fruits such as mangos, durians, pineapples, guavas, longans, rambutans, custard apples, pomelos and jackfruits. Thailand produces about 7 million tons of fruit each

Food

year, and only about one per cent of it is exported.

For the Thais the 'king of fruits' is the durian. Oval in shape, it is about 20–25cm long and almost as wide. Its olive-green yellowish skin is covered with a fearsome armour of thick sharp-pointed spines up to 2cm long. Inside, the flesh is 'custard-like' – creamy and yellow – and *extremely* pungent. Don't be put off by the smell, it really does taste good. There are at least five varieties of *mamuang* (mango), which is often eaten with glutinous rice, and topped with coconut cream, as a dessert. *Lamyai* is a marble-sized fruit with a hard brown skin which peels away to reveal a firm translucent flesh surrounding a black seed.

The lychee is similar to the *lamyai* but slightly larger with a pinkish flesh. The *mangkhut* (mangosteen)

Mae Hong Son's early morning market, Northern Thailand

season lasts from May until July. It is a small dark purple fruit with a white flesh which is sweet but slightly tart. Thais are fond of trying to guess the number of seeds they will find inside.

Thais will eat bananas when they are fully grown, but not yet ripe, fried and seasoned with sugar and salt, as a snack called *kluai chap*. If they are ripe, they can be made into all kinds of sweetmeats, including *kluai ping*

> << In May the Songkhla festival has an annual fruit-carving competition. >>

(grilled banana soaked in syrup), *kluai buat chi* (pieces of banana boiled in coconut milk and seasoned with sugar and a pinch of salt) or *kluai khaek*, which Westerners will recognise as banana fritters. That does not end the banana's role in the Thai kitchen. They are also turned into wrappings, cooking utensils or plates. The flowers will be put into a soup or a salad, and the leaves and trunk used for flower arrangements.

The presentation of food is extremely important. Meals are sometimes served with vegetables carved into the shape of blossoms and leaves. Puddings and salads may be garnished with roses or orchids.

Regional dishes The northeast speciality, som tam, is a salad made from grated unripe papaya, mixed with sliced tomatoes, chopped garlic and chillies, with pounded dried shrimps, fish sauce and lemon juice. Northeasterners usually like to take it with sticky rice and salted beef (the beef seasoned with pepper, marinated in garlic and soy sauce and dried in the sun).

The north is the best place to savour vegetables, taken raw or very slightly cooked, with *nam phrik ong* which is a thick dipping sauce of tomatoes, ground pork, garlic and chilli, seasoned with soy sauce and sugar and served with streaky pork. Many of the **central** Thailand dishes have already been described.

Chicken green curry would be very typical, served with salted egg and *yum*, the Thai salad which does not use oil.

In the **southern** provinces there is an even wider range of curries, using all kinds of green, yellow or red curry paste. Some of them are very hot indeed. Southerners also enjoy fried fish, often coated with turmeric and other herbs and spices, deep fried and served with an aromatic sauce. Western food is served in Thailand, along with many other cuisines, in restaurants and hotels, and there is a huge variety of Chinese restaurants to patronise. But don't leave Thailand without trying Thai food. Even if you find your first Thai meal a little too hot, too spicy or too strong, don't give up. There are so many kinds of dish that it is worth persevering – you will certainly find some that you really enjoy.

A mouth-watering market display

■ **The Thai language is one of the oldest in the Orient, but the Thai script is more recent. Thailand has epic folk tales drawn from mythology and modern award-winning writers. Classical works of art are often based on Buddhist religious texts, but modern works have experimented with abstract forms. Thai music is very different from the West's, using different instruments and tones. The classical orchestra accompanies the traditional *khon*, or masked dramas. .....■**

44

Language The spoken word is tonal: the same sound can have different meanings according to the tone with which it is pronounced. There are five tones – low, high, mid-pitch and rising and falling. Westerners find it difficult to learn when one word – *ma* – can mean 'horse', 'dog' or the verb 'to come' depending on pronunciation.

Epic tales Thai folk tales draw on Indian mythology, using themes of romance or the feats of divine heroes. They were usually written in verse form. *Khun Chang Khun Phan*

Painted fishing boat, Songkhla

is a Thai epic about a love triangle of a woman with two lovers and is often recited with a rhythmic percussion accompaniment.

Another classic is the *Ramakian*, the Thai version of the famous Indian epic *Ramayana*. The version current in Thailand today was written by the first two kings of the Chakri dynasty. It records the state ceremonies and traditions of the Thai royalty and is the theme of the large murals which adorn the walls of Wat Phra Keo, the Royal Chapel of the Emerald Buddha in Bangkok.

The *Jataka* are popular folk tales relating to the previous lives of the Buddha, mixing traditional folklore and pre-Buddhist legend with down-to-earth wisdom and high spirituality. One of the most popular, which teaches the virtue of generosity, is the tale of Prince Vessandan (a previous incarnation of the Buddha) who gives away everything, including his wife and children. Its thousand verses are usually chanted at temples over a three-day period in October, at the end of *Phansa*, the Buddhist Lent.

Modern literature A journalistic heritage is reflected in modern social realism novels which deal with problems such as poverty, prostitution and corruption, as well as the formulaic themes of cops and robbers, romance and ghost stories. Thailand's most famous novelist is Kukrit Pramoj, whose career as writer, critic and left-of-centre politician eventually led him to become Prime Minister in 1975. One

<<   Thai script was developed by King Ramkhamhaeng in 1283. The King is said to have been responsible for the first Thai literary work, a famous stone inscription, supposedly of the late 13th century, extolling the glories of the Sukhothai kingdom. Thai script reads from left to right, although vowel sounds may be written after, before, above or below the consonant they follow.   >>

of his best known works is **Red Bamboo**, the conflict between two boyhood friends in a remote village: one becomes a Buddhist monk, the other a Communist cell organiser. Both have a zeal for improving the village but disagree totally on how to do it. They finally unite to drive out a rapacious landowner.

One of the most celebrated of the new- wave writers is Pira Sudham, a Thai who writes in English about life in poverty-stricken Isan, in the northeast of Thailand. His *Monsoon Country* portrays the odyssey of Prem, an outcast in his own village. He is taunted by the other village children who call him 'Tadpole'. Prem manages to escape his village to attend university in Bangkok, and wins a scholarship to study in England. His quest for knowledge leads him to become thoroughly Westernised, leading a life of luxury in Germany and even winning poetry prizes in Western languages. But Prem never forgets his roots in Isan. Eventually he rejects Western materialism, burns his Western clothes and goes back to his village to become a Buddhist monk.

Films There is a trend towards social realism in recent Thai films. One film, *American Surplus*, details the discrimination against a girl born of a Thai bar-girl and a black American GI. *Thongpun Kokpoh* (The Citizen) portrays the struggles of a taxi driver from the northeast trying to make a living in Bangkok in the face of powerful and corrupt officials. *The Hunt* portrays the lives of a group of girls who have been raped, and their quest for revenge against their assailants.

Painting The theme of much Thai painting is the *Tosachat*, the name given to the last 10 of the Buddhistic *Jataka* tales. You see it on wall murals, temple banners, canvas paintings, manuscripts and carvings on bookcases. Some of the best examples are at Wat Suwannaram in Thonburi where formal gestures and religious symbols are skilfully blended with naturalistic observations of people working, relaxing, gossiping and even flirting. Modern art made its appearance with the heroic realism of the Italian sculptor Corrado Feroci. He was invited to the court of King Vajiravudh and commissioned in Thailand's first

<<   Recent research has shown that the Thais may have been the originators of many Oriental styles of ceramic which later developed in China, not the other way around. Some pottery kilns date back to AD900.   >>

flush of 'democracy' to sculpt the Democracy Monument (1939) and the Victory Monument (1941). During the 1960s and 1970s many Thai artists experimented with abstract forms. King Bhumiphol is an accomplished artist. The style of his more abstract works has been compared to that of Expressionist artists Edvard Munch and Oskar Kokoschka.

The Arts

Lop Buri is famed as the birthplace of a distinctive and highly developed school of sculpture specialising in both Mahayana and Theravada figures of the Buddha in bronze and later, sandstone. The best Lop Buri Buddhas are marvellously authoritative with diadems enclosing a conical *ushnisha* – the protuberance on the crown of the head symbolising enlightenment.

Music Traditional Thai music, pentatonic in origin, is sometimes difficult for Westerners to appreciate. It is a rich polyphony of subtle variations in tone, texture and mood, tuneful and often played at a fearsome pace. Behind the strange melodies lies an eight-note octave, but unlike Western music the stress is on full note intervals without semitones.

One common instrument is the *pi*, a woodwind instrument with a reed mouthpiece. You can hear it being played at Thai boxing contests. The

classical shadow theatre (*nang*) and dance-dramas, khon.

Khon or 'masked' drama is one of several traditional forms which were revived by the early Chakri kings. It is believed to be about 400 years old

<< '…[in Thai music] not a single note between a starting note and its octave agrees with any of the notes of the European scale.'
– Sir Hubert Parry (19th-century British composer. >>

and is almost always an enactment of the *Ramakian*. It developed from the ancient Thai arts of *nang yai* ('shadow play') and *krabee-krabong*, which is a form of theatrical fencing. Originally all the actors wore masks and mimed one of the 138 *Ramakian* episodes to the music of a *piphat* orchestra. Over the centuries the costumes and headdresses have

Thai musicians

pin is similar to the Indian banjo (*vina*), while the *ranad ek* is like a wood-block xylophone. Bamboo pipe instruments are common in the north and northeast. In some of them several bamboo pipes are bound together to form a sort of mouth organ called a *khaen*.

The Thais have developed their own version of a classical orchestra called a *piphat*, which can include as many as 20 players. The *piphat* was the traditional accompaniment to

become more and more stylised. There are also established musical idioms for moods such as anger and grief and actions such as weeping. One of Thailand's most famous pop stars is not actually a Thai at all. Billy Ogan is the son of a Catholic Filipino father and Thai mother and still carries a Philippine passport, though he calls himself a Thai and appears on stage with jasmine garlands draped round his neck. He began as a model and film star, but made singing hits with 'Billy, Billy', in 1987 and 'Billy Khem' in 1988.

■   The ancient art of Thai massage – *nuat phaen boran* – is quite an experience. Like other Eastern forms of massage, it balances the body's energies by working on the acupressure points and meridians – *sen* – in a similar way to acupuncture. It can be quite vigorous, but it feels wonderful and it's certainly a great cure for sitting in any one place too long. ....■

The beach is a good place to find a massage. Pattaya and Phuket in particular are home to the bands of blue-shirted women who have cards of accreditation; most hire out their services individually. Hotels and guesthouses will also provide facilities and the larger ones, such as The Pearl in Phuket, will have specialised staff.

<< *Caveat emptor!*
Watch out for the distinction between the ancient and 'modern' massages. The latter is a quaint euphemism for sexual services, and some establishments, such as the Jansom Chumphon (sister of the famous Jansom Thara in Ranong) offer both! >>

Where to go In Bangkok, **The Society for Ancient Massage** is located on the River Chao Phraya on the northeast side of Krung Thep bridge, and **The Two Doctors** apothecary shop is on Ha Prachan Road near Wat Mahathat. Here are preserved some traditions of the Thai masseur such as the prayer to Jivaka Kumarabaccha, the Buddha's personal physician and early disciple. The scriptures mention practices which bear a striking resemblance to those of today.
The home of traditional healing, Wat Po, has two pavilions of 20 beds each and a cool marble floor. **Buatip Thai Massage** opposite the Landmark on Sukhumvit Road is among the modern-looking places that just do the ancient massage.

Several blind masseurs are employed for their heightened tactile sensitivity.
The Patpong area has **Plazazone** on Patpong Soi 2 and **Marble House** on Soi Surawong Plaza. Small cubicles are provided, and at the latter, voluminous cotton trousers.
The price for having your body pummelled may vary between 100 (or slightly less) and 200 baht, including a tip for the masseur. The supposedly higher quality Buatip charges 300 baht.

Pleasure or pain? Thai massage

47

■ **Thailand is well served with internal flights – Thai Airways has a large number of flights to all important cities and major tourist resorts – and a railway network extends into most regions of the country. Buses run in and between most towns and cities, but in city centres the traffic can be chaotic. River boats are the favourite means of travel from Bangkok up river – to Ayutthaya, for example. .....■**

In the early days The first rickshaw was introduced to Bangkok about 1871, and within a generation it became so popular that the government had to regulate its control and safety. Horse-drawn trams arrived in 1888, later converted into electric trams. Just after the beginning of the new century Prince Rabi, one of King Chulalongkorn's sons, could be seen driving the first motor car.

Railways The first railway was completed in 1900, between Bangkok and Nakhon Ratchasima.

On the road, Southern Thailand

Major railway lines now connect the cities of Chiang Mai, Nong Khai and Ratchathani with Bangkok. Trains also run directly into Malaysia and Singapore. Before the Indochina war there were trains to Cambodia too,

and these are being resumed. Trains are often more comfortable than buses over long distances – but tickets must be booked several days (at least) in advance.

Bangkok was full of k*hlongs* (canals) up until the 1950s, with many small boats plying up and down. Although that network has collapsed, the mayor of Bangkok is organising a new limited service of river and canal taxis, along those waterways that remain. The Chao Phraya express service is great fun and can be picked up from many points on either side of the river. There are also long-tail boat taxis which are shared with other passengers.

Buses running regular routes in the city are reliable and cheap, once you get the hang of how to use them. The conductor keeps tickets and

<< Bangkok traffic averages only 4 kilometres per hour; hardened international travellers will tell you that only Lagos, in Nigeria, is worse. >>

loose change in a metal tube about 40cm long. The hinged metal lid of the tube is used to clip off tickets from the roll.

Although buses are frequent and convenient the signs are seldom in English and can be confusing. Local passengers will often help if you get lost or confused.

There are three kinds of bus in Bangkok: the regular public buses follow a more or less standard timetable along fixed routes; air-

conditioned buses connect the main bus stations and centres and private air-conditioned bus services are available at many hotels and offices with a deluxe service. Most journeys within Bangkok cost 2 to 5 baht, depending mainly on whether buses have air-conditioning. The public bus station in north Bangkok serves Chiang Mai and Ayutthaya; in the east is a bus station for Pattaya; and there is one in the northwest of the city for Phuket and the south.

Alternatives in town Many *tuk tuks*, motorised trishaws (*samlors*), are cheaper than taxis over short distances – provided you bargain a little. The original non-motorised *samlors* still survive in the provinces, but were banned in Bangkok some years ago. In Chiang Mai and other

> << People often complain that when Thai civil servants take out their scissors to cut red tape, 'they cut it lengthwise'. >>

Samlors *in the rush-hour*

regional centres there are *songthaews* – small pickup trucks with two rows of seats – which pursue a more or less fixed route. Taxis, where all the windows can be tightly closed and some air-conditioning turned on, afford a little more comfort but can be expensive.

> << Until the 1930s trains and canal boats were the only practicable means of communication between Bangkok and the provinces. >>

If you take a taxi, it is essential to negotiate the fare at the beginning of the journey – 60 baht might be a typical fare for a short journey within the centre of Bangkok during the daytime.
The swampy nature of Bangkok's site prohibits the building of an underground transport network, and long-standing plans for an overhead transit system have still not been been realised. Thai red tape takes years to unravel; meanwhile, the traffic pile-ups get worse.

■ **The King is the most famous person in Thailand. His portrait appears everywhere, his name is endlessly invoked, his appearances attract huge crowds. Besides the king, there is a host of former prime ministers, military leaders and businessmen and women who have high profiles. Other well-known figures include authors, Buddhist monks, a beauty queen and a pop singer. .....■**

50

Royalty and politics On one of his regular walks through remote villages the King discovered that people knew in advance that he was coming and would 'get things ready' for him. He decided not to tell anybody where he wanted to go, so that his fairly large retinue would set out with no idea of their destination. However, this proved too chaotic in terms of logistics, so now the King compromises. Half of the visits are a surprise, half are planned ahead – a very Thai solution!

The King's daughter, Princess Sirindhorn, who frequently deputises for him on public occasions, is also a celebrated figure, as are former prime ministers like Thanom Kittikachorn, Kukrit Pramoj and his brother Seni Pramoj, Prem Tinsulanond and Chatichai Choonhavan. Prem was the epitome of the traditional-style consensus politician, ready to wait a long time to win unanimous approval before going ahead with any decision. Chatichai's moment of fame, before his premiership in the late 1980s, was in defusing an Arab hijack of hostages from the Israeli embassy in Bangkok. Chatichai, then a Foreign Office Official, persuaded the Arabs to change their Israeli hostages for Thai volunteers, including himself. He flew with the hijackers and the Thai hostages to Cairo.

Chaovalit Yongchaiyudh is probably the most energetic and active general on the retired list; he suggested that corrupt politicians should be beheaded.

At a slightly lower level, General Chamlong Srimuang, the Mayor of Bangkok and a Buddhist ascetic, has endeared himself to the Bangkok population. He has foresworn sex, meat and liquor, sleeps on the floor and is regular in his Buddhist prayers.

<< Kukrit Pramoj was a graduate of Queen's College Oxford, where he was renowned for having a barrel of beer always open in his room. He insists that he knows all the 2,000 fish in his fish pond by name. He is also very proud of the two chicks he reared personally when the mother hen died . >>

Pop star Billy Ogan

The King visits his people

Popular entertainment In the world of Thai entertainment the name of Billy Ogan, a pop singer who has a Filipino father and a Thai mother, ranks very high. Ogan is Catholic, not Buddhist, but he was an extremely popular model during the late 1980s and became an adulated pop star.

Writers Thailand's most famous writers are Kukrit Pramoj, author of *Red Bamboo*, and the new-wave writer Kampoon Boontawee. Kukrit also wrote *Four Reigns*, a fictionalised story of the royal family, of which he is a minor son. Since he founded the newspaper *Siam Rath*, one of the few successful radical publications, he is also highly regarded among journalists. He also portrayed the Prime Minister of Sarkis in the film, *The Ugly American*, in which Marlon Brando was the star.

Well-known women Many of Thailand's famous women have made their name in the business world: Phornthip Narongdej is Senior Executive of Siam Motors; others include Lersak Sombatsiri, owner of the Hilton Hotel, and Sirilak Patanakorn, a graduate of the London School of Economics, who was president of the Bangkok Stock Exchange.

Religious figures Some Buddhist monks have become celebrities in Thailand, such as Phra Bodhirak, the former TV producer and singer, who is now the flamboyant and controversial leader of the radical Santi Asoke sect. Buddhadasa, the founder of the Suan Mokh movement. is well known throughout the country for preaching 'dhammic socialism' (see page 31).
In the world of industry and commerce Dhanin Chearavanont and

<< Phornthip Narkhirunkanok is Thailand's most successful beauty queen, who became a national heroine after winning the Miss Universe competition in 1988. The Thais did not seem to care that she had spent almost her entire life abroad in California. >>

Chatri Sophonpanich, heading the Charoen Pokphand group and the Bangkok Bank respectively, are the leaders. In both cases their father emigrated from China, and they represent the first generation to be Thai-born. Both are famous for having key friends in the leadership of the political parties and the army, and they can swing very big deals indeed.

Pontala

Langur
Linbon
Fache
Dame

Lassa or Bar
ancole

SEM

Cha
nay

Osul

Men"in

Younin in

Me ng

Bao

TONQUIN

Ta R.

PART

CHINA

Can

Leng
LAOS

Kemarat

xia nge

AVA
Liactore

Tia
into

Kian
Biang

hai

Bacan
Aria

Pegu R.

anque
tone

Porceloune

R. etay
Kihoy
Cuadag

Cuabu

Cuabang

Guian
Cua
Guasay
Behoa

Reccio
Ketru

Yn R.
Louitcheon

I. de Tai

Bay Quantch

The Best
Port

Gulf of

Lineato
van

Aman I.

P. Tay

Tinchos

Prom
PEGU
Pegtu

Moro
Dougon

Syriam

Cosmin

Dala

Menamhiau R.

Lenching

Chaitai
Corazu

Ountouni

Prabat

SIAM

Cochinchina

Dourg or
Chi

Falso

Ca China
La Don
El Potego
Baubon
Diuhae

I. de Bai

The Sh
of Par

aman
Isl.

St Clara I.
Great I.

Chitte
Andaman

Canicubar

Miroi

Siam
D. Fac

Pieri

Blantock

Siam

Cam
bo
dia

Binda

Quinin

Cambo

Ciampa

I. Cambi

umbrire

Iunsia
lem I.

Dich
ling
Lone

Cima
erina

Chan

Ling

Laxo

Perry

Cam
dia
Po.F.

Baban

vejen Bay
P. de Ma
P. de Ter

P. Cecir

Ambra
The Brothers

Lapanga R.
bequaume R.
P. Condor

Canicubar

Iunsia
lem I.

P. Sammay

P. Cara

I. Ligor
P. Cosin

Ligor

na

BAY
OF
SIAM

R. vay
P. Uby

C. ier

C. Tom

Str. of Malacca

P. Bouton

Ouda ya
D. Ja

na

P. Riodang

Slackenburg

SUMATRA

Diamond I.
Penia
Dely

Bancali.

Tegs I.

P. Nayos

P. of y

MALACCA

Bara
Patan

Mal.
accaB.

Lohor

Str. of Singapora

C. Romania

a Pas

Poncians

P. Capas

Natuna

China
R

Arramba

Bor

BORN

INDIAN

Origins and Settlements

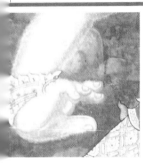

■ The origins of the Thai people themselves are obscure. It is generally accepted that the ancestors of the Thais were, by the 7th century AD, living in the kingdom of Nanchao, in what is today China's Yunnan province. The slow migration southwards began in about AD900 and was probably speeded up by the Mongol invasions of China in the mid-13th century. .....■

Beginnings Before the Thais reached Thailand there had already been sophisticated Mon and Khmer civilisations, influenced by India, in the region. Some artefacts remain from these early cultures, in the form of Indian Gupta-style Buddhas, terracotta heads and some stucco reliefs on the walls of the few remaining buildings from antiquity. Theravada Buddhism may have been introduced to these agrarian city state cultures by Indian missionaries as early as the 2nd or 3rd century BC.

<< Rama Tibodi I is noted for the promulgation of the first recorded Thai legal system. >>

The early Thais practised a rice agronomy, and their religion was a mixture of Buddhism and animism. This was a country ruled by a monarchy with periodic corvée (forced) labour; as yet there were no instances of peasant revolt or class warfare. In the 12th and 13th centuries the Thai migrants from China, by now converted to Theravada Buddhism, set up little fiefdom states in the upper reaches of the Chao Phraya valley. These began to impinge on the Khmer empire to the south and the Mons to the west in Burma.

The Sukhothai period Many histories mark the beginning of the Thais as a distinct people with King Phra Ruang's capture of Sukhothai in

Khmer ruins in the Chao Phraya valley

1253 from the Khmers; and the Sukhothai period is often seen as the golden age in Thai history.
The Thais were strongly influenced by the Indianised culture of the Mons especially their art, sculpture and literature. From the Khmers the Thais borrowed Brahminical doctrines of political organisation, a written script and improved agricultural technology. Sukhothai reached its peak with the late 13th-century reign of Ramkhamhaeng (the first Thai king to be called 'the Great'), who extended his kingdom to the Bay of Bengal, Luang Prabang and the Malay peninsula.
The second Thai capital was founded at Ayutthaya in 1350 by Rama Tibodi I, who captured Khmer and Sukhothai territories until his realm extended from Laos in the north and as far as the Malacca straits in the south.

<< Paul Benedict (in *Austro-Thai Language and Culture*) has speculated on linguistic evidence that the Thais came from Indonesia and Southeast Asia before migrating northwards into China. >>

It was during the Ayutthaya period that elaborate royal rituals and the Khmer ideas of the king being a god were introduced. However, in spite of all the pomp and tribute the Thai kings' power was actually quite limited until the great centralising reforms of King Trailok (1448–88), who set up the Thai civil service and stipulated carefully the amount of land to which each rank of official was entitled. He also codified the bemusing complexity of royal household etiquette and introduced the idea of having a second or vice-king to simplify succession problems.

From outside Thailand Thailand's first Western contact was with the Portuguese at the beginning of the 16th century; a century later, French, English, Japanese, Dutch and Spanish mercenaries, missionaries and traders were visiting Ayutthaya in considerable numbers. They were stunned by the wealth of the city. Thai tolerance of Westerners became strained after a charismatic Greek adventurer, Constantin

Phaulkon, achieved such a high status in the Thai court that he began to take over Thailand's foreign policy, favouring the French at the expense of the Dutch. He was executed in 1688 – probably the last and perhaps the only Westerner ever to have been executed in Thailand. Throughout this period Thailand was fighting wars against the Burmese and Cambodians. After several defeats in the mid-16th century Thailand became for a time little more than a vassal state of Burma. The Burmese invaded again in 1765. After a two-year siege the Burmese razed the great Thai metropolis of Ayutthaya to the ground and carried off an immense amount of booty and 30,000 prisoners. The sack of Ayutthaya and the loss of all her cultural treasures was a terrible blow to the Thais, who have never completely forgiven the Burmese.

A temple mural from the 18th-century Wat Phra Keo, where the Emerald Buddha is contained

■ **Chao Phya Chakri became King Rama I of the new Chakri dynasty (reigned 1782–1809). His many achievements included the founding of a new royal palace and temple and the construction of Bangkok, originally designed to be an exact replica of Ayutthaya. He also reformed the Buddhist *sangha*. He repelled a full-scale invasion by Burma in 1785 – and fought four more wars with Burma before his death in 1809. .....■**

Before Rama I Phya Tak, or Taksin, was a general of mixed Thai-Chinese parentage, who showed great courage in fighting the Burmese. As King Taksin he established a new capital further down the Chao Phraya river at Thonburi (on the opposite bank from Bangkok), and eventually brought the provinces and large areas of Laos, under Thai control. Taksin's descent into madness and increasing cruelty eventually led to a rebellion in Thonburi in 1782. The King's most trusted general Tongduang (Chao Phya Chakri), was summoned back from military campaigning in Cambodia to take a lead. It was decided that both the

A Wat Phra Keo mural (below); and (above) King Rama I

<< The first printing press was set up in Bangkok in 1835. The future King Mongkut (Rama IV) was the first Thai to set up his own press, which he used to print Buddhist books. >>

King and the rebels should be put to death. Taksin was put into a sack and beaten to death with sandalwood clubs. So Chao Phya Chakri became King Rama I and founder of the Chakri dynasty.

The 19th century By the time Rama III was crowned, the Burmese were engrossed in fighting the British colonialists on their western frontier, leaving Thailand free to build up an empire to the east in Indochina. The early 19th century was also a time when European nations began to make a real impact on Thai life: trade treaties were signed with Britain (1826) and the USA (1833) – the first such American treaty with an Asian country. By the late 1840s there was increasing diplomatic and military pressure to revise earlier trade agreements, but Thailand scented the threat of Western imperialism, to which its neighbours were fast succumbing.

<< During King Taksin's 1778 invasion of Laos the 2,000-year-old sacred Emerald Buddha was recaptured and installed at Thonburi. >>

Two Remarkable Kings

■ In 1851 King Mongkut ascended the throne of Thailand for a reign of 17 years, during which the foundations of the kingdom's modernisation were firmly laid. He was succeeded by his 16-year-old son, Chulalongkorn, who instituted many reforms and succeeded in keeping the European colonial threat at bay. .....■

King Mongkut At the age of 20 Mongkut had been ordained as a Buddhist monk, and before becoming king he spent 27 years in the monkhood. This gave him the opportunity to tour the country, discovering the people's needs and complaints, and learning much from the foreigners who had begun to reside in Thailand. In particular, he learned English from American missionaries, which he later used to advantage to correspond personally with Queen Victoria and President Lincoln.

Mongkut's achievements Mongkut had to agree to new treaties with Britain and the US, giving foreigners extraterritorial immunity from the Thai courts. These treaties allowed Thai trade with the West to expand.

> << A *Bangkok Post* editorial called *The King and I* 'patronising, ignorant, stupidly comic and an affront to the Thai people'. It is still officially banned, although videos circulate clandestinely in Bangkok. >>

He entirely reformed the taxation system, modernised the armed forces and police, and built roads and canals.
Mongkut was the king who hired Mrs Anna Leonowens, an English widow from Singapore, to teach his 82 children in the palace in the 1860s. It was her books, *An English Governess at the Siamese Court* and *The Romance of the Harem*, which formed the basis of the musical *The King and I*, in which Yul Brynner caricatured the part of King Mongkut.

Having studied astronomy, Mongkut astonished foreigners by correctly predicting the eclipse of the sun in 1868 – but while making the calculation in a remote part of southern Thailand, he caught malaria, and died soon afterwards. His 16-year-old son, Chulalongkorn, succeeded him.

King Chulalongkorn Once Anna Leonowens' star pupil, Chulalongkorn's long reign (1868–1910) allowed him to fulfil his father's plans and bring Thailand to the point of modernity. He travelled to Singapore, Java (in Indonesia) and India, and twice to western Europe, intensifying his desire to continue the Westernisation of his kingdom.

Chulalongkorn's achievements Chulalongkorn abolished the practice of perpetual prostration in the royal presence, and simplified the court dress and hairstyle. He abolished slavery, reformed the Buddhist *sangha*, formed a council of state and privy council to regularise the government, and set up 12 ministries to carry out government functions. The king himself wrote more than 200 books of history, archaeology, literature and public affairs. Modern schools were started, one of them destined to become Chulalongkorn University. Until then boys – but not girls – used to study informally under the monks in the Buddhist temples.
The first railway was opened, and currency was improved with modern minting. Everything in this absolute monarchy depended on a royal lead, so Chulalongkorn's reforming zeal was indispensable. The affection which Thais still feel towards this

great king may be observed every 23 October when people pay homage to his statue at the Royal Plaza.

Apart from the continuous and systematic modernisation of the country along mainly French, British and German lines, the most important achievement during these two crucial reigns from 1851 to 1910 was the preservation of Thai independence. In the second half of his reign the king was under constant pressure from the British and French colonial advance in neighbouring territories. He had to cede Laos, parts of Cambodia and control of the four Malay states of Kedah, Perlis, Kelantan and Trengganu to those two European powers. This was agreed to reluctantly, and only because it fended off the threat of one or both of these European powers taking over the whole of Thailand.

This was the high tide of European colonialism. The British slowly nibbled away at the Malay states and

Opposite page: King Mongkut (Rama IV); and (above) King Chulalongkorn (Rama V)

had started to overrun Burma in 1824, while the French established a foothold in Vietnam. Thailand thus faced European imperialism on three sides: to the east, west and south. The 'open door' treaties of the 1850s postponed the threat to the kingdom's independence by satisfying the short-term commercial ambitions of the French, British and others. Luckily, the appetite for further conquest began to wane in the 1890s, and there was an agreement between Britain and France not to annex Thailand.

>> '*Never having been colonised, we can only blame ourselves for our problems.*' – Former Prime Minister Kukrit Pramoj. >>

■ **Chulalongkorn's immediate successors were neither as able nor as wise. The relative unpopularity of Prajadhipok led to discontent, which strengthened conspirators during the depression of the 1930s. When fighting broke out between democrats and loyalists in 1935, King Prajadhipok abdicated in disgust, leaving only his 10-year-old nephew as next in line. ...■**

King Vajiravudh (reigned 1910–25) succeeded his father, Chulalongkorn. He tried to continue the reforms of his father and grandfather, although he lacked their charisma and character. The new king tried to promote nationalism by creating the Wild Tigers' Corp and the Village Scouts organisations. But this 'praetorian guard' made Vajiravudh unpopular with the army and navy.

More changes Government ministries continued to be reformed and Vajiravudh introduced surnames for Thai people – who had not hitherto felt the need of them. After his stay in Britain he introduced soccer, Western-style dancing and Western hairstyles for women. He made Siam (as Thailand was then known) the first Asian country to bring in compulsory education, and opened the country's first boarding public school. He wrote copiously, under various pen names, translating many of Shakespeare's plays, and giving his views on the Chinese in

> << Vajiravudh was the first king to have been educated at Oxford University, where he wrote a book in English on *the* War of the Polish Succession. >>

Thailand in a book called *The Jews in the Far East*. He was so generous and extravagant that the national budget was gravely overspent. Sympathetic with the Allied cause in World War I, Vajiravudh declared war on Germany in 1917. In 1921 the Americans agreed to a new treaty

foregoing their former extraterritorial demands, thus setting an example for other Western powers to follow in respecting Thailand's independence. This was King Vajiravudh's greatest achievement. Whereas Mongkut had 39 wives and 82 children, and Chulalongkorn had 36 wives and 77 children, Vajiravudh preferred male company. Marrying late, his only child was a daughter; he was therefore succeeded by his younger brother, Prajadhipok (reigned 1925–35).

King Prajadhipok The new king, who had studied at Eton College in England, also lacked the strong will of his earlier predecessors, though he proved conscientious and thrifty, and retrenched government officials by hundreds in order to balance the books. When visiting the United States in 1931, King Prajadhipok shook hands with several Siamese students. This was the first time that any Siamese had ever touched his monarch without being punished. The world depression of 1929–30 meant that the king had to reduce official salaries again, as well as raise taxes, and this emboldened a group of ambitious army and navy officers and civil servants to change the regime.

The bloodless revolution On 24 June 1932 the People's Party, whose leaders were almost all European-educated, led a *coup d'état* to remove the absolute powers of the king and introduce democracy. The king agreed to become a constitutional monarch and the revolution succeeded without bloodshed. A new constitution set up a national assembly, with power to name the prime minister. But the conspirators soon fell out. Their economic spokesman, Pridi Panomyong, a French-trained left-winger, was unable to persuade them to back his utopian plans to nationalise land and enterprises and put everyone on a state payroll. When King Prajadhipok abdicated in 1935, retiring to exile in England, he left no son. The succession thus passed to his nephew, who was then a boy of 10, and in no position to withstand the ploys of the revolutionary democrats.

Offerings lie at the feet of the statue of reformer King Vajiravudh (Rama VI) in Bangkok

One of the early acts of the revolutionaries was to celebrate the arrival of democracy by changing the name of the country from Siam to Thailand. Nationalists among the 'democratic' group argued that Siam was not a Thai word but one used by foreigners to describe Thailand and therefore unsuitable for a free and independent country. They also reasoned that the 23 million Thai-speaking people beyond the frontiers, in southern China, French Indochina and Burma, needed to be reflected in the kingdom's name. One of the *coup* leaders, Phibul, decided on Thailand as the new name, although many criticised it as being a bastardised conjunction – 'Thai' meaning 'free', and 'land' being an English word.

■ **Two men dominated Thai public life during the quarter-century following the 1932 revolution – Pridi Panomyong and Phibul Songkram. Pridi was a brilliant Doctor of Law from the University of Paris, who served as Regent while King Ananda Mahidol was a minor, and then later as Prime Minister. Phibul became Prime Minister and Army Commander in Chief, surviving difficult times to stay in power for some 20 years. ....■**

Pridi Panomyong Part Chinese, Pridi had extremely egalitarian views – bordering on Marxist – although he was acquitted of being a Communist by a high-powered committee including a royal prince, the Chief Justice and a British legal adviser. He became Foreign Minister and tackled the further revision of treaties with foreign countries, something high on the agenda of the revolutionaries. After Thailand declared war on Britain and the US in 1942, Pridi organised an underground resistance movement against the Japanese. When the Japanese surrendered, Pridi, in his capacity as Regent, officially repudiated the earlier declaration of war on the US and Britain, an action which saved Thailand immense trouble in the post-war period. In the following year Pridi became Prime Minister. At this point Pridi seemed to be in the ascendant, triumphing over his conservative opponents. But an unexpected tragedy snatched the prize from his grasp. The young King, who had returned from Switzerland, where he had been studying, was found dead in bed in the Grand Palace on 9 June 1946, a revolver by his side and a bullet wound in his head. The story behind his death has remained a puzzle, in spite of public investigations. Meanwhile the economy had suddenly plunged, with high prices and scarcity of food, and this encouraged the right-wingers to act. There was another bloodless *coup d'état* in November 1947, as a result of which Pridi had to flee from the country, leaving his rival Phibul as the new Army Commander-in-Chief, poised for a prolonged domination of the country's politics.

Pridi Panomyong poses with his family during his years of exile

60

Phibul Songkram was one of the leaders of the 1932 revolution. He had led the army again in the *coup d'état* of 1933. In 1938 he was made Prime Minister on a platform of national reconstruction on progressive lines. In the immediate

> << Phibul decreed that men and women should wear Western clothes, kiss each other in public, give up chewing betel-nuts and learn Western dancing. >>

aftermath of World War II, Phibul was in semi-disgrace, having backed the Japanese side. But he soon made a comeback, being confirmed as Army-Commander-in-Chief in 1947 and resuming the premiership in 1948.

Phibul excluded Chinese from many occupations (including farming, taxi-driving and hairdressing), and made Chinese schools teach the Thai language and culture. Following a visit to many Western countries, his hitherto autocratic regime became more liberal; he had come back deeply impressed by the way in which democratic government was carried out in the West.

He encouraged public debate, passed many labour laws and recognised the Trades Union Congress. The result was that the government's manipulation of the general elections of 1957 was exposed and denounced, where before it would have been endured in silence.

Phibul himself was no money-grabber, but others in his cabinet were hugely corrupt, especially his Minister of Defence, Sarit Thanarat. In July 1957 disaffected army officers led by Sarit deposed Phibul, and he fled to exile in Japan.

Phibul's resilience was legendary. He was once shot in the neck and shoulder at a football match, but recovered. A couple of years later his family dinner was poisoned, but again he recovered. He escaped from a ship where he was being held by rebels in the middle of the Chao Phraya river. His side strafed the vessel and everyone jumped overboard but he swam to the bank held by rebel soldiers. Later, a prince who had witnessed the scene asked why he hadn't made for his own side. Phibul replied that no one

> << Pridi's great memorial is the Thammasat University, which he founded, and which remains a centre of radical thinking in Thailand. >>

would have recognised him in the dark and anyway his side were better shots!

Both of these two leaders remained in exile. Pridi spent many years in Canton, in the People's Republic of China, and later lived just outside Paris. He made several soundings to successive Thai governments for a return, but none of them felt the risk was worthwhile, given the former prime minister's powerful personality and radical views.

THAILAND WAS *At War*

■ **The great international wars of the 20th century have been crucial in the formation of Thai policy and the alignment of the kingdom in its regional and global setting. Thailand entered World War I on the side of the British and French; the position in World War II was more complicated; while the Vietnam War was far closer to home and much more dangerous.** ....■

World War I In spite of the trouble she had experienced at their hands in the colonial period, Thailand backed the British and French in the Great War. This was largely because King Vajiravudh had become an Anglophile, with many English friends from his years at the Sandhurst military college and at Christ Church, Oxford. The decision enabled Thailand to participate in the conference of Versailles in 1919 and to lobby effectively for the abolition of the unequal treaties with Western countries.

World War II saw fierce fighting going on in neighbouring countries and a seemingly unstoppable Japanese advance. There was no reason for Thailand to become involved in the European war, but

Thai soldiers help a released prisoner of war in Vietnam

Thailand and Japan had the distinction of being the only Asian countries to be independently represented at Versailles, and they had naturally formed some ties. When Japan sent her armies into China and Southeast Asia, attacking European colonies, the Thais had mixed feelings. The Japanese could hardly restrain themselves from occupying Thailand, after their success in Vietnam, and there was no effective British or French force available to protect Thailand. Temptingly, the Japanese offered to restore some of the territory which Thailand had had to give up to France earlier. The Thais actually had a short war with France in early 1941 and lost a naval engagement.

One of Phibul's advisers warned that Japan's intention was 'to chase away the white men from Asia and put itself in their shoes'. But Phibul's government declared war on the

Allies, though it allowed a degree of ambiguity as to whether the declaration had been effectively delivered to them. Thailand continued technically independent and sovereign throughout the war period.

The presence of more than 50,000 Japanese troops made it impossible for Phibul to act against Japan. All the same, he was no puppet: he would not enter the Japanese Co-Prosperity Sphere, or attend the Greater East Asia Conference, or

was defeated in 1945 a new pro-Allied government was able to take over in Bangkok. This was the moment for Pridi, who was able to persuade the Allies not to treat Thailand as an enemy, but almost as a friend. There was no formal occupation by the British army, as might have been expected.

The Vietnam War The Thais had already in 1954 joined Pakistan and the Philippines with the Western powers in the South East Asia Treaty

A US pilot makes contact

send his children for schooling in Japan. A measure of real independence was maintained. Meanwhile, Thais who disagreed

> << '...like a fox arbitrating a dispute between two rabbits in a cabbage patch, preparing to fatten them before eating both of them.' – An American critic of the Japanese offer.
> 'What would you do if you were a rabbit?' – A future Thai Prime Minister. >>

with the Axis alignment started a Free Thai Movement in the USA which linked with pro-Allied agents within Thailand, so that when Japan

Organisation, under which Thailand provided bases from which American bombers wreaked havoc on Vietnam in the 1960s and early 1970s. Thailand had little option but to join the United States in contesting Vietnamese Communism, which was loudly hostile to Thailand. The Queen's Cobra Regiment of Thailand actually served in South Vietnam, fighting the Communists. Yet Thailand's other neighbours were mostly neutral in the conflict.

When the Vietnam War ended in 1975 it was followed by the Vietnamese invasion of Cambodia. This was also a threat to Thailand, and the Thais collaborated in helping those resisting Vietnamese occupation, including the Khmer Rouge, whose brutal treatment of their own population shocked the world.

■ After the two dominating personalities of Pridi and Phibul came three more generals who tried to play the same role, though less successfully. Field-Marshal Sarit Thanarat was succeeded by the weaker Field-Marshal Thanom Kittikachorn and his portly, pugnacious deputy, Field-Marshal Praphas Charusathien. .....■

Field-Marshal Sarit Thanarat Sarit was half Laotian. He had the temerity to bundle Phibul out of the country, largely because the former dictator had interfered with Sarit's improper profits from the state lottery. In spite of his corruption, however, he proved to be rather popular. He reversed many of Phibul's unpopular reforms, including those dictating the style of dress; he even tried to bring down the prices of electricity, sugar, charcoal and other items. The Chinese were encouraged, during his dictatorship, to feel that they were an accepted part of Thai society. He brought the young King Bhumiphol forward and gave him a bigger role in public affairs – something which the King fully exploited – as a symbol of Thai nationalism and traditional culture. Sarit could also be tough: he closed down the weekly dance at the Lumphini Garden; arrested men with long hair, tight trousers or flashy clothes, made rock-and-roll and the twist illegal and ordered summary executions of arsonists.

Sarit often expounded the idea that democracy needed to be adapted to the Thai genius in order to succeed. Political parties were abolished. Sarit governed without a parliament and managed to postpone indefinitely the writing of a new constitution. He set a new precedent in Thailand for open army rule. He never studied abroad and did not share the ideals of those who promoted Western-style parliamentary democracy. His direction of the economy proved invaluable, since he turned away from the state-enterprise ideas of both Pridi and Phibul to encourage investment of private capital, both domestic and foreign. Sarit's First Six-Year Plan (1961) provided the basis for the economic development that was to astonish observers later. Everyone knew that Sarit had a strong appetite for sex, and that he had many mistresses. Only after his

<< Thanom's son, Narong, married Praphas's daughter and become particularly hated as a crude implementer of the dictators' commands. The three were nicknamed 'father, son and wholly gross'. >>

death in 1963, however, did it come out that he maintained 100 mistresses in great style, using illegal income from various official funds and using government influence for private financial gain. Sarit left an estate of US$140 million on his death, and everyone knew that it could not have come from his salary.

Field-Marshal Thanom Kittikachorn Sarit's successor was reticent by comparison. Under Thanom's rule, from 1963 to 1973, the army had to come to terms with the idea of a constitution. After many years of drafting, a new constitution was proclaimed by the King in 1968. This made the Prime Minister responsible to parliament, and a general election was held in 1969: Thanom's party won a majority. But the various parliamentarians were so demanding and so unwilling to collaborate with the government in administering the country, and there was such insurgency in the border

areas, that Thanom abrogated the constitution and proclaimed martial law in 1971.

Thanom and his deputy, Field-Marshal Praphas Charusathien, were then faced with renewed demands for democracy and a constitution, and this came to a head in a bloody confrontation in 1973.

The student rising in 1973 (see also pages 66–7) The students' revolt was sparked by the refusal of Premier Thanom's government to speed up the drafting of a new constitution. When 25 democrats protested near Thammasat University, half of them were arrested, and this brought 100,000 students into a rally and protest march to the police headquarters.

The explosion came on 14 October 1973, when the soldiers and students made bloody battle, leaving 69 dead and more than 800 wounded, while the police HQ was burnt down. Thanom and Praphas resigned, and were advised by the King to leave the country in order to prevent further violence.

The era of Thanom and Praphas was beneficial for Thailand in economic affairs and in many other respects. Sarit's policies were broadly followed especially within the economy. But a harmful precedent was created in asserting the army's right to rule, and it did nothing for the concept of clean government.

Field-Marshal Sarit Thanarat (centre), one of the Thai Generals

■   The students who had been so successful in 1973 sought to consolidate and extend their new-found power. They formed an alliance with workers and peasant groups, and also to some extent with the Communist Party of Thailand. The army leaders were demoralised by the exposure of corruption, and the new senior general showed no desire to enter government. The proliferation of political parties made democratic government ineffective. The King therefore filled the power vacuum. ....■

The King came into his own after Thanom and Praphas had fled, appointing as new Prime Minister a British-trained judge, Sanya Dharmasakdi. The first civilian head of government for more than two decades, he and the King between them organised a large National Convention to elect a new Legislative Assembly.

The students and workers were forming groups and unions without police registration, contrary to the law, but Sanya persevered and a general election was held at the beginning of 1975. The first elected Prime Minister under the new

An anti-Generals statement

constitution was Kukrit Pramoj, a minor royal who is also a brilliant editor and novelist. Kukrit's chief success was in diplomacy. He was the first Thai Premier to visit the People's Republic of China, where he secured the opening of diplomatic relations between the two countries. But his parliamentary support was unstable, and another election was held in 1976, which led to his elder brother, Seni Pramoj, becoming Prime Minister.

A rash of strikes broke out in factories, often supported by the students. In the rural areas, the new phenomenon of landless tenant farmers threw up peasant organisations to lobby for improvement. The Farmers' Federation of Thailand was set up with student help, to become a large and powerful body. In November 1974 about 50,000 students and farmworkers, led by young Buddhist monks, demonstrated in Bangkok. While the army had been willing to take a back seat in the political arena after the scandals of previous military dictators, it was greatly concerned by the growth of radical and sometimes Communist-influenced pressure groups in the country. The students seemed oblivious of the backlash which their actions were inviting.

Right-wing backlash Just as the students had sponsored new radical groups, so now right-wing military officers countered by sponsoring or supporting rightist movements.

Some of them had wide popular support in the middle class and lower-middle class. The most famous of these was the Red Gaurs, organised by the controversial Major-General Sudsai Hasdin, who commanded the Army's Internal Security Operations Command. The Red Gaurs became in effect a paramilitary group, recruiting former mercenaries who had fought against the Communists in Laos. Also among supporters for Red Gaur were vocational students in Bangkok, who had distanced

> **<<** A charismatic monk supported Navapol, preaching that it was not a sin to kill Communists. **>>**

themselves from the more radical university students, being more concerned about jobs than political ideals.

Another group was Navapol, also established by right-wing army officers. It stood for a commitment to the Thai monarchy, nation and Buddhism.

In 1974–5 the leadership of the farmers' movement was systematically assassinated, and in 1976 some 30 leading personalities of left-wing parties were killed. The 1976 elections produced a weak civilian coalition government which was not able to prevent the army from arranging for the former dictators, Thanom and Praphas, to return to Thailand.

Two students distributing posters for the expulsion of Thanom were arrested in September 1976, and later found hanged. This sparked large-scale student protest, and on 5 October a group of students staged a mock hanging to publicise the murder of their two comrades. On the next day large numbers of Navapol, Red Gaurs and other right-wing organisations launched an assault on Thammasat University.

Massacre Many students were brutally murdered. Some were lynched, burnt alive, beheaded or had their eyes gouged out. When the apparently gentle Thai turns nasty the results can be horrifying. This prompted yet another *coup d'état* by armed forces leaders, and the King installed as the new Prime Minister a strongly anti-Communist judge, Thanin Kraivixien.

The right-wing reaction to student radicalism now set in.

The 1973 uprising

■ **Judge Thanin turned out to be the most repressive Prime Minister in Thai history and was soon ousted by the army leaders, who put one of their own men, the pipe-smoking moderate General Kriangsak Chomanan, into the premiership. He could not retain the support of the army and stepped down in 1980. Another general, Prem Tinsulanonda, took over, and he was to transform the face of Thai politics entirely. ....■**

Judge Thanin was an ideological rightist who banned political parties and student groups, made strikes illegal, imposed strict censorship and made thousands of arbitrary arrests. He even ordered Thomas More's *Utopia* and George Orwell's books to be burnt. Many of the student leaders involved in the 1973 uprising now left Bangkok in fear of their lives. They went 'to the forest' (the jungle) to join Communist Party guerrillas. (See page 185.) There they

> << General Kriangsak Chomanan invited the returned leftist students to his house and cooked breakfast for them. >>

were disillusioned to find that the Communist leaders in Thailand were mostly Chinese, and ardent Maoists, many of whom could not even speak Thai. Eventually, when the fury of the right-wing backlash had subsided, most came home to Bangkok.

The 1982 bicentenary of the Chakri dynasty – one of Prem's public relations successes

During this period of right-wing backlash in the late 1970s, Thailand had to cope with the withdrawal of the Americans from Vietnam and the fall of South Vietnam, formerly capitalist, to Communist control. It was a time of nervousness and danger, because the Vietnamese Communists, free from engagement with US forces, were able to turn their attention to Laos and Cambodia on the Thai frontier.

When Thanin was ousted, **General Kriangsak Chomanan** came to power, and he returned to a more open style of government and removed many of the restrictions, even holding elections in 1979. But in spite of his efforts, General Kriangsak could not command the support of the army. He gave way to General Prem Tinsulanonda.

General Prem was no great intellect, and had no strong power base of his own apart from the support of some other generals. Instead, he offered a style of leadership which was calm and consensual. He began as a serving officer heading the government, and ended eight years later as a Prime Minister nominated by the elected National Assembly.

In the 1980s the Thai economy first began to sprint, especially from 1987, when Thais sensed that they could become the next Newly Industrialised Economy in Asia – and double-digit growth was maintained for four years running.

Perhaps the vital thing for Thailand was that General Prem listened to

the technocrats in the civil service and followed their advice, particularly about the economy. Prem brought his senior planners and Finance Ministry officials into regular consultation with private businessmen, under his own chairmanship, to resolve disputes between the private and public sectors which were harming the economy. He agreed to a substantial devaluation of the baht, something which is always difficult for non-economists to accept.

He did not lack rivals and enemies within the armed forces. Two *coup d'états* were attempted during his premiership, and many physical attacks made on him. When General Arthit Kamlang-ek opposed the baht devaluation and called Prem a liar Prem dismissed the army commander.

Prem's genial manner endeared him to almost everyone, from the King down to ordinary citizens. He ensured the success of the double celebration in 1982 of the bicentenary of the Chakri dynasty and of the foundation of the new capital at Bangkok. Both events heavily publicised the King. The royal gratitude was expressed when King Bhumiphol gave his personal protection to General Prem during one of the unsuccessful *coup* attempts. But the King was gravely ill in 1982, and out of public life for three months.

By allowing the constitutional political process to resume, providing him with an elected cabinet, Prem satisfied the liberals, while his stern attitude to crime and corruption pleased the right wing. This formula might have gone on for longer, but after almost a decade, one of the MPs threatened to reveal secrets of the bachelor Prem's private life. At that point he stood down, leaving the political parties in the National Assembly to find their own candidates.

Prem will take his place in history as the man who served as leader of a civilian administration longer than anyone else, and who gave technocrats their lead.

General Prem sings for Thai TV

■ **The man who stepped into Prem's shoes as Prime Minister in 1988 was a former cavalry general turned diplomat and businessman, Chatichai Choonhavan, leader of the Chart Thai party, which was the largest in the elected Assembly. For three years Chatichai set a rather different style of government from the passive Prem's. .....■**

Under Chatichai the economy began to develop rapidly, with 10 per cent annual growth and the private sector leading. It was no coincidence that businessmen occupied many of the party leadership and cabinet positions during the Chatichai era. Many new development projects were started, and there was fierce controversy about alleged corruption. By this time the amounts of money

Chatichai (above), and his former Deputy Prime Minister, General Chaovalit Yongchaiyudh (below)

involved in election-time vote-buying and bribery had multiplied. The political parties needed more and more funds to be sure of doing well in elections, and ministerial corruption – a bribe in return for official approval of a big project – was the easiest way to get them. The army in particular urged changes in the constitution to make elected MPs resign their seats if they joined the cabinet.

Coup In February 1991 the army leadership united to depose Chatichai, complaining of his bad treatment of the army and army interests, as well as the corruption that was rife in his cabinet. In the early morning of Saturday, 23 February 1991, soldiers left their barracks to take control of key government buildings. In most cases they numbered only 50, or even less. They were not resisted, there was no fighting, and no blood was shed. Prime Minister Chatichai was arrested later that morning. There was no struggle and the Premier was later released unharmed but left for exile in England.

That afternoon, the Supreme Commander announced the total seizure of power by his armed forces. The constitution, Senate and House of Representatives were all summarily abolished. In the evening General Sunthorn and his deputy,

<< The Supreme Commander of the armed forces was well known for his tight-fitting uniforms and passion for flying helicopters. >>

General Suchinda, flew north to explain their action to the King. The King endorsed the *coup* in a slightly lukewarm manner, though he apparently sympathised with the criticisms of the civilian government's corruption. Yet he recalled Premier Chatichai from England to present him with a royal honour, and afterwards the military junta gathered at Chatichai's house to pour holy water over his hands for the Thai New Year, in the customary tradition.

Chatichai and other politicians were later investigated for corruption, but the special investigators appointed by the military junta could not find the evidence they wanted and the matter was turned over to the civilian courts.

The army installed a caretaker government under an ex-bureaucrat, Anand Panyarachun, and he in turn named a cabinet of technocrats and businessmen. Free from political

commander and Deputy Prime Minister in the Chatichai government. NAP became the third largest party, with 72 seats in the new 1992 parliament. Other senior army officers organised another party (Samakki Tham) These officers were the real brains behind the 1991 *coup* although ostensibly they had been supporting General Suchinda Kraprayoon. The Samakki Tham won 78 seats in the 1992 elections, to become the biggest in the House of Representatives. The Chart Thai

General Suchinda Kraprayoon

pressures, this administration was able to clear some of the backlog of difficult decisions left by Chatichai. The military junta held elections in March 1992 under a new constitution, and army generals formed political parties to contest them. One party (New Aspiration Party) was the creation of General Chaovalit Yongchaiyudh, former army

party of Sombun Rahong opted to make common cause with the group of generals around Suchinda. It came second in 1992 with 73 seats. Within months, demonstrators were filling the streets of Bangkok to call for a democratically chosen prime minister, rather than one named by the military. The ensuing violent clashes between army and protestors made headlines around the world.

BANGKOK

0   1/2   1   1 1/2 km
0   1/2   1 mile

BANG PHAT

Kblong Sam Sen
NAKHON CHAISI
KRUNG THON BRIDGE
RATCHAWITHI ROAD
SAMSEN ROAD
Kblong
Mae Nam Chao Praya
Kblong
CHARAN SANITWONG ROAD
PRAPINKLAO ROAD
Kblong Bang Yikhan
Bang Yikhan

National Library
Wimanmek Palace
National Assembly
Dusit Zoo
Chit Pal
RAMA ROAD

Bank of Thailand
SI AYUTTHAYA ROAD
King Chulalongkorn State

Khlong Bangkok Noi
Wat Suwannaram
Royal Barges
PHRA PINKLAO BRIDGE
Wat Indraviharn
PHITSANULOK ROAD
Wat Benchamabo
RATCHADAMNOEN ROAD
RATCHADAMNOEN ROAD

CHAKRAPHONG RD
WISUTKASAT RD
National Gallery

Govt House
Royal Tu Club

ARUN AMARIN ROAD
BANGKOK NOI
PHRAN NOK ROAD
Thonburi Station
National Theatre
Thamasat University
Sanam Luang
National Museum
Wat Mahathat
Silapakorn University
Wat Phra Keo
Grand Palace
Lak Muang Shrine
SANAM CHAI RD
MAHARAJ RD

Ratchadamnoen Boxing Stadium
Tourist Office
LANLUANG ROAD

RATCHADAMNOEN KLANG RD
Wat Rajanada
Giant Swing
Democracy Monument
Golden Mount (Wat Saket)
LANLUANG ROAD
MAHACHAI RD
WORACHAK RD
RATCHADAMNOEN
Phadung

CHARAN SANITWONG ROAD
ISARAPHAP ROAD
Kblong Mon
Wat Arun (Temple of Dawn)
WANG DOEM RD
Wat Kalayanimit

BAMRUNG MUANG RD
Wat Suthat
Wat Rajabophit
CHAROEN
Wat Pho
Khlong
TRIPHET RD
Nakorn Kasem
KRUNG KASEM
Chinatown (Yaowarat)
KRUNG KASEM ROAD
Kblong
Phdung

PHRA BUDDHA YOTFA (MEMORIAL BRIDGE)
PRACHA THIPOK ROAD
CHAKKRAWAT RD
PHRA POKKLAO BRIDGE
YAOWARAT ROAD
KRUNG ROAD
Mae Nam Chao Praya
Wat Traimit
Hualamp Main Stat
Bangko Centre
MAHA PHRU THARAM RD

Kblong Bangkok Yai
SOMDET CHAO PHRAYA RD
CHAROEN
SIPHA

PHET-CHAKASEM ROAD
INTRAPHITHAK ROAD
Kblong Bang Sai Kai
LATYA ROAD
GPO
SURAW
KRUNG ROAD

THA PHRA TAKSIN ROAD
TAKSIN ROAD
Wongwain Yai Station
WONGWIAN YAI
KRUNG THONBURI ROAD
Bangrak Market
SIP
Kblong Samre
TAKSIN BRIDGE
TALAT PHLU
KHLONG SAN
Wat Yannawa

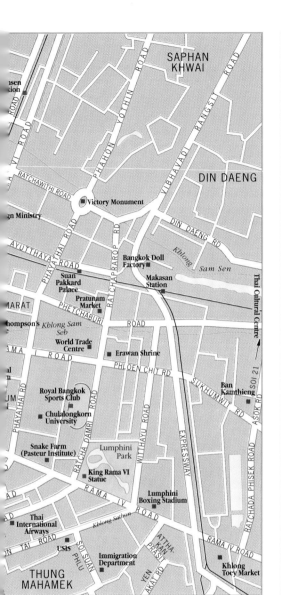

BANGKOK

SAPHAN KHWAI

DIN DAENG

...sen ...tion

...n Ministry

Victory Monument

RATCHAWITHI ROAD

AYUTTHAYA ROAD

DIN DAENG RD

Khlong Sam Sen

Bangkok Doll Factory

Makasan Station

Suan Pakkard Palace

Pratunam Market

PHETCHABURI

Thai Cultural Centre

MARAT

...hompson's ...e

Khlong Sam Seb

World Trade Centre

ROAD

Erawan Shrine

RAMA I ROAD

PHLOEN CHIT RD

SUKHUMVIT RD

ASOK RD

SOI 21

Ban Kamthieng

Royal Bangkok Sports Club

Chulalongkorn University

WITTHAYU ROAD

EXPRESSWAY

RATCHADA PHISEK ROAD

Snake Farm (Pasteur Institute)

Lumphini Park

RATCHA DAMRI ROAD

King Rama VI Statue

Lumphini Boxing Stadium

RAMA IV ROAD

Thai International Airways

Khlong Sathon

USIS

SOI SUAN PHLU

Immigration Department

ATTHA KAN PRASIT

YEN AKAT RD

Khlong Toey Market

THUNG MAHAMEK

Lumphini Park

▶ ▶ ▶ BANGKOK

Sometimes it is hard to find a good word to say about Bangkok. The air is thick and the roads clog up with traffic. The oppressive heat is unrelieved by trees or greenery and after walking for half an hour you can become seriously dehydrated. Visitors ask themselves how it is possible to live like this.

Yet amazingly a great many people come to love the place – or at least to develop a love-hate relationship with it. The basic rule to beat the heat is to remain calm. Bangkok does have its cool oases, and it is the focal point for the rest of Thailand, with which most people get on famously.

Contrasts Unlike old-established Western capitals, Bangkok has the exhilarating feeling of growth at a breakneck pace. The population will smash through the 10 million barrier in less than a decade and foreign capital moves freely, creating employment. All of this contibutes to Bangkok's charm. It is a modern city

where almost anything can be obtained, and at the same time it has a strong sense of history and an unmistakable identity.

The dark side to this is evident in the acres of leaky timber shacks that form a vista from the expressway as it flies over Khlong Toey port. The people are cheerfully resilient; out of the tourist areas they will always smile and say hello. The phrase *ot thon*, 'to endure' finds an equivalent in the Buddhist lexicon, *ubekha*, 'equanimity'

Bangkok may be relatively young – just over two centuries – but it has a firm foundation in the heritage of the ancient city of golden Ayutthaya. The official name, 'Krungthep Manakhorn' (Bangkok Metropolis) once prefixed Ayutthaya's name. The sumptuous spires and roofs of the Grand Palace are Thailand's best-known symbol to the outside world; this section will guide you through the major monuments one by one.

But Bangkok is not just about monuments, it is vibrant, alive and full of hope. It gives a strange feeling that anything might be possible – and it usually is.

Bangkok is still growing fast, and its traffic grows at the same pace – making life in the city dirty and dangerous

Temples and Shrines

▶▶ Arun, Wat

Arun Amarin Road

The 'Temple of Dawn' is built on the site of Wat Chang, the focus of King Taksin's Thonburi. Taksin was paranoid about his status as an outsider king and alienated the court, who had him executed. King Rama III raised the main *prang* (tower) to its present height of 104m.

The locals frighten their children with a tale of the guardian *yaksha* of *wats* Arun and Po slugging it out in the Chao Phraya.

As you come up the river, the glittering tower is an impressive sight. Nowadays dwarfed by skyscrapers, there is still an interesting view from halfway up the main *prang*, reached by a very steep and narrow staircase. A representation of Mt Meru, the centre of traditional Indian cosmologies, it depicts the first 33 heavens immediately above it. The four small accompanying *prangs* are dedicated to Phra Phai, the god of the wind. Mosaics made of broken Chinese porcelain cover the *prangs*.

A pavilion in the compound has images of important stages in Buddha's life: birth, enlightenment, the first five disciples and his death or Parinibbana.

It is probably best reached by *reua kham fak* (river ferry) from Tha Tien.

Open: daily.

◀◀◀ Benchamabophit, Wat

Si Ayutthaya Road

Built of Carrara marble, this is also known as the 'Marble Temple', and is the last *wat* of comparable size with Arun to go up in the modern era (1901). As at Wat Niwet Thamprawat, King Rama V commissioned stained glass representations of Thai and Buddhist themes. The main image is a copy of the reputedly flawless *Phra Phuttha Chinnarat*, the original of which is to be found in Phitsanulok.

The most interesting aspect of the temple is its bronze Buddha images – 53 of them line an inner courtyard.

The temple is easily found on Si Ayutthaya Road near Chitralada Palace, and could usefully fit in a day tour to Wimanmek and/or Dusit Zoo.

Open: daily. Admission charge.

◀ Erawan Shrine

Ploen Chit Road

The Erawan Shrine, at a busy crossroads on Ploen Chit Road, is always milling with people. They come here to seek favour of the Brahmin god, Phra Pom; such favours may be as simple as help with winning a lottery. There is a resident dance troupe which starts performing at 07.00hrs and many of the supplicants commission the dancers to give a performance by way of an offering.

Spirits were said to inhabit the site of the shrine, which was built in 1956 at the same time as the Erawan Hotel – which has now been demolished and replaced with a much larger, modern structure.

Grand Palace see pages 79–81.

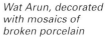

Wat Arun, decorated with mosaics of broken porcelain

Indraviharn

Wisut Kasat Road

Wat Indraviharn (full name Wat Indra Mavasihara) on Wisut Kasat Road has a huge (32m) statue of a standing Buddha. There is also a lifelike image of Luang Phor To, cradling his alms bowl and housed in an air-conditioned, hollowed-out *stupa*. Only a short bus ride north from Banglamphu (western end of Khao San Road) into Sam Sen Road.

Mahathat, Wat

Sanam Luang

This extensive wat of the mid-Victorian era is centrally located on the west side of Sanam Luang and extends back to Maharaj Road and the river. The home of Mahachulalongkorn Buddhist University, it is also renowned as a place where lay people can go to get instruction in meditation.The higgledy-piggledy *kuti* or monks' quarters make up most of the floor area.

What makes it especially worth visiting is the market which is held here on *wan phra*, the Buddhist holy days (full, new and half moons), although unfortunately the future of the market may be in doubt. Stalls offering herbal medicines, old Buddhas and symbolic figures jostle with strange foods and fortune-tellers. Outside, by Sanam Luang, conjurors perform bizarre acts, such as putting nails into their cheeks.

Open: daily, 09.00 – 17.00hrs

People gather round the Lucky Sara Tree (Buddha's Birth Tree) at Wat Mahathat

BANGKOK TEMPLES AND SHRINES

► ▶ ▷▷ **Lak Muang**

Sanam Luang

Variously named the 'City Axis' or 'City Pillar', Lak Muang dates from the time of the city's foundation when Bangkok was only a village. This pillar, protected by a little shrine, is over the road from the east wall of Wat Phra Keo and was originally erected by Rama I to commemorate the establishment of the new capital city. The symbolism for such pillars is multifold, the Sivaic *lingam* or phallus being very important. It is difficult to recognise the pillar's origins, however, since it is covered in gilt, as well as flowers and other offerings.

Likay performers – classical Thai dancers – are available to be commissioned to perform by Thai worshippers. As part of the ceremony the people read their fortunes with the *siem sii* and light the obligatory joss sticks and candles to put themselves in the right mood.

There is a public park near the shrine, as well as several ministries, the Defence Ministry easily spotted by the cannon outside at Sanam Luang's southeastern corner.

Wat Pathum Wan

► ▶ ▷▷ **Pathum Wan, Wat**

Siam Square

Situated on the banks of the Chao Phraya, in Pathumthani, this cultural diversion and peaceful oasis from the modern mêlée of Siam Square is worth a visit for its entertaining murals. The story of Sri Thanonchai, the artful trickster, takes up the lower walls. The upper walls, meanwhile, show the stately procession of royal barges in the rare royal *krathin* ceremony.

Siam Square is a gathering place for university youth, drawn by the movie theatres and bookshops. The British Council library recreates perfectly the instantly recognisable ambience of an English municipal library.

▶ ▶ ▶ **The Grand Palace and Wat Phra Keo**
Sanam Chai Road
Nowadays open to an endless stream of visitors, the Grand Palace was once a city within a city, residence and last bastion of the Chakri dynasty. It covers 218,400sq m and the perimeter walls are 1.9km long. Each of the Ramas from I to VI added his own buildings. The principal elements are described below.

The harem Guarded by women, no men apart from the King had any right to enter, on pain of severe punishment. Anna Leonowens' books (see page 56), give a rare inside picture of the harem, which played an important role in feudal politics.
Unlike the characters in the fanciful production *The King and I*, Leonowens' books present an intellectual woman, with a dry sense of humour. Although the harem was disbanded and the King moved out to Chitralada, the buildings still stand, and some still have important ceremonial functions.

The seated Buddha at Wat Phra Keo

Wat Phra Keo (The Chapel Royal) This is the building containing the image of the **Emerald Buddha** (see below), the holiest shrine in all Thailand. The chapel was completed in 1784 and is unique among Thai temples in having no resident monks; it also functions as the monarch's private chapel. To that end there is a partition to either side of the image that serves as a retiring room. Murals inside the chapel depict Buddha's life, besides medieval cosmology and stories of the Buddha's former lives.

The Emerald Buddha was discovered in 1464 when a lightning bolt hit a temple in Chiang Rai. It remained in the possession of the northern Lanna kingdom until a Lao king was offered the vacant Lanna throne – from there it went to Wiang Jan (Vientiane) in Laos. When Chao Phya Chakri, later to become King Rama I, made an expedition to Vientiane, the small, green jade image was the prize among the spoils.

Note: the image is only open to public view on certain days of the week.

A curiosity just outside the chapel is a model of Cambodia's famous Angkor Wat, built by King Rama IV. Next to it are the Royal Pantheon (1903), the large *chedi* (pagodas where holy relics are kept) modelled on Phra Si Sanphet, Ayutthaya, and the Repository of Scripture.

The compound is an eclectic and dazzling jumble that some have called the 'Siamese Disneyland'. Statues of white elephants vie with the reliquary *chedis* and mythological giants (*yuk*) and the half-bird, half-woman *kinnaree*. The entire epic story of the *Ramakian* is depicted in mural form along the galleries which enclose the chapel compound.

In the palace itself, the audience hall of Amarindra is open to view. It is part of the 'Mahamonthien' where kings are crowned in the room that is home to the country's guardian spirit, *Phra Siam Deva Dhi Raj*. Behind that is the Chakrabardiman, where kings traditionally stay the night after their coronation.

The audience hall of the Dusit Maha Prasa was the first brick building in the compound, completed in 1789. It is a cruciform plan of pure Siamese design, where kings lie in state.

The Chakri palace (1882) is of architectural interest for its efforts to combine Western and traditional Siamese styles (a trend taken to greater extremes at Bang Pa-In, Ayutthaya). King Chulalongkorn, the creator of all this whimsy, conceived the Italian colonnades. A conservative faction at court insisted on the Thai roofs. The spires hold royal ashes; kings in the middle, princes to the left.

Galleries depict diplomatic endeavours of the past, such as missions exchanged between King Narai and King Louis XIV of France, and King Rama IV's delegation to Queen Victoria. Today, foreign ambassadors present their credentials here to the King.

The Grand Palace Museum, a stone building to the northeast of the palace complex, provides invaluable explanations of the methods used in the construction and restoration of the various monuments. Upstairs an array of artefacts can be contemplated in air-conditioned

The Emerald Buddha's robes are changed three times a year by the King to symbolise the passing of the seasons – cool, hot and rainy. Many of the yearly rites such as the ploughing ceremony (see page 94) start with his blessing.

The Temple of the Emerald Buddha

A temple guard (above) and a young Buddhist (below) at Wat Phra Keo

silence. These include two detailed models which give a startling pictur e of how the palace has been changed and added to in the course of its 200-year history.

Visiting heads of state might banquet at the Sala Sahathai and stay in the Boromabiman building, which was richly decorated by King Rama VI with a square dome and the written listing of the 'ten kingly virtues'

Numismatists may be interested in the **Coins and Royal Decorations Museum** near the ticket office. Exhibits date from the 11th century onwards.

Open: The Grand Palace: daily, 08.30–12.00 and 13.00–15.30hrs; The Chapel Royal compound: daily to 16.00hrs (tickets also gain access to Wimanmek Palace); Coins and Royal Decorations Museum: daily to 15.30hrs. Admission charge.

The 10 kingly virtues: Giving, ethics, self-sacrifice, honesty, humility, concentration, patience, avoidance of wrong-doing, non-anger and non-violence.

*A Chinese guard,
Wat Pho*

▶ ▶ **Pho, Wat (Wat Phra Chetuphon)**
South of the Grand Palace
This large *wat* of 16th-century foundation took about 12 years for King Rama I to restore in the 1780s. Many come from far and wide to see the massive reclining Buddha, 46m long. The mother-of-pearl inlay on the feet represents the 108 marks whereby a Buddha is recognised.
More mother-of-pearl is used on the chapel doors to depict scenes from the Thai epic *Ramakien*, also shown on Ayutthaya-period tapestries that were literally snatched from the flames when the city was destroyed by the Burmese in 1767. Rubbings are sold of the sandstone bas-reliefs around the chapel's base.
Inscriptions and treatises on medicine, botany and massage are left over from a host of other subjects formerly on public view, which earned this *wat* the epithet 'great storehouse of knowledge', and made it a forerunner of the modern university.
Herbal medicine is still practised and taught here and Wat Pho counts as the foremost institution in the training of Thai masseurs and masseuses. By the east wall is a massage area where anyone feeling aches and pains can try the Wat Pho version, which costs around 140 baht per hour (see page 47) .
Open: daily, 08.00–17.00hrs. Admission charge.

▶ ▶ **Rajabophit, Wat**
Off Atsadang Road
A fair way south of the Lak Muang, this *wat* of radical circular architecture was built around 1870 by King Rama V or Chulalongkorn. The tall, gilded *chedi* is in a concentric cloister, and both are decorated with porcelain and chandeliers. Inside, the Buddha image is seated on a naga or dragon-headed serpent, which originated in Lop Buri.
The bot (chapel) has mother-of-pearl doors and windows bearing the insignia of the five royal ranks conferred by the king. The interior is vaulted and four chapels lead off from the central gallery. All in all this is an unusual and interesting *wat*.
Open : 08.00hrs–20.00hrs.

▶ **Rajanada, Wat**
Off Mahachai Road
An otherwise ordinary 19th-century *wat*, this temple is distinguished for its amulet market. The amulets or *phra phim* depict images of the Buddha and also Thai deities and the more prominent or famous monks.
The amulets reputedly have magic powers and can protect the wearer – the more expensive ones are worn by soldiers and these can cost thousands of baht, although not all come so dear. There are various classes of amulet, each with its own special purpose: some are love amulets; some have many eyes to protect the wearer from all directions. This is not the cheapest place to buy any type of amulet, which are often made of terracotta and are usually worn around the neck on a gold or a silver chain.
Open: daily.

► ► **Saket, Wat**

Off Worachak Road

Once a charnel house, after a plague which claimed 30,000 lives in the reign of King Rama II, this *wat* is distinguished by the 80m-tall Phu Khao Thong (Golden Mount), which was started by King Rama III. Rama IV had 1,000 teak logs piled into the foundations to prevent it from collapsing because the underlying ground was too soft to support the structure.

The *chedi* was added in 1863 by Rama V and relics were brought from Nepal in 1897, a gift of the British viceroy. The spire is worth the climb – the view from the top affords a surprisingly panoramic vista over the Bangkok rooftops and beyond.

Every November there is a large festival in the grounds of this *chedi*, during which there .is a candle-lit procession up the Golden Mount. Food stalls and stage shows appear by the dozen and the mount is lit up with different coloured lights.

Open: daily. Admission free (charge for summit of the Golden Mount).

Elaborate symmetry at the 19th-century Wat Rajanada, site of an amulet market

▶▶ Suthat, Wat

Facing the Giant Swing

Look closely at the doors here: they are said to have been personally carved by King Rama II. There are some Jataka murals of an informal style, but most notable is the 8m-tall main Buddha image, which comes from ruined Wat Mahathat in Sukhothai and was brought down the river by King Rama I. The peculiar statues of generals, scholars and sailors were brought in as ballast for Chinese rice hulks.

The *bot* (chapel) is reputedly the tallest in Bangkok and the *wiharn*, where the sacred objects are kept, is also very large.

Reclining at the feet of Wat Suthat's Golden Buddhas

Giant Swing Wat Suthat's most famous asset is the Sao Ching Cha or Giant Swing. Every January up until the 1940s men would grab for bags of gold off a 15m pole in an often fatal Sivaic rite. The place where people used to hit the deck is now the 'land of pigeons', with a Brahmin temple (Wat Suthat) opposite.

Open: The *wiharn* is open 09.00–17.00hrs, weekends and public holidays only.

▶▶ Traimit, Wat

East of junction between Yaowarat and Charoen roads

This *wat*, said to date from the 13th century, is a good place to visit if you have a three-hour wait for a train from nearby Hualamphong Station. Bags can be checked in at left luggage, and the Wat Traimit is a short stroll away down the road of the same name.

Vendors and schoolchildren crowd the entrance where the star exhibit, the Golden Buddha, is marked with signposts and a small entry fee is collected. This Buddha is the largest solid gold image in the country; if it were melted down its five and a half tons would be worth US$14 million at today's prices. Its discovery is said to have been an accident. Like many valuable images in times of warfare and civil strife, it had been camouflaged in stucco. Only some 30 years ago the image was rediscovered when the casing cracked while the image was being moved by crane.

Open: 09.00–17.00hrs. Admission charge.

Chinatown

■ **The Chinese quarter in Bangkok is of huge size and influence, tracing its beginnings to a river-station – Bangkok – used for the building of Krung Thep. The identity of the Chinese Thais is blurred by intermarriage and assimilation, but most are only a few generations removed from the original immigrant *Tia* (Father). The predominant group speak *tae-jiw*, a branch of Cantonese, although Hokkien is also important. Around the turn of the century, the Chinese quarter gained a reputation for vice. .....■**

Yaowarat Road, with its forest of Chinese signs, could be taken for Hong Kong or Singapore. Off the busy thoroughfare are timeless alleys and elaborate temples. Gold shops abound and others sell gaudy paraphernalia such as paper houses and the Benzes burnt in the Kong Teck ceremony. Old men hang around the tea-houses.

Because of the debilitating heat, the area is best explored on foot as the one-way system is a nightmare. Soi Wanit 1 to the south – better known as Sampheng – runs parallel to Yaowarat. Wat Patuma ,at its eastern end, was once the royal execution ground. Continue east to the old market, *talat gao*. This is an early morning experience. Ancient Wat Chakrawat, with its pond of crocodiles, is about halfway along Sampheng.

North from the old market is a new version, set up along Soi Issaraphap, which also leads to Wat Mangkon Kamalawat (Neng Noi Yee) on Charoen Krung (New) Road. This is the largest Mahayana temple in Bangkok ,where laity can consult oracles and worship the Buddha Matreiya. A glimpse of the classically proportioned and decorated monks' quarters is permitted. Mayanist monks are vegetarian and do not collect alms.

Turn right down Plapachai Road behind this temple to reach Li Thi Miew. This is a Taoist shrine decorated in ancient style. Yaowarat is also home to the 'Thieves'

Market', up Boriphat Road near the canal. Soi Wanit leads across the canal to Pahurat, Bangkok's Indiatown ,which is famous for its textile markets.

Catching up with the news in Chinatown

In Jim Thompson's House (see opposite) every room contains a treasure. Look out for a 6th-century Buddha image in the study and a cute Chinese 'mouse house' in the bedroom. The shop is highly recommended for its authentic souvenirs: paintings of Siamese cats, the rice goddess – even the whole Thai zodiac.

▶ ▷▷▷ **Ban Khamthieng**

131 Soi Asoke (Soi 21)

This fine old house is headquarters of the Siam Society, a scholarly organisation devoted to researching obscure aspects of Thai culture. Their journal is a widely respected source material for academic writing of all disciplines. An invaluable venue for any serious study of Thailand, there is a reference library and books on sale. Originally constructed in Chiang Mai some 200 years ago, Kamthieng House was moved to Bangkok in the 1920s and rebuilt on its present site in attractive grounds.

There is also a museum of folk art, covering areas not represented in the national museum; exhibits tend to concentrate on humble aspects of daily life such as fishing and cooking.

Open: Tuesday to Saturday, 09.00–12.00hrs; 13.00–17.00hrs. Admission charge.

▶ ▷▷▷ **Bangkok Doll Factory**

85/2 Soi Rachada Phan

Bangkok Doll Factory is situated on Soi Rachada Phan, winding down the *soi* 800m from Rajaprarop Road. It is entirely the creation of Khunying Thongkorn Chanvimol, who set up the current factory and showroom in 1961.

The attached international dolls' museum has over 700 exhibits which demonstrate the doll-maker's craft. Khunying Thongkorn has specialised in miniature representations of Thai life, from the colourful hill tribes to tableaux from the classics of Thai literature.

The delicate figurines are hand-made from cloth and painstakingly detailed. They have received royal favour as gifts for foreign dignitaries. The most famous subjects are the *Khon* dancers, whose distinctive painted masks in small scale have become popular in their own right.

Commissions and special occasions have, on the other hand, produced representations of figures as diverse as Miss Universe and the Pope. Other interesting themes covered include rural life, the history of Thai dress, the national dress of neighbouring countries, various regional dances and a host of others.

Check about opening hours and the details of special exhibitions on 245-3008.

▷▷▷ **Chitladda Palace**

Sri Ayutthaya Road

This is the official residence of His Majesty the King: casual visitors are not welcome, and soldiers will not hesitate to shoot on sight. The wooden palace itself is sited in the middle of spacious grounds and is therefore virtually invisible from the road.

All in all, a disappointment. However, the imposing moat around the compound cannot be missed.

▷▷▷ **Dusit**

This area around the National Assembly contains Thailand's 'corridors of power', being HQ to the powerful defence establishment. It is, unlike the rest of the city, spread out and leafy. The imposing Ananta

Samakhom throne hall, formerly the parliament building, has a big dome. Behind it is the current parliament, while next door is the city's main zoo – **Khao Din**. It is more of a park than a zoo, and the entrance fee is modest.

Another public resort in the vicinity is **Suan Amphorn Gardens**, frequently the site of exhibitions.

▶ ▶ ▶ Jim Thompson's House

Soi Kasem San 2, off Rama I Road, opposite the National Stadium

This is well hidden at the end of Soi Kasem San 2, but a delightful surprise awaits. This remarkable haven, overlooking a characterful if odour-laden canal, is one of the most appealing places in Bangkok.

The former owner, Jim Thompson, is something of a local legend. Arriving with the US Army in 1945, he soon adopted Thailand as his permanent home. He made both name and riches promoting Thai silk, but his interest was in the Thai fine arts, as these buildings, his monument, attest.

The ingenious structure, cobbled together out of six old red teak structures, is a series of small rooms, with a surprise in each. The place has bags of charm and the personality of its former owner still pervades. The collection is an outstanding one and a lesson in good taste.

Open: Monday to Friday, 09.00–16.30hrs. Guided tours in English. All admission fees are donated to good causes.

Fine arts at Jim Thompson's House

BANGKOK OTHER SIGHTS

▶ ░░░ Lumphini Park
Between Rama IV and Sarasin roads
A smallish green lung at the meeting of 'port' and 'downtown' – Lumphini, named after the Buddha's birthplace, is distingushed for a standing statue of King Rama VI at its southwestern corner.

By day it is pleasant enough, with a fitness and recreation park used for *tai-chi*, jogging and *tagraw* (see pages 110–13). There is also a boating lake. It is one of the places that stops moving when the national anthem is played at 08.00hrs and 18.00hrs.

Beware of it at night, however, when the story is different – the dark acres are irresistible to the violent and seedy element from Patpong to the south and Sarasin to the north.

▶ ▶ ▶ Pipitaphan (National Museum)
Off the Na Phra That Road to the north of Sanam Luang, by Thamasat University.
A few baht will get you into this treasure trove of art and culture. Try to arrive by 09.00hrs to take advantage of one of the guided tours which are provided at no extra charge and are excellent.

The nucleus of the collection was first put on show in 1874, and was organised seriously as a national collection from 1933. The museum is housed in several different buildings, themselves fine examples of Thai architecture.

The oldest buildings in the compound date from the 1780s and were built as a palace for the second or deputy king. When the office of second king was abolished by King Rama V, the buildings were given over to become a museum.

The palace originally included an extensive park, which covered most of what are now the northern grounds.

The Pavilions The main acreage is spread out in pavilions behind the **Buddhaisawan Chapel** (1795-7). Built by the second king for his personal use, the chapel contains formal murals depicting 28 scenes from the Buddha's life. The main image, **Phra Buddha Sihing**, is anointed in the official celebrations of Songkran in April.

Halls behind the chapel are devoted to various themes; the large **Atsaraavinitchai Pavilion** is used for travelling and other temporary exhibitions. The emphasis is on artefacts and arts from Siamese history. Gold, palanquins, shadow puppets, ceramics, mother-of-pearl, ivory, weapons, royal regalia, stone inscriptions, wood-carving, textiles, Buddhist utensils and musical instruments each have their own room among the sprawling whitewashed cloisters. Of the ceramics, there are Chinese (Ming Dynasty) examples and native Thai Benjarong (five-coloured) ware.

The rear porch of this hall has models of ships and a large doll's house. One prize exhibit is a model train presented to King Rama IV by Queen Victoria. The Textile Hall has examples of classical Thai patterns, including those picked out with gold thread. A portico at the end of this hall has some delicate silk embroidery – pictures of In-Jan, the original Siamese twins.

Lumphini Park: a pleasure by day, a danger by night

The **Mahasurasinghanat Building**, to the left of the main structure, is devoted to pre-Thai art and work of non-Thai civilisations. The Mon-Indic culture of Lop Buri is to the fore, along with art from Dvaravati sites. The Mon are presumed heirs of Dvaravati culture, which appears to have been a peace-loving society occupying the Chao Phya basin some 900 years ago.

Meanwhile in the south, the Javanese influence , as yet untamed by Islam, was very strong. Sumatra next door was centre of the Srivijayan empire which overran the Malay peninsula, leaving a wake of cultural objects across southern Thailand.

The **Prapas Pipitaphan**, to the right, tells the story from the 13th- to 14th-century kingdoms of Lanna (Chiang Mai) and Sukothai onwards. The introduction of writing had meant that Thai history could at last begin to be recorded. Various alliances and royal houses contested

'The ruler does not collect *jagthor*p (a Khmer tax)' – Part of the inscription of King Ramkhamhaeng of Sukhothai from which, it is said, the Thai script is derived.

89

the supremacy of Siam.

Of course Siamese art reached its high point in the Ayutthaya period, and although temporarily subdued by the Burmese, arose phoenix-like in the early Bangkok period. This hall also has special sections for coins and Buddha images.

Sivamokkhaphiman Pavilion is the main building and houses the proudest exhibit – the 1283 inscription of King Ramkhamhaeng of Sukhothai setting forth the prospectus of the Thai nation. It is referred to by some as the first Thai constitution.

Bangkok's National Museum

Suan Pakkard Palace

A smaller gallery of Thai prehistory is located here at the back of the same building. The most interesting exhibits here are the Bronze-Age whorl-patterned pots produced by the Ban Chiang civilisation, and also some unusually shaped Stone Age vessels.

Other small buildings are scattered across the compound. A fine collection of cremation chariots has its own pavilion on the right and a Chinese house of the court service is tucked away behind exhibits of Thai art.
Also of interest is the Red House, or Tamnak Daeng, which was once the residence of the older sister of King Rama I. Once upon a time it was situated in the grounds of the Grand Palace, and nowadays it is home to a collection of furniture which was once used by royalty.
A small bookshop in the foyer of the main gallery of Thai history has many titles in English explaining the exhibits. Guided tours in English start at 09.00hrs. Thai art and culture (Tuesday), Buddhism (Wednesday) and pre-Thai art (Thursday).
Open: 09.00–16.00hrs. Closed for lunch. Admission charge.

 **Suan Pakkard Palace**

352 Si Ayutthaya Road

A convenient *tuk tuk* ride from Pratunam, 'the cabbage garden' is Bangkok's serious rival, in sightseeing terms, to Jim Thompson's House. Five traditional houses were brought here in the 1920s by Princess Chumbhot Nagara Svarga and set in a landscaped garden.

The main reason to visit must be the splendid lacquer pavilion, which was discovered in Ayutthaya, its inner walls portraying the life of the Buddha, among other themes.

Other noteworthy exhibits are the gold and lacquer manuscript cabinets besides a good collection of Ban Chiang pottery and Khmer statuary.

Open: 09.00–16.00hrs. Admission charge.

▶ ▶ ▶ **Thonburi**

Wongwien Yai

The best way to see Thonburi is undoubtedly by canal.

The floating market in Wat Sai, Bang Khun Thien district, was the first to attract tourists and has now become commercialised; permanent shops have been set up along the banks, which would seem to contradict the 'floating' spirit.

There are long-tailed boats to this market from near Wat Arun; tours are often advertised in local hotel lobbies. Wat Arun is Thonburi's main attraction.

The left bank at Thonburi is gradually assuming the character of the modern day Bangkok. Ribbon development along main Charan Sanitwong Road parallel to the river, has many market gardens behind it; Wongwien Yai (Big Roundabout) boasts an impressive statue of King Taksin, Thonburi's founder. The immediate environs, the narrow streets, canal bridges and *wats* preserve much atmosphere from King Taksin's temporary capital.

91

A victim of commercialisation: Thonburi Floating Market

▶ ▶ ▶ Wimanmek Palace (Phra Thi Nang Wimanmek)

On Ratchawithi Road by the National Assembly

'The palace in the clouds', is claimed to be the world's largest structure made entirely of golden teak and contains over 80 rooms. On the orders of King Chulalongkorn (Rama V), the palace was 'moved' in 1900 from Si Chang island in Cholburi province. The work was finished in seven months, and set a trend that brought more royalty to the area to build their homes.

Wimanmek was designed by Prince Naritsaranuwattiwong; two wings, each measuring 60m long, each contain three floors. There are 31 rooms, not including balconies. His Majesty would come here with his queens, favoured concubines and daughters. The Amporn Sathan extension was added in 1907 to accommodate these influxes. The Queen gave orders for it to be made into a museum, and it now contains some of the king's personal effects and *objets d'art*.

After the reign of Rama VI the palace was used merely to store things and its condition deteriorated. It was opened to the public in 1982 to mark the 200th anniversary of Bangkok's foundation.

It has the appearance of an island, being partly flanked by pools of water. A jade pool, green with vegetation, lies to the south, and beyond is a Thai house built for the use of visiting guests. The silver room has much detailed original work, such as a silver tree with woven leaves. On the wall are photos of various royals and aristocrats. There is a metal room with bronzes, models of warships and steamships belonging to King Rama VII. Two trophy rooms contain swords and guns and the traditional colonial elephants' feet.

Open: daily, 09.30–16.00hrs. Free if you use a ticket already purchased for the Grand Palace.

Once one of Thailand's greatest natural resources, teak made particulaly good house-building material. A hardwood, its naturally occurring teak-oil made it durable and weather resistant. The teak forests have been felled drastically, but new propagation techniques are being tried (see pages 244–5)..

92

State coaches at Wimanmek Palace

Royal Barges

■ **These ceremonial barges are brought out only on very special occasions. Intricately carved, they are used in a traditional journey along the river when the King makes his way to Wat Arun. Here he presents the *krathin* robes and gifts from the Grand Palace to the monks as a symbol of the end of the rainy season and the Buddhist 'Lent' in October. .....■**

A colourful spectacle Over 2,000 men straining at the oars, chanting ancient hymns and all dressed in brilliant costumes make quite a sight. Although the practice was discontinued for a while, it was revived in 1982 for the celebration of the 200th anniversary of the Chakri dynasty. Only a big occasion will get them out again – the last time was in 1987. The spectacle is usually announced a year in advance; the last time was for the King's 60th birthday.

They might well come out again for his 70th or more probably 72nd (Thais mark age in 12-year cycles) in 1999.

Sneak preview In the meantime visitors can visit the Royal Barge Museum on the bank of Bangkok Noi Canal. Best reached by boat (the regular long-tail from Tha Chang), vehicles can also gain access at 80/1 Rim Khlong, Arun Amarin Road.

The principal barges The King's barge, named *Sri Suphannahong*, is obviously the biggest (about 44m, with 54 oarsmen) and is also the oldest and most ornately carved. It takes the form of a golden swan with a great bauble dangling from its beak. This is the *hong*, an important national symbol used on coinage. His Majesty sits under a golden central canopy, tiered umbrellas of state set along the mid-line. Ceremonially dressed crews pull the angular swan's head forward and there is a special crew member whose job it is to chant the rhythm of the oars.

The next biggest barge is *Anantanagaraj*. This has a seven-headed serpent prow and like the others, elegant carvings along the sides. The full-blown ceremony uses 50 barges in all.

Open: 08 30hrs–16.30hrs. Small admission charge.

Royal Barges at night

Bangkok Festivals

■ Festivals and fairs are celebrated with gusto in Bangkok. Thais will celebrate at the drop of a firecracker, at almost any time of year, although dates will vary according to the lunar calendar. Below are some significant occasions. .....■

Buddhist festivals Magha Puja, in mid-February, celebrates the spontaneous gathering of 1,250 disciples to hear Buddha's sermon. There is mass merit-making and *wian thiang*, which involves worshippers circling round a *bot* three times.

Visaka Puja, in May, commemorates Buddha's birth, enlightenment and death. This is the most fervently celebrated Buddhist festival; structures are erected in Sanam Luang for the faithful to listen to sermons. This immediately precedes the ploughing ceremony.

The ploughing ceremony – the royal ceremony known in full as *jarot hangkhai raek na Khwan* – has its roots in the Sukhothai period. The exact day is chosen by astrologers, usually in May, the start of the rains. After the procession, the king and queen appear and the 'lord of the first field' comes out to greet them. A white bullock is then yoked to a plough and the lord makes three furrows in each direction. Astrologers can then predict the next year's harvest. Before leaving, the King asks the lord for some rice seeds to sow in a special patch at Chitralada palace, to provide the new seed for the next year's ceremony.

Asalha Puja, in July, commemorates Buddha's first sermon to his five original disciples. A few days after this festival, the Buddhist Lent, **Khao Phansa**, marks the start of the rains. **Kathin** is held during the rainy season, when banknotes attached to 'money trees' are presented to *wats*; and Ok Phansa, in October, marks the end of the rains.

Wat Saket The 'Golden Mount' hosts a lively fair in November. Typical of *wat* fairs all over the country, this has amusements and side-stalls, loud music and lots of people milling about, even all the way upstairs to the top of the *chedi*.

<< In September the Chinese community makes offerings of food to the moon goddess. Special altars are crammed with goodies, including 'moon cakes', which passers-by are invited to try. There are also dragon dances and fireworks. >>

The King's Birthday On 5 December the Sanam Luang area becomes a feast of neon, and outdoor movies play all along Rachadamnoen Klang Road. It is also 'Father's Day' (The Queen's birthday on 12 August is 'Mother's Day'). Every fifth year in the 12-year animal cycle is considered to be particularly auspicious; 1987 saw a fine spectacle.

Making a splash at the Songkran Water Festival

River and Canal Tours

■ Trips on the Chao Phraya river or its connecting canals (*khlongs*) give the visitor a glimpse of how the city must have appeared to the Europeans, who dubbed Bangkok 'the Venice of the Orient'. The picturesque *khlong*-side life with its glittering wats and cool palms is being replaced by the concrete mayhem that is Bangkok today. .....■

Regular services The Chao Phraya express boats or *reua duan* are cheap but can get dangerously crowded. They start between Krung Thep and Taksin bridges on the right bank and run north to Nonthaburi. Remember the last boat leaves Nonthaburi at 17.45hrs. (If stranded, buses 64 and 203 go to Banglamphu.) The trip north from Nonthaburi goes to Ayutthaya and beyond. The pier (*Tha*) for that popular tourist area is Tha Phra Athit on the Phra Athit Road. The southbound boat from there stops at Thonburi railway station (the starting point for a trip to Kanchana Buri).

Special trips and charter boats The Express Boat Co runs a Sunday excursion to Bang Pa-In, stopping at Bang Sai, which leaves Maharaj Pier (by Wat Po) at 08.00hrs. About 900 baht would be required for a sumptuous vessel to Ayutthaya such as the *Oriental Queen* or the *Ayutthaya Princess*, leaving from the

Tha Oriental. A buffet lunch is included in the price.

Those wishing to explore the canals of Thonburi can use the regular service or charter a long-tail (*reua haang yaao*) for around 500 baht per day. This is cheap for a group. The best place to take canal buses is from the pier on the opposite bank to Wat Po: for a modest fee, a one-hour return trip can be taken – one of the great Bangkok bargains.

Travelling by river

Regular Long-tail Routes		
Pier	**Destination**	**Direction**
Tha Saphan Phut	Wat Lat Lao	S
Tha Saphan Phut	Bang Waek	SW
Tha Tien	Bang Noi	W
Tha Chang	Bang Chuak Nang	SSW
Tha Chang	Bang Yai*	N
Tha Chang	Pratunam Chimpli	NW
Tha Maharaj	Bang Phrom	WNW
Tha Maharaj	Bang Ramat	NNW
Tha Maharaj	Pratunam Chimpli	NW
Tha Chang-Bang Yai goes by the southern bus station		

Outside Bangkok

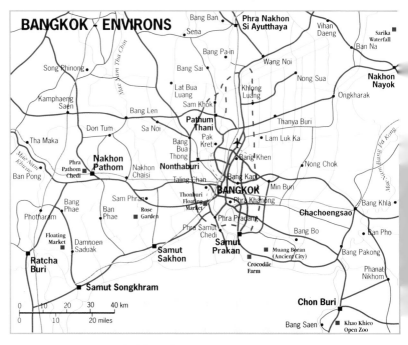

BANGKOK - ENVIRONS

▶ Muang Boran (Ancient City)

Sukhumvit Road, Bang Puu, Samut Prakan Province

What did Thailand's ruins look like when the buildings
were new? This question may be answered at Muang
Boran, a collection of reproduction buildings, most of
them scaled down to one-third size.

Muang Boran is the brainchild of one man with a great
love for the architectural fabric of his country. It is
situated near the Crocodile Farm, 33km to the east of
Bangkok; the drive out takes about two hours. Be careful
when asking for 'Muang Boran' as it means 'ancient city'
and this could be interpreted to mean a real ancient city
like Ayutthaya.

This fascinating attraction presents Thailand's major
monuments modelled in over 81 hectares of attractive
gardens, which are laid out in the same shape as
Thailand itself. Vehicles are available to explore the big
site so this could be a short-cut to appreciating the
country's cultural diversity.

Hop from province to province in Muang Boran, from the
distinctive That Phanom in Nakhon Phanom to Wat
Mahathat in Sukhothai. Ayutthaya's Royal Palace, long
ruined, has been recreated from old chronicles. The
moslem minority has not been forgotten: there is also a
model of the famous Pattani mosque. More humble
scenes abound, such as a floating market, and the overall
attention to environment and detail is remarkable. There
are a variety of refreshments in a pleasing *khlong*-side
ambience.

The Ancient City Company can give more details about
the Ancient City; its office is at 78 Democracy
Monument Circle, Rachadamnoen Avenue (tel: 222

8145/224 1057), in the shadow of the *Democracy Monument*, a reproduction of another famous structure. Weekend and holiday tours can be booked here.

A similar development, **Mini Siam**, has sprung up in Pattaya, although on a much smaller scale. Muang Boran itself had a predecessor in King Rama's VI's 'Dusit Thani'. This 'tushita heaven' was the king's idea of Utopia; it has now been dismantled.

Open: daily, 08.30hrs–18.00hrs.

Samut Prakarn
Sukhumvit Highway (Highway 3) South of Bangkok
Samut Prakarn (Affairs of the Sea) has traditionally welcomed marine visitors on their way up the Chao Phraya river. The most hostile of these were the French in 1893, who sailed over the bar at Paknam ('river mouth') and shelled the *porm* (fort) on the western shore.

The foreign minister at the time, Prince Devawongse, hurried down here to placate the French commander, a diplomatic move that may in itself have saved the much-valued Siamese independence.

Samut Prakan was one of the first Siamese towns to be connected to Bangkok by road. Big ships still make their way over the bar *en route* for the modern port at Khlong Toey.

Crocodile Farm, 30km south of Bangkok on Highway 3, is the place to see domesticated *saurian*. Hundreds of individuals from a variety of both saltwater and freshwater species can be inspected or even fed here from a raised walkway. There is a croc-catching show daily and a shop selling crocodile skin products including handbags and belts. Not for conservationists.

▶▶ Suan Sam Phran (Rose Garden)
Off Highway 4, one hour west of Bangkok
The banks of the broad Thachin river in Nahkon Pathom provide the setting for the Rose Garden resort. Visitors pay a small admission charge to get into the landscaped gardens, lakes and bridges. Choose either to picnic, dine in the riverside restaurant, swim, play bowls, boat, waterski or look at the model village. A longish afternoon show at extra charge, depicts some costumed aspects of Thai culture, rites of passage, dancing, with shows of Thai boxing and *krabee krabong*, sword and stave fighting.

The endangered crocodile was among the most dangerous jungle predators during the 'bad old days'. Thai respect for this savage old monster can be found in the folk tale of *Kraithong*, the eponymous hero being the only 'crocodile doctor' skilful enough to catch the diamond-toothed *Chalawan*.

97

A keeper entangled with a Siamese estuarine crocodile at the Crocodile Farm

Shopping

A useful gift would be a brightly coloured sarong. It is an ideal garment to take swimming and can double as a sheet. A man's *ph-khao-ma*, for bathing and generally lazing about the house, is identified by large checks.

A Bangkok street vendor

City for shoppers Whether you are shopping in the colourful, lively but swelteringly hot markets or the glitzy space-age department stores, one thing is clear: a cornucopia beckons that can empty your purse more quickly than you can say *thii-raleuk*, the Thai word for souvenir.

There are two tiers of prices in Thailand: 'basic' and 'luxury'. The basic includes anything the Thais consider essential for daily life and most things actually made in Thailand. These cost approximately 30–40 per cent of their equivalents in Western homes. Thus food, cigarettes, petrol, clothes, candles and incense are affordable by the majority. Luxury, imported goods – electronics and the like – are roughly comparable with prices in the West.

Clothes These are obviously popular with visitors. Indeed, the resourceful traveller could take just one change of clothes and purchase a holiday wardrobe going along. The holiday wear is of the casual, brightly patterned 'Hawaiian' variety, but bargains do not stop at casual wear; Thailand is justly famous for its bespoke tailors. They might offer some standard styles to choose from, but it is possible to get any style run up from a sketch or photograph. A man's formal suit should cost upwards of 1,000 baht and at least 48 hours should be allowed for fitting and adjustments. A word of caution: there are some tales of people being fobbed off with shoddy workmanship, so be sure of your purchase.

The fabrics available for shirts and dresses are legion. **Cottons** come in brilliant hues and prints. Batik in particular, is enjoying something of a boom. Some shops sell only cloth, huge bolts of it waiting to be cut. The famous Thai **silk** is still cheap, and you will notice that it is, for many women in Bangkok, just regular office wear (see page 203).

Souvenir shops Most people understandably want some souvenir proof of their visit. Although Oxfam has done sterling work promoting village handicrafts, major credit for the currently booming Thai handicraft scene should go to Queen Sirikit, whose 'Support' foundation saved many of the traditional Thai crafts from extinction.

Common everywhere are baskets and furniture made of **bamboo and rattan**. These 'wicker' goods are surprisingly cheap. and the *yan lipao* vine from the south can be woven into elegant accessories. The north is famous for intricate **wood-carving** – either figurines or scenes in bas-relief. It is unlikely that the average visitor will have space in their luggage for furniture, but it can be shipped anywhere in the world. Whether ornamental or functional, it is all very reasonable.

Markets These are everywhere. The streets of the city are in themselves one huge market, selling anything from silk artificial flowers to a job-lot of barbers' scissors. The grand-daddy of them all is Chatuchak, up by the Northern Bus Terminal on Phahon Yothin Road. Open only on Saturday and Sunday, it has become known as the 'Weekend Market'. China, wood, pets, books (including cheap second-hand paperbacks), fabulous food displays and, of course, clothes are sold at stalls cheek by jowl over a huge area.

It can get hot, but the experience is worth it. Other popular markets include **Sampheng** in Chinatown, **Nakorn Kasem Road** by the canal, **Pahurat** and **Penang Market** in Khlong Toey, near the port. In Pratunam, a large covered area on Ratchprarop Road covers the down-market clothes scene fairly comprehensively.

Department stores For shopping in comfort, try any of the air-conditioned department stores which have sprung up all over the place. These are great for Western food items and the more up-market clothes. The **Siam Centre** and nearby **Mabunkhrong** on Rama I Road were among the first. The biggest is **Central** at Lard Phrao or perhaps the **Zen** on Ratcha Damri Road. **Pata Pin Klao** in Thonburi boasts a zoo and monkey theatre!

Jewellery and handicrafts Jewellery is another of the luxury goods which Thailand exports in large amounts, and which is correspondingly cheap locally. Thais love gold and still buy it by the baht, showing the origin of their money (a baht of weight is 15 grammes of gold). Local production alone provides pearls (from farms in Koh Samui & Phuket), rubies and blue sapphires to be set into gold and made into jewellery. The factories are concentrated around **Soi Mahesak** to the west of Silom Road. Look for TAT accreditation to make sure the stones are what they say they are; there are a lot of

Lard Phrao department store

Every colour of the spectrum is available in Thai silk including some fabulous shot-silk which could be called the 'Thai hologram', warp and weft shimmering in alternate colours. Enough to make a skirt will set you back anything from 500 baht upwards. The *mudmee* pattern is made by tie-dying the threads before they are woven. Not all of it is the real thing, so beware. Learn to distinguish between the real and the fake by feel.

SHOPPING

Second-hand goods
In the back of Phanthip Plaza, a shopping mall in Phetburi Road, is a second-hand mart, bursting at the seams with odd rubbish. This is a 'must' for fans of flea markets in general, as are Wat Mahathat, the canalside and Chatuachak. Wat Mahathat is host on holy days to a market of herbal medicine and Buddha amulets.

Fake designer goods
Tourist areas have encouraged the growth of several peculiar retail phenomena. The fake, whether a designer garment, a watch or a video or music tape, hovers on the fringes of legality. Tapes are the best bargain, but outside pressure may well stop the trade.

fakes about and 'amazing bargains' will probably turn out to be cons. To be on the safe side, ask for an independent test at the Asian Institute of Gemological Sciences (700–1,000 baht).

More down-market, but still very attractive, is silver jewellery set with turquoise. Like wood-carving, it is considered to be a northern craft. Many hill tribespeople trek down to Bangkok selling their distinctive tribal designs.

Another fine handicraft is lacquerware. After a block of teak has been transformed with the shiny black lacquer, patterns are either appliquéd in gold leaf or just painted on.

Other crafts Alternative options of Thai handicrafts include hand-painted blue celadon ware, a craft taught them by the Chinese. Cushions, whether the triangular *morn khwan* or the square *morn kit* are ornately embroidered. Also from the north come hand-painted paper umbrellas.

Narai Phand, on Ratcha Damri Road, is a government-sponsored store with the widest selection of handicrafts from all over the country. Perhaps the saddest stalls of all are those selling paintings of rural scenes and dead insects in glass frames. All these stallholders are deaf and dumb.

Unusual shops Banglamphu has some odd shops, the like of which are not to be found elsewhere, as well as its wholesale clothes market. Handy snack stalls abound everywhere. The tourist emporia in Khao San have selections of music tapes (many pirated), which are the best to be found anywhere. There is also one of Bangkok's few co-operatives, good for traditional cooking utensils and also the Buddhist bookshop opposite Wat Boworn, with a selection of English books. The traditional musical instrument workshop can be found on the corner of Tanao and Ratchadamnoen Klang Roads and a huge government school supplies shop on Ratchadamnoen Klang by the bus stop is fascinating.

Traditional Thai crafts are well in evidence in Bangkok: this stall offers models and dolls

■ **Thailand is a hospitable country and this is reflected in its attitude to foreigners. Almost every nationality can be found, especially in Bangkok. Businessmen form one of the largest groups, and Englishmen, like David Tarrant of the Inchcape Group, can become very influential in the economy. ....■**

Westerners The archetypal *farang*, the term reserved for Western foreigners, was Jim Thompson, the American who set up the Thai silk industry in a big way after the war. He mysteriously disappeared in the Cameron Highlands of Malaysia in 1967, but his company is still active. His famous Thai house, full of the most beautiful Thai paintings and *objets d'art*, is open to the public. Some Westerners are attracted by Buddhism, and some become Buddhist monks. There is one *wat* in the remote forests of Ubon Ratchatahani which has 20 permanent monks and branches in England, Australia, Switzerland, Italy and New Zealand. A few foreigners teach at the universities and colleges.

Asians Most of the foreigners living in Thailand are from other Asian countries. In addition to the Chinese, there is a big Indian community, many of whom used to work as butchers, because the Thais, as Buddhists, preferred to avoid this occupation.
Many Indians have become extremely successful in business, like Sura Chansrichawla, a second-generation Punjabi Sikh, whose real estate, valued at US$650 million, makes him one of the biggest landowners in Bangkok.

Far Easterners Some 40,000 Japanese troops were based in Thailand during the Pacific War. Today there are probably 25,000 Japanese living in Thailand, mostly factory managers and technical advisors in joint enterprises. Although there is little resentment against Japan's wartime activites,

there are many left-wing critics of Japanese investment and management methods. The more negative segments of Japanese society also appear, notably the *yakuza* or gangsters, who are quite active in Thailand.
The large refugee population of Vietnamese and Cambodians still living in the border areas of Thailand is a significant legacy from the Indochina War .

Silk was Jim Thompson's fortune. This collection can be seen at Jim Thompson's House (see page 87)

101

Food

Western foods such as Wiener schnitzel or burgers will make serious holes in your cash, whereas the local Thai food, which may be pricey at home, is very cheap – and genuine.

Bangkok really is a gourmet's paradise. The Bangkok posting is a major prize for master chefs of the big hotel chains. Like any large city which opens its doors to all nationalities, it is host to a plethora of international cuisines.

Thai food can be a real assault on the Western palate. To them, Western food is *jeuut* – tasteless. To Westerners, Thai food may be divided into varying 'degrees of difficulty'.

Isan (northeastern) food is a good example of these variations. The *som tam*, or papaya salad, a speciality of the region, can be made sweet with sugar and peanuts and one chilli. *Tam thai* is made with tiny prawns, and cooked this way most Westerners would find it delicious. The average Bangkok Thai would move up to *tam puu*, with the diminutive freshwater crab and two or three extra chillies, whereas a northeastener might add the vile-smelling fermented fish they call *plaa raa*, and employ a 'scorched mouth' policy with regard to the chillies! With this in mind, it might be a good idea to memorise the phrase *phrik neung met* – 'one chilli'.

The most international Thai dish must be khao phat or fried rice. With either beef, chicken, pork or squid and an egg, you can get it almost anywhere.

Shophouse restaurants These also do fried noodles with *phat sii iw* (soy sauce) and the *phat thai* of increasing international fame. The *phat gaprao* (sweet basil fry) on rice has a unique pungence, but probably best avoided by those with a sensitive stomach.

Much more healthy and traditional are the 1001 varieties of *gup* – 'with'. With boiled rice, that is: the main food of the central plains. *Gup* restaurants are distinguished by rows of pots or aluminium trays. Pointing at the dish of your choice alleviates the language barrier; the order *raat khaao* will get your choices 'on the rice' as one dish.

Up-market eating places Those with a bit of money to spend can go to the class 'restaurant' as we understand the term. It can be interesting to order one of the exotic dishes and see what appears.

European sensibilities may be offended by *khai yio maa*, – literally 'horse-piss eggs' – which have been steeped in goodness-knows-what for so long that they are quite black when they hit the table!

This sort of restaurant charges upwards of 50 baht for a dish, and is mainly frequented by the professional classes. Note the Thai tradition for picking up the tab: one person pays all. If a boss is dining with his underlings, 'face' requires that he is the one who must oblige.

Street food In recent years the profusion of street food stalls, night markets, charcoal burners, noodle shops and kitchenettes in Bangkok has turned the city into one huge open-air restaurant. The Thais enjoy wandering around to find out what is cooking in the next street.

Certain distinctly Chinese items have found their special niche on the street. Boiled noodles, whether *nam* (soup) or *haeng* (dry) sell from carts which are often open all

Bangkok vegetable market

night. *Ba'mee*, the yellow wheat-flour noodles, are especially recommended.

From the many rich dishes, try *khao muu daeng* (red pork in a special sauce with hard-boiled egg) or *khao man kai*, white chicken in a fatty rice with dark soy.

The bone-shaped golden crispy *Paa thong go* is a Thai version of hot buttered toast, often eaten after being dipped in sweet Thai coffee.

Sweetmeats The sweet-toothed have a bewildering choice of *khanom* or sweetmeats. There are the cheap street kind, from the sticky Islamic *roti* to the delicate *khanom beuang*, a coconut cream crisp.

The restaurant diner may opt for the coconut milk/sticky rice concoction; this is easily the best way to appreciate the notorious durian, while mangoes are more well known. Try the *pheuak* – an Asian tuber called taro with a vanilla-like flavour – or the honeydew melon, diced and covered with shredded ice.

The other way to round off a great meal is with fresh fruit. Most kinds are seasonal, like *ngo*, the red hairy rambutans and *malagor*, the fleshy orange gourd papaya, but familiar pineapple and bananas appear all year round.

Spotted on menus:
Spicy bowel salad
Fried ash with ginge
Ear lice and Thai pepper on pork
Spicex semi biled fish
Fried fish bowel with combination
Boiled crap
Farce [stuffed] with omelette
Fried mice pork

103

Freshwater crab – a Bangkok delicacy

Nightlife

'The world seems tarnished the next morning.' – observation after drinking Mekhong whisky.

They say it was American soldiers looking for some recreation who got the petite farmers' daughters dancing to loud rock music, wearing bikinis and holding on to firemens' poles. That was 20 years ago. Tourists may have more than made up for the departing GIs, but the fear of AIDS is changing the scene somewhat.

The area around Patpong Road and Soi Cowboy is full of murky dives, mainly catering for men. On the whole this is a concentrated area of spectacular sleaze. The road is named after a Chinese millionaire, Phat Phong, who owns nearly everything thereabouts.

The other side of the coin can be seen in the victims of poverty, bad education, pimps, deserting husbands and irregular papers among a host of other woes. Patpong *et al* represent the visible tip of an iceberg of suffering. While the women there enter into voluntary arrangements with the bars, in other establishments their rights are not nearly so well respected.

It will still be a long time before Bangkok shakes off its reputation as 'the brothel of Asia' but entertainment of the regular sort is booming right now, and women or men who don't care for degrading spectacles have a wide choice of venue to while the night away.

One of the more disturbing aspects of the tourist trade: Bangkok's notorious nightlife

Pubs and clubs Middle-class Thais thinking along similar lines opened the first 'pub', **Brown Sugar**, on Sarasin Road. This proved to be a wild success and pretty soon the area behind Lumphini Park – Lang Suan – was a festival of music and drink. Professional bands pump out jazz, rock, reggae and Latin rhythms. The drinks tend to be overpriced, however; it has this in common with Patpong. Most establishments are open until 02.00–03.00hrs.

Particularly recommended are **Round Midnight** (mostly Latin), and **The Old West** (Santana-type rock). If you want to talk, feel free to sit outside. Pubs have now opened in many other areas. The **Gypsy** in Banglamphu is near the New World department store. Sukhumvit Road, and Soi 55 (Thonglor) especially, has more than a few. One which helped popularise jazz here is **The Saxophone** by the Victory Monument.

Not to be outdone, there are 'ladies' clubs' such as **Chippendales** in (fairly remote) Huay Khwang. Wealthy women tired of errant husbands get their revenge here with a selection of toyboys.

Bangkok has yet to lose the label 'brothel of Asia'

If the restaurant you are in looks like closing,there are several late openers to choose from. The Isan places are the best, their *som tam* and *nam tok* being renowned drinkers' appetisers.

105

Discos Another Western-inspired fixture on the night scene is the discothèque. While small and intimate dancehalls thud in the basements of large hotels like the **Shangri-la** (Talk of the Town), the **Dusit Thani** (Bubbles) and the **Ambassador** (Flamingo), there are a few mega-palaces, whose clientele is mostly students. The most impressive of these is **NASA Spaceadrome** on Ramkhamhaeng Road (turn left at the end of Phetburi New Road).

Mars Party House in Patpong is five floors of dancing. The Superstar is being renovated, but the pride of the gay scene is just around the corner. Straights are welcome at the **Rome**, with its hipper-than-hip music and decadent décor. A Pattaya-style transvestite revue, **Calypso**, has opened in its own large theatre on Sukhumvit Road near the Washington cinema. Either of the two nightly performances will cost around 300 baht.

Drinking Licensing laws are non-existent and almost any little restaurant can oblige with either beer or Mekhong whisky (foreign spirits being mainly confined to the pubs and discos). Check out the rum-like Saeng Thip, with coke, for a smoother drink than Mekhong, which can have lethal after-effects. Of the beers, Kloster lacks the formaldehyde tang of the more popular Singha.

Finally, you may be tempted to try out one of the many cafés, a very Thai institution. Off the tourist track, entertainment is provided by a roster of male and female singers in elaborate evening dress. They sing requests and are rewarded by garlands of jasmine – altogether very civilised!

■ Never really an art form for mass entertainment, the traditional *khon* performances survive mainly thanks to the Fine Arts Department. Each takes the form of a masked dance-drama and can last for up to eight hours when the fuller versions are staged. Designed originally for performance at court for the pleasure of the King, *khon* drama, like all classical performances, can be a bit heavy going, even for the Thais. However, the programme is leavened with music, from classical (both Thai and *farang*) to folk and popular and the costumes are very extravagant. Actors will happily pose for photographs after a performance. ..■

National Theatre This is a large building where plays and *khon* drama in Thai are staged. As befits the theatre's status, the performances are most often adapted from such literary classics as *Phra Lor* or the *Ramakien* epic. This is the Thai version of an Indian legend (the *Ramayana*). There are tales of battles and even comedy where various colourful characters act out the parts. One of the all-time favourites is the monkey-god Hanuman, who is easily distinguished by his white face. The troupe regularly participates in the joint Asian Ramayana festival.

The dancers move with slow, deliberate formality and it is an interesting spectacle, but hard – even for those who understand a little Thai – to follow. The theatre itself is large, its lush decorations and facilities mainly patronised by schoolchildren being dragged through their set texts, although the material of *Phra Lor* is very salty. Entry to the National Theatre is never more than 40 baht and English-language programmes can be obtained from the Thailand Cultural Centre. These also contain a wealth of other 'arty' activities, current details of which can mostly be found

Bangkok's National Theatre

in the *Bangkok Post* and the *Nation*.

The Cultural Centre This is way out of town on Rachadaphisek Road. It offers much more accessible attractions such as recitals, mime, ballet and singing contests. Here they also stage performances of *Likay*, a lively folk theatre. This is much more in the popular vein of entertainment and relies on pratfalls and bawdy lyrics rather than on long or complicated dialogue. The comedy of the early evening gives way to more *risqué* material and the air is thick with *double entendres* until the small hours of the morning. It is easy to see *Likay* in its spontaneous environment all over the country at provincial temple fairs. *Khon Sot* (fresh) is halfway between *Likay* and court *khon*. Charity concerts, featuring music from the current Thai hit parade and old crooning standards, are sometimes televised.

The Thai classical music performances are put on at the beginning of every month. These ensembles, somewhat cacaphonic to the untrained ear, are tuned on an a seven-note scale and much improved by vocals.

More accessible may be a *Luuk Thung* performance. This folk-with-modern-instruments gives concerts of old favourites sung by the top commercial stars.

Other cultural activities In Bangkok these are clustered around the British Council, the American University Alumni, the Alliance Française and Germany's Goethe Institut. The Alliance puts on some excellent films, while the others encourage modern Thai artists of all disciplines.

The **Visual Dhamma Gallery** is where to catch the best of the plastic arts. Universities and hotels likewise plug the high-culture gap; the **Imperial** and the **Monthien** in particular stage regular concerts and plays, while the Auditorium of **Chulalongkorn University** presents a similar programme to the one put on at the National Theatre.

Traditional Thai dance

Accommodation

Ten years ago Khao San Road was an ordinary thoroughfare in the heart of Bangkok's historical district. The first guesthouses, such as the VS and PB, were basic affairs – cheap but welcoming. The road's heart is a row of wooden shophouses, and a few leftovers from the old days which now compete for space with up-market tailors.

New guesthouses, cafés, shops and moneychangers open almost daily and souvenir stalls line the pavements. Khao San Road itself has become saturated and the guesthouses have spread out into adjoining streets, mainly around Wat Chana Songkhram up to the river. They are moving north up Samsen Road and east along Ratchadamnoen.

Guesthouses The popularity of the guesthouse is explained by a combination of low tariffs and informal atmosphere. Budgeteers now have a huge variety to choose from and newer developments have raised the general standard.

Shophouses all down Tanao Road soi (west) have opened as guesthouses recently. However, some disturbing incidents have been reported at the Orm, so perhaps this is better left alone.

Central Guesthouse, 59 Tanao Road soi (east) is a basic, moderately comfortable wooden house with a shared bathroom. **The Apple** is a basic but laid-back guesthouse on the other side of Wat Chanasongkhram (an interesting walk through a wat that looks after animals).

The **Ngaam Pit** and **Rose Garden** guesthouses (among others) are opposite the temple's further wall, a fine situation of tall shophouses with quiet courtyards outside.

Straight along the soi to Phra Athit and the distinctive **New Siam**, recently opened, is another comfortable alternative. Also quite comfortable is the **Peachy** guesthouse, on Phra Athit Road, and organised much more like a hotel.

These houses are all convenient for the Express Boat pier at Tha Phra Athit.

Anyone with the misfortune to find themselves stuck at an unplanned stop in the back of beyond can take comfort from the fact that every province and many districts can be relied on to have at least a small hotel, often under Chinese management.

A communal toilet – including a pot and water to use instead of toilet paper

Other budget areas In Bangkok these include Thonburi (around Pata Pin Klao) and Rama IV Road. While the former area is a Khao San offshoot, the latter dates from Vietnam. The **Grace** and **Malaysia** hotels in particular are surviving icons of the era.
As a base for provincial travel the guesthouse scene has one major advantage over conventional hotels. Up-country relatives of the proprietors usually advertise in them with enticing notices and business cards, so providing a ready-made basis for somewhere to stay further down the line. This way, too, there is more chance of finding an English-speaking place that understands how Westerners like to relax.

Moving up-market Above all the Thais are keen hoteliers and so the choice is great. Hotels in the moderate to expensive bracket are scattered about the city in a bewilderingly random fashion. If you find yourself in Banglamphu, the **Viangtai** is in the luxury bracket.
Moving 'downtown', many moderate hotels have the advantage of being open 24 hours a day. One such is the **Reno** in Soi Kasemsan, Rama I, which also has a pleasant swimming pool. The **Honey Hotel** (Sukhumvit Soi 11) and the **Rex**, prominent on the south side of that road, are establishments of very similar calibre.
A long way out north onPhahon Yothin Road is the **Lost Horizons House**, a bed-and-breakfast establishment. If you have ever wondered what it is like to live in the classical old Thai house, find out by reserving on 279-4967.

> The atmosphere on the streets may be like a mini-United Nations, but curiously enough houses often become favoured by a specific nationality. Nevertheless, English remains the universal contact language.

109

At the top end Of up-market hotels, the **Oriental** is a tourist attraction in itself, its former building carefully preserved with details of the famous writers who have stayed there, such as Conrad and Somerset Maugham. The tradition is kept alive with an award ceremony every year for writers in the Southeast Asian languages.
Gargantuan riverside neighbours such as the **Shangri-La** offer a similar service. There's the **Siam Intercontinental**, the **Regent**, the **Imperial**, the **Dusit Thani**, the **Monthien**, the **Ambassador** and international chains such as the **Hilton** for five-star diners or guests. The Regent has a light and airy lobby and the Hilton has refreshingly green gardens.

The Imperial Hotel

Sports

Thai boxing is supposed to have developed from hand-to-hand combat with the Burmese. King Naresuan the Great was himself a skilled fighter and made it compulsory training for his troops in the 16th century.

110

'Vicious and little controlled' was how one visitor described Thai boxing and certainly it is not hard to believe that less than 60 years ago *Muay Thai* – as it is known to its adherent – was illegal. Until the 1920s horsehair strappings were used instead of gloves and rules were non-existent.

Kick-boxing

Thai Boxing The main stadiums for this part-sport, part-martial art are Ratchadamnoen and Lumphini. The audience will bet furiously but won't take a *farang* wager.

There is a lot of bleeding and lost consciousness, with legal blows including such charming moves as the elbow thrust and drop-kick. Looking at the fanatical level of interest in this national sport today, it comes as no surprise to discover that when it was outlawed prior to the 1930s an unregulated underground scene flourished. Eventually a set of rules was adopted: a fighter can use his feet , elbows, legs, knees and shoulders, in fact almost any part of his body. However, butting, biting, spitting and kicking an opponent when he is down are all forbidden. Kick-boxers fight in bare feet and are drenched with buckets of water in between rounds, when they are also pummelled by their masseurs almost as hard as by their opponents.

The kick-boxing ring has proved a successful training ground for regular boxing, Thai fighters consistently taking world honours in the lighter-weight divisions. Junior Bantamweight champion Khaosai Galaxy has stayed the course longer than most. The Isan lads produce *Muay Thai* champions like Rambo. Size is not a decisive factor and is not necessarily a measure of potential. Skill and dexterity are more important and a well-delivered kick can floor an opponent.

Tension is heightened by a band which plays drums and the oboe-like *pii chawa*. Before a fight commences, fighters pay homage to their teachers and then start with an elaborate dance. When the fists start flying, the band crashes with the action. There are usually five three-minute rounds, and the referee has the power to stop the fight if one of the contestants is seriously injured.

If you want to sample the frenzied atmosphere of a bout, Lumphini on Rama IV Road is open Tuesdays, Fridays and Saturdays, while the stadium on Ratchadamnoen Nok is open on the other days. Tickets for home defences are hard to come by! Ticket prices vary from around 500 baht for a ringside seat to 140 baht for the outer ring.

*Kites in Sanam
Luang*

Kites Kite fighting as a sport survives today from its origins in the Sukhothai period. Nowadays it tends to be an after-work activity that starts at around 16.30hrs, when the larger offices close for the day.

The large star-shaped 'male' *julaa* is pitted against several smaller square 'female' *pakpao*. The *julaa* are sometimes as long as 2m and take up to 10 men to fly; the *pakpao* are smaller and faster and can usually be flown by an individual. For the purposes of a match the 'male' and 'female' teams face each other from opposite ends of the field. The object is to force the opponent out of the sky. The *julaa* tries to cross the boundary and capture the *pakpao*, bringing it to the ground back in its own territory. This is achieved by flying a series of skilful loops and sometimes by putting powdered glass on the strings.

Although the days of grand tournaments sponsored by kings are now over, the Mecca for Bangkok fliers is Sanam Luang, the Royal Field. This is a large open expanse between the Grand Palace and Ratchadamnoen Avenue. Ornamental and specialist models are hung up across the paths for sale.

Prime season for kites is between March and May when the southerly winds are blowing regularly. Watching this colourful spectacle is really a very pleasant way to pass the time.

The best vantage point for watching the kites in action could well be the benches which are found under leafy shade to the north of Sanam Luang. The ubiquitous mobile snack-sellers are usually on hand to ply the visitor with hard-boiled eggs and chilli fish broth noodles.

The children have kites of their own which are usually in the form of dragons and bats, which they fly for the sheer fun of it, leaving the serious fighting to the grown-ups.

First records of kite-flying as a recreational activity traditionally come from the Sukhothai period. Ramkhamhaeng's father, Sri Intharadit was a major enthusiast. Legends tell how he met the daughter of Phaya Eua retrieving a kite from her roof in the dead of night.

SPORTS

Three levels of the sport of sword fighting are practised: with real weapons, with toy weapons for a striking game, or with decorated toy weapons for a dancing game.

Tagraw is a national sport and men of all ages spend their time playing in their off-duty moments. Skilled players make the movements look effortless and dance-like as they use different parts of their bodies to keep the ball in the air.

Sword Fighting Hand-to-hand combat with swords has been successfully turned into a spectator sport by the exponents of fencing and a little-known variant with the traditional Thai battle sword called *krabee krabong*. Also involved are the long, spear-like *ngaao* and the stave, *phlorng*, which gives it a resemblance to *Tai-kwondo*.

The sword (the straight-handled *daap*) is used double-handed, or with a shield. The *krabee* with its proper hand-guard is used alone. The *mai san* are short shields for the forearms, which link the sport with Thai boxing. Another similarity is the band which accompanies the fighting, as are the ceremonies paying respect to the masters which start a 'bout'.

In the sport version, players are arranged in suitable pairs, often matching one weapon against another of a different type: so the stave may be pitted against the arm-shield, for example. There is no firm deciding test of victory – the players attempt set pieces in the roles of 'attack' and 'defence'.

Many children still learn the art at school and demonstrations are included in cultural shows put on for tourists at such places as the Rose Garden.

Tagraw or *takraw* is a sport in which a special touch-sensitive rattan ball is volleyed between two teams who face each other over a badminton-like net. The object of the game is to keep the ball aloft and to this end any part of the body can be used except the hands. Whether the game originated in Thailand or Malaysia is a moot point. Malays take it very seriously; their word for it, *sepak* (kick), is added in the combined name *sepak-tagraw* in the Southeast Asian games.

Formal matches can be watched at Hua Mark or the National Stadium on Rama I, although it is very much a participatory sport, with matches going on everywhere. Another version, *Takraw Buang*, resembles basketball. Those without equipment stand around in a circle and anyone who wants to develop their skills can have a go.

Advertisement for a Thai boxing match

Other Sports

Boat racing Numbered among the many popular minor sports in Thailand, boat racing involves crews of 20–100 paddling brightly bedecked hardwood canoes. The occasional Thai vs Lao contest on the Mekong river is a far cry from Oxford and Cambridge universities' crews battling it out in the annual boat race on the River Thames! Inside Thailand, the Phichit Regatta at the beginning of September is well known, but there are races in provinces as far afield as Nan, Buri Ram, Ratchburi and Korat (Phimai).

Fighting fish Buddhist fish-lovers may be appalled at the bizarre fighting fish which tear each other to pieces in a jam jar to satisfy a wager. On their own they are quite attractive and show no signs of their aggressive potential, but it is a different story if they are allowed to see one another. Two fish in separate jars must be shielded from each other's view .

Golf The Thais are great fans of Western sport. While their football pitches struggle with floods and droughts, golf courses are well looked after. Courses spring up everywhere as the focus for suburban development. Golf is tremendously popular with the leadership élite. Recommended courses in the Bangkok area include the **Navatanee** at Bang Kapi (par 72), **The Rose Garden** at Nakhon Pathom (par 72), the **Royal Thai Air Force** at Don Muang (par 68) and the **Krungthep Kritha** at Hua Mark (par 72).
Of provincial courses, the **Royal Hua Hin** (par 72) is the oldest, having opened in 1924. The **Thaai Muang** (par 72), north of Phuket in Phangnga province, features an 18th which is parallel to the beach.

Back in the city, a golf driving-range has been built on Rama IV Road at soi 26, where it is possible to practise your swing without the tedious long walk afterwards.

Snooker This went through a boom here after the success of James Wattana Phu-Ob-Orm in Britain (see panel). For the less elevated, a casual frame can be had in Khao San Road at the PB Guesthouse.

Thai chess The board-game fanatic may well enjoy a board of Thai Chess (*Mark Rook*) which is often played on the pavement. The moves are played faster than in the Western version of the game.

Bull fighting takes place in the south, but the Thai version is bull versus bull, rather than man versus bull

James Wattana, or 'Tong', as he is known at home, was Thailand's first snooker player to have major success in world tournaments. In 1986 at the age of 18 he beat three former world champions, Steve Davis, Denis Taylor and Terry Griffiths, to win the Camus Masters' Trophy. He scored the highest break in the 1992 British Open Tournament.

Golfing in Bangkok

Practical Points

Thailand is divided into 73 provinces –*jangwat*– which in turn are subdivided into districts – *amphur* – then communes – *tambon* – and then groups – *moo*. A group of houses –*moo-ban*– is the Thai for village. Each province (*jangwat*) has a hospital, hotels, banks and specialist shops. Districts (*amphur*) may have a hospital or bank, *tambon* and *moo-ban* will have at least petrol and food.

Getting about In Bangkok it can be a nightmare. Pollution is high on the list of Bangkok's troubles. It is worsening and masks are now a common sight on the streets. As cars increase, the roads can't cope, and road budgets are a political football. Trying to drive in Bangkok itself is an unpleasant experience – slow, dangerous, smelly, confusing and best avoided. Getting out of Bangkok is a blessed relief. Up-country driving has its drawbacks but jams are not often among them, although there is a shortage of dual carriageway.

Driving at night, especially for motorcycles, is best avoided. Cars must put up with heavily insect-smeared windscreens, particularly around dusk, and motorcyclists must put the visor down or endure an unexpected diet of flies.

Motorcycle taxis, whose drivers know the backstreets and can squeeze down alleys, are cheaper than personal vehicle hire, and although their bikes are not all that powerful, they are usually quicker than taxis.

Tuk tuks, as a practical form of transport do not rate too highly, being uncomfortable, dangerous (unless you are wedged in), noisy and polluting. They are good, though, for loads such as backpacks and giant baskets of fruit.

Taxis are clean and air-conditioned and have drivers who will often complain in English about the traffic. They can get expensive. *Songthaews* are pick-ups or low trucks with two long benches. Nowadays these ply along *sois* rather than the main roads.

Buses are improving. Bangkokians squash into the 2 baht (blue/white) and 3 baht (red/white) buses but the cost efficiency of such a low fare for the route's entire length cannot be denied. Even the little green buses, a back-up system that operates the normal routes, are usually quite packed.

The air-conditioned buses, identified by the Thai letters saying *por*, or on the board, operate a sliding scale, from 5 baht upwards. They can also fill up to bursting but by getting on near the beginning of the route it should be possible to get one of the precious seats.

Crews personalise their vehicles with Buddhas, and Buddhist monks have an unassailable right to the back seats, so leave these alone. Many frown on the backpacker habit of blocking the gangway with their backpacks.

The system shuts down around 23.00hrs However, there are a few all-night buses which charge a staggering 3.50 baht. The most useful must be the No 2. from Sanam Luang all along Sukhumvit Road.

Provincial Buses Operated by a sprawling state enterprise calling itself the Transport Company, the Thai system is cheap and extensive. Getting out of Bangkok, the three main terminals are sensibly sited on the major routes out of the city. Provincial fares recently went up by a third; for this the passenger gets accident insurance.

The non-aircon buses (*rot thammada*) are referred to

unkindly as the 'orange crush'. While they are absurdly cheap (less than 200 baht for 1,000 km) and correspondingly popular, leg-room is severely limited. This service will stop to pick up or set down anybody anywhere along the route.

Blue and white air-conditioned coaches are fast, with comfortable reclining seats and a toilet, and hostesses plying the traveller with soft drinks and sweets and, best of all, perfumed 'cold cloths' to wipe the face and arms. Fares are very reasonable (less than 500 baht for 1,000 km). At night the air-con system becomes so chillingly efficient that a woolly or jacket will be needed to supplement the blankets provided.

Even with the comforts, a long journey is still gruelling, and a train berth or aeroplane seat can seem more attractive.

Private-sector buses service popular routes such as Bangkok–Phuket and 10–15 vehicles per time may leave the Saai Tai in the high season. A further spin-off are minibuses (*rot tuu*) which can be faster even than a tour bus, though not as comfortable.

North/northeast terminal, Morchit, Phahon Yothin Road: Ayutthaya, Bang Pa-in, Khao Yai, Lop Buri, Nakhon Nayok, Nakhon Sawan, Petchabun, Saraburi, Suphan Buri, Chiang Mai, Chiang Rai, Fang, Kamphaeng Phet, Lampang, Mae Hong Son, Mae Sai, Mae Sot, Nan, Phitsanulok, Phrae, Sukhothai, Tak
From a separate northeastern terminal: Khon Kaen, Loei, Mukdahan, Nakhon Ratchasima, Nong Khai, Roi Et, Sakhon Nakhon, Surin, Ubon Rachathani, Yasothorn

South terminal, Sai Tai, Nakhon Chaisri Road: Damnoen Saduak, Hua Hin, Kanchana Buri, Nakhon Pathom, Phetcha Buri/Cha-am, Chumphon, Hat Yai, Krabi, Nakhon Si Thammarat, Narathiwat, Phang Nga, Pattani, Phuket, Prachuap Khiri Khan, Ranong, Songkhla, Sungai Kolok, Suratthani, Trang, Yala

East terminal, Ekamai, Sukhumvit Road, Chantha Buri, Ko Samet, Pattaya, Si Racha, Trat.

Some of the more useful air-conditioned buses:

6 Sanam Luang, Indra Vihan, Nonthaburi, Pak Kret

11 Sanam Luang, Ploen Chit Road, Sukhumvit Road, Ekamai (eastern bus terminal)

12. Sanam Luang, Phetburi Road, Ramkhamhaeng Road, Bang Kapi

44 Sanam Luang, Phaholyothin Road, Chatuchak, Morchit (northern bus terminal), Lat Prao Road

7 Phrakhanong, Rama IV Road, Lumphini, Hualampong Station, Sanam Luang, Thonburi, Saai Tai (southern bus terminal).

115

Everybody wants to get everywhere quickly. The traffic light sequence in Thailand is red – stop (or red when it's clear of other cars and police – go); amber – go; green – go . The normal response to a changing green-to-red signal is to speed up. Only the traffic jams are effective in bringing vehicles to a halt.

CENTRAL THAILAND

Nang Khruan Waterfall

Phop Phra

2194m

Khlong Lan

Khlong Lan N P

Ban Bang Khao Saan

Um Phang

Kamphaeng Phet Hist Park

Kamphaeng Phet

Sai Ngam

Phichit

Wang Sai Phun

Bang Krathum

Taphan Hin

Pho Thale

Thap Khlo

Bang Mun Nak

Khlong Khlung Res

Khlong Khlung

Khanu Woralaksaburi

Chumsaeng

Banphot Phisai

Kao Liao

Mae Wong Res

Lat Yao

Nakhon Sawan

Krok Phra

Bung Boraphet

Nong Bua

Tha Tako

Phaisali

Pra Chedi Sam Ong

Three Pagodas Pass

Sangkhla Buri

Khao Laem Dam

1810m

Srinakarin Dam

Thap Salao Dam

155-m

Esa Waterfall

Sai Poe Waterfall

Khlong Pho Res

Lan Sak

Thap Than

Huai Kot

Uthai Thani

Chai Nat

Phayuha Khiri

Takhli

Tak Fa

Kh Charc

Khok Samrong

Ban Mi

Sing Buri

Lop Buri

Ban Samo Thong Hot Spring

Ban Rai

Hankha

Sanphaya

Thong Pha Phum

Than Lot Cave

Chaloem Rattanakosin N P

Si Siwat

Hin Dat Hot Spring

Dan Chang

Lao Khwan

Doembang Nangbuat

Don Chedi

Si Pratham

Chaiyo

Phra Phutthabat

Sena

Sarabur

Erawan Waterfall

Sai Yok Yai N P

Khao Pang Waterfall

Bo Phloi Sapphire Mines

Bo Phloi

U Thong

Wat Visoe Chi Chan

Suphan Buri

Ang Thong

Tha Rua

Phra Nakh Si Ayuttha

Ban Nam Tok

Hellfire Pass

Prasat Muang Singh Hist Park

Ban Kao

Tha Muang

Kanchana Buri

Phanom Thuan

Kamphaeng Saen

Song Phinong

Bang Pa-in

Sa Noi

Prathum Thani

N S

Andaman Sea

BUR

Photharam

Suan Phung

Nakhon Pathom

Nonthaburi

Bang Khen

BANGKOK

Pra Khanong

Floating Market

Damnoen Saduak

Rose Garden

Samut Prakan

Ratcha Buri

Pak Tho

Khao Yoi

Ban Laem

Samut Sakhon

Crocodile Farm

Ban Sae

Ban Hin See

Nong Ya Plong

Khao Luang

Samut Songkhram

Bight of Bangkok

Si Rach

Ko Sichang

Kang Kra Chan Dam

Tha Yang

Cha-am

Phetcha Buri

Ban Lamung

Ko Phai

Ko Lan

Kaeng Kra Chan N P

Marukkha Thaiyawan Palace

Klai Kang-Won Palace

Hua Hin

Ko Khram

Sattahip

Ban Pa La-u

Pran Buri Dam

Pran Buri

Ban Yang Chum

Khao Sam Roi Yot Mountain

Kui Buri

Gulf of

Khao Sam Roi Yot N P

Prachuap Khiri Khan

Huai Yang Waterfall

Thap Sakae

Mae Nam Ping

Mae Nam Nan

Mae Nam Khwae Noi

Mae Nam Khwae Yai

Mae Nam Tha Chin

Mae Nam Chao Phraya

Bangkok's hinterland, the Chao Phraya Basin, is the most densely populated and agriculturally productive of the country's main rural regions. For the purposes of this book it includes the eastern coast of the Gulf.

The **central plain** is drained by the Chao Phraya, the Tha Chin and the Bang Pa Kong rivers, and is very fertile. When the Thai people first arrived here from the north they found civilisations that offered them useful lessons in city-building, administration and statecraft.

The 9th-century Dvaravati culture passed on the strain of Theravada Buddhism that remains Thailand's official religion. Some say Nakhon Pathom may have been the chief city of Dvaravati, although most come to see the 19th century chedi.

A Buddha's head encased by a tree in Ayutthaya

When the Mon withered under Khmer pressure, Thai chieftains took the lead. During this time Lop Buri was a Mon-Indic centre offering valuable tutelage. The foundation of Ayutthaya soon afterwards hastened the Thai adoption of Indic rituals and mythologies.

The name 'Siam' dates from the Khmer (10th–11th centuries), who employed Thai mercenaries. Khmer sanctuaries are scattered far to the west. For 400 years the focus of Siam was Ayutthaya (although King Narai decamped briefly to Lop Buri). Although it weathered innumerable vicissitudes, the Burmese finally put paid to its dreams. Rallying quickly, the Siamese drove them out, and Bangkok replaced Ayutthaya as the regional trade hub. Of the many ancient cities in the central area, Suphan Buri, Kanchana Buri and Phetcha Buri deserve special mention.

While the western mountains are still fairly wild, an important government project, the Eastern Seaboard, is developing a natural gas complex. Meanwhile the 'rice basket' is being quietly undermined. The scant returns from rice are encouraging increasing numbers to sell up, as the price of land shoots up, putting a question mark over the classic scenes of buffaloes and straw-hatted bending figures.

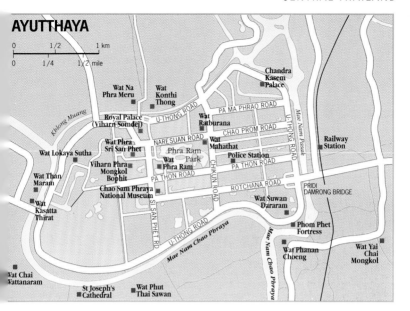

AYUTTHAYA

▶ ▶ ▬▬ **Ayutthaya**

76km north of Bangkok. Trains and buses (northern terminal) from Bangkok

A pleasant day trip from Bangkok, especially by boat or train, the ancient city is littered with the remnants of its former glory. In its heyday, Ayutthaya was one of the biggest cities in the world, the centre of a civilisation that had diplomatic relations with Louis XIV of France. (His Jesuit mission built Siam's first observatory.) This vast area, scattered over the large modern town, is really too much to attempt on foot, but there are fleets of *tuk tuk* drivers on hand to guide people round for half a day.

History In 1350, when it was newly founded, Ayutthaya was just another Thai city state in the Chao Phraya basin. There was Lop Buri, still a centre of Mon-Indic culture, and there was Sukhothai, the overlord. Less than 100 years later, in 1438, Ayutthaya wrested control of the lower Chao Phraya basin from Sukhothai and did not yield it for another four centuries. Whereas Sukhothai represented a rebellion from the Angkor (Khmer) yoke, Ayutthaya's kings, in particular King Boromtrailokanat, sought to consolidate their power through the reimposition of Khmer social controls like slavery.

By the early 16th century the first voyages of exploration had led to the establishment of European trading settlements. The remains of these can be found to the southeast. Portuguese and Dutch were the most persistent settlers, although the English and French had an important presence.

It is quite easy to imagine Ayutthaya as a bustling city at the hub of an empire. Tourists come to see the ruins, but may be disappointed with the sandstone stumps – all that remained after the Burmese had finished with the capital; their destruction of the city in 1767 was total.

When they sacked the city, the ostensibly Buddhist Burmese took pleasure in beheading Ayutthaya's Buddha images. Hundreds of defiled images still sit as mute testament to senseless destruction.

119

Wat Yai Chai Mongkol

The monuments The most impressive monument to Ayutthaya's past is **Wat Lokaya Sutha**, with its large reclining Buddha. This has only recently been renovated in gleaming whitewashed cement.

The oldest temple is **Wat Phanan Choeng** to the south of the city, which predates the city's foundation by 26 years. Near by, and also beyond the river, is **Wat Yai Chai Mongkol**.

King Narai built the **Suriyat Amarin Hall**, to the north of the city, to review boat races. **Banyong Ratanat Hall** was built by his son Phetracha a few years later in 1688. There are altogether the ruins of some 375 monasteries, 29 fortresses and 94 city gates. On the island is the ancient palace, **Viharn Somdej**, attributed to King Prasat

Thong. Nearby **Wat Phra Sri San Phet** is the classic shot many take home with them of three large *chedis* standing in a row. Further south of this is the tall (12m) bronze image of **Viharn Phra Mongkol Bophit**.

Certain sites, including this one, charge entrance fees; the two-tier system that charges the foreigner twice as much as a Thai.

Wat Mahathat (1384), with its tall Khmer-style tower, is picturesquely reflected in the pools of centrally located **Phra Ram Park**. Near by is impressive old Wat Ratburana (1424). South of the river, and now restored to immaculate condition, is **Wat Phut Thai Sawan**.

Museums There are two national museums in Ayutthaya: at **Chao Sam Phraya** and **Chandra Kasem** palace. While the former has the more exquisite exhibits, the latter sells an excellent guide to the old city. In addition to this there are the high-tech displays of the **Ayutthaya Historical Study Centre**, which opened two years ago on Rotjana Road, near the Teachers' Training College.

King Narai the Great had a bodyguard of mercenary Samurai. The Japanese built their own village in the same area, which is now marked with memorials.

121

Staying over There is not much in the way of guesthouse accommodation here, but the **Pai Tong** guesthouse, on the river near the station is said to be friendly. It is worth distinguishing between the old and new **BJ** guesthouses. The old one, which is off Naresuan Road (tel: 251512), comes recommended; the new one is a rogue imitator.

Of the hotels, the **U Thong** and **Cathay** are of no more than an average standard.

Making 'historical'
figures in Ayutthaya

CENTRAL THAILAND

Before Cha-am on route 3203 is a turning for Hup Kraphong Cooperative. This agronomists' treat is a royal experiment with a 'Thai kibbutz', drawing on Israeli expertise. Villagers sell handicrafts fashioned from a local variety of hemp.

Creative topiary at Bang Pa-in

▶▶ **Bang Pa-in**

Buses (northern terminal) from Bangkok; boat from Maharaj Pier at 08.00hrs, returning at 17.30hrs

The famous **summer palace** of King Chulalongkorn was originally built by King Prasat Thong of Ayutthaya and abandoned when the city was sacked. King Chulalongkorn used the place to indulge his love of eclectic style. The formal Siamese element jostles with Greek, Italian and Chinese influence.

Most bizarre of all is perhaps **Wat Niwet Thamprawat**, reached by a cable car, which proves that the beauties of Gothic cathedral architecture can just as well be used to praise Buddha. The place is nonetheless sombre and unsettling – Westerners may expect to see a black-clad minister in this setting, but all around are monks in their orange robes.

The grounds are pretty and have some curious topiary.
Open: daily, except Mondays, 08.30hrs–12.00hrs; 13.00hrs–16.00hrs.

▷▷▷ **Cha-am**

Buses from Bangkok, Hua Hin and Phetcha Buri. Off Highway 32

Like Hua Hin (see page 125), Cha-am is a resort with a history – though its future is perhaps looking even more high-rise. A mere 20km north of its royal neighbour, Cha-am's beach lies 1km off Highway 4.

The long beach here is Bangkok's closest on the western side of the bight, which accounts for its rapidly developing popularity. The **Rung Arun Bungalow** on Ruamchit Road is at the bottom end of pricey resorts.

▶ **Chantha Buri**

Buses from Bangkok (eastern terminal) and Pattaya

This ancient port is about 330km from Bangkok, south along Highway 3 and the eastern coast. Popularly known as Muang Chan, it is replete with natural resources. The rainy season feeds the waterfalls and the lush forest; the dry season is the time to take to the province's beaches; and the best time of all is the fruit season.

Laem Sadet Khung Kraben has long, clean beaches. It is off Sukhumvit Road (Highway 3) at km 301, a right turn 27m along a laterite road. Coconut palms add to the tranquil atmosphere and many of the restaurants have bathing rooms for swimmers. The town itself is interesting and includes Thailand's largest Catholic cathedral, built by an emigré Vietnamese community.

Few rubies are left in Thai mines...

The Gem industry 'Chan' (as Chantha Buri is locally known) is more famous for its position as a centre of Thailand's booming gem industry. The most convenient gem mining region for the casual visitor is **Tha Mai**. It is reached along Highway 3 and day tours are organised from Pattaya. Twelve kilometres along the route is the small peak of **Phloi Waen**, with **Wat Khao Phloi** at the top. Thai miners have more or less worked out the reserves; jewellers say the last big area for rubies is Phailin, in Cambodia. Beware of the rip-offs and false guarantees that plague the gem trade; see page 260.

Somdet Phra Chao Taksin Maharaj Public Park is a 60-hectare public park in the centre of Chantha Buri town (opposite the provincial court). Boats can be hired for punting. In the middle of the park is an island with a statue of King Taksin, who rallied Siamese troops here in their darkest hour against the Burmese.

Laem Sing, too, is worth a visit, on the left of the river mouth. It can be reached in 10 minutes by boat from one of the fishing villages. A walkway passes an ancient fort called **Phai-rii Phinat** and there are fine views to be had from this hill. To the west of Laem Sing is a clean yellow beach with great views of the islands **Koh Chula**, **Ko Nom Sao** and **Ko Pehrit**; a pair of old cannon remain by a sentry post. In town there are three budget hotels awaiting independent travellers.

Along the road to Laem Sadet Khung Kraben, a right fork leads to the smaller beach of **Khung Wiman**; just before the beach is a large standing Buddha, 'subduing the ocean'.

...but panning continues in some areas

CENTRAL THAILAND

Apart from Damnoen Saduak (see below), other floating markets of interest include Wat Sai in Bang Khun Thien, Thonburi, whose over-popularity spoiled the original atmosphere. In Samut Songkhram province there are Bang Nok Khwaek and Amphawa, the latter being a district next-door to Damnoen Saduak, where the market is held at night. The turn-off from route 35 is very clearly signposted, while route 325 from Nakhon Pathom is the usual alternative.

National Parks Khao Khitchakut National Park is reached by a metalled road (Highway 3) 21km from Sukhumvit (km 324). It is mostly forest and spots well worth visiting include the nine-level Krathing Falls. Great care should be exercised when climbing the levels.

There are two National Park dormitories, capable of sleeping 10–15 people each; a large camp here takes 100 people. A fee is collected on the way in.

Wat Khao Sukrim, a further 10km from Krathing Falls and about 16km from Chantha Buri, is fairly new. This 'reformist' *wat* has a 24-hour supply of free food and a library for overnight stays: a *wat* for the devotee rather than the tourist.

Phliw is a particularly charming, three-stage waterfall at the end of a metalled road 16km from town. There are some *chedis* 200m up, dating from the reign of King Rama V, and a pyramid contains the remains of one of his queens.

About 4km further on are **Trork Nong Falls**. The 'twin peaks' of **Khao Soi Dao** are thickly forested with beautiful mountain views, and a vast wildlife reserve is home to Soi Dao Falls, a 16-level waterfall said to be the biggest and most beautiful in Eastern Thailand (65km north on the Prachin Buri road).

Damnoen Saduak's floating market

Damnoen Saduak
104km southwest of Bangkok; service from southern terminal
Buses run regularly to Damnoen Saduak, a popular tour destination, starting at 06.00hrs.

Visitors go to see the floating market – most popular of the many that have grown up in the region. All over the navigable system women paddle their little boats, selling food to householders on the banks. The market is held early to avoid the midday heat. The classic Thai peasant's straw hat is much in evidence among the women who mostly trade in fruit and vegetables, visitors looking on from the bridge spanning the canal.

124

▶ ▷▷▷ Hua Hin

South on Highway 4, about 230km from Bangkok

Hua Hin is a historic resort, the site of King Rama VII's palace, Klai Kangwo or 'far from worries'. Of period interest are the royal golf course, the railway station and its hotel, which are now in private hands. The spacious Edwardian verandahs are quite impressive.

Hua Hin is well endowed with other hotels and guesthouses – budgeteers can shop around for a homely atmosphere – but maybe this 'endowment' has gone too far, as blocks of flats and apartments crowd out the skyline; Hua Hin is bidding to become Pattaya without the nightlife, but with hill tribe trekking. The beach is pleasant enough, but lacking in shade.

▷▷▷ Kaeng Kra Chan National Park

Off Highway 4 Phetburi (Phetcha Buri) Province

Covering an area of 2,500 sq km, Kaeng Kra Chan is the biggest National Park, located 60km from Phetburi (Phetcha Buri) town. The park office is a futher 8km from Kaeng Kra Chan dam, built to service a smaller dam further down the River Phet. Its reservoir has 20–30 islands and supports waterfowl and fish. Boats can be hired for 10–12 people.

The Thor Thip waterfall Boasting 18 stages, this dramatic spectacle is to be found 15km from Khao Phanoen Thung, the tallest peak in the park at 1,207m; the peak is 20km from the park office.

Walkers might go another 99km along the dam to the Paa Son Khao Thammachat, a mountain pine forest. Rewards take the form of viewpoints, cliffs and rock gardens. The park is not greatly developed and treks off into the jungle are best undertaken with national park guidance.

Staying over There is an accommodation service at usual National Park rates and it is advisable to make a reservation on 579-0529 or 579-4842. Alternatively, there is a moderate private sector development, **Kaeng Kra Chan Resort**, which can be booked on 513-3238.

The Karen village of Pa La-u, a 40km jaunt from Hua Hin, has two stunning waterfalls. If camping, take every precaution against malaria. Attractive features in town include a thriving night market. Walkers can have a go at the stairs up Khao Tagiap (chopstick mountain), which has a monastery, a band of monkeys and tremendous views of the coast.

125

Hua Hin – tranquillity under threat from development

■ **Despite huge losses of natural habitats in the second half of this century, Thailand is still rich in wildlife of all kinds. This ranges from the exotic insects that you can see in town gardens to the giants of the jungle – tigers, elephants and (possibly) the Sumatran rhinoceros (which has not been spotted for over 20 years). These are the creatures most visibly under threat from the desecration of jungles and other habitats – a problem which Thailand is trying to counter. .....■**

Thai wildlife: fighting a losing battle? A female firetailed sunbird...

White elephants were regarded as supernatural omens of divine favour, and became a symbol of prestige for the royal families of both Thailand and Burma. The king today has six such elephants in his stable, but each one can consume more than 6kg of sugar cane, 30 kg of bananas and 300kg of grass in a single day. The feeding bill is colossal. That is why the English phrase 'white elephant' means an expensive encumbrance.

Threats Loss of habitats is not the only threat to Thailand's wildlife: in settled, heavily populated regions, it's neither safe nor convenient to have large, potentially dangerous animals wandering around. Hunters and poachers take a huge toll; the rarer some species become, the more desirable they are to unscrupulous collectors, and the prizes to be gained are therefore very high. Several species of mammal, bird, plant and even insect have been brought close to extinction by poachers and collectors. Trading in the meat of wild creatures is commonplace, as you can see by visiting the Chatuchak Weekend Market in Bangkok. Not only are wild birds and wild pigs sold for their meat, but even protected species like barking deer. The Wildlife Protection Division, which apparently has only nine permanent officials, faces a grave shortage of funds and manpower to carry out its job.

Variety Thailand is at a geographical crossroads, and has 'captured' species from the Indian subcontinent, northern Asia and Australasia, as well as southern Asia. This diversity is particularly noticeable in its birdlife; around 850 species have been recorded, making this one of the most exciting places in the world for birdwatchers.

When it comes to insects, the species are literally innumerable. It is possible that they become extinct even before they are recognised, as forests tumble under the loggers' chainsaws.

Optimism The Thai authorities are anxious to preserve and enhance the country's wildlife, if for no other reason than its appeal to tourists. Already there are 50 or so National Parks, protecting more than 25,000 sq km of unspoiled areas. One of the best and most accessible is Khao Yai (see pages 134–7), which covers a huge area of tropical rainforest. The rainforests are Thailand's greatest natural treasures, with staggering diversities of plants and creatures. Also of great interest and beauty are the coastal regions, with mangrove swamps, forested islands, salt pans, marshes and beaches.

Elephants The elephant is Thailand's most revered animal and national symbol, once featured on its flag (see panel). But that doesn't deter the poachers. A chief warden at a national park recently committed suicide in desperation because his rangers were repeatedly attacked by elephant poachers, armed with M-16s and other sophisticated military weaponry. The maximum fine for poaching is so small as to be derisory.

At the beginning of the century there were about 100,000 domesticated elephants here. They were used in war, to carry logs and to open up virgin forest. You will still see them used commercially even in the towns. A very small proportion of them are 'white' elephants. These are not actually white all over, but have lighter patches of skin here and there.

The former flag of Thailand was unintentionally flown upside down at the Versailles Peace Conference and people said it looked like 'a small domestic animal', so King Vajiravudh changed it for stripes

127

In 1991 a raid on a wildlife farm in Damut Prakan province revealed a grisly haul of 40 bear's paws. These are a particular delicacy in the Chinese and Korean cuisines and are believed to enhance sexual prowess..

...and white water buffalo

CENTRAL THAILAND

Railway Trip to Nam Tok

Two trains daily make this two-hour trip along the 77km that remain of the Death Railway. Booking is not possible. Near the end, the train grinds slowly along a wooden viaduct with views over the river and surrounding mountains. At Tham Krasae it is possible to break the journey and lunch at the bungalow resort below. At the end of the line, *songthaews* leave Nam Tok for Sai Yok Yai, a roadside waterfall. There are frequent buses back to Kanchana Buri.

128

The Bridge over the River Kwae

▶ ▶ ▶   **Kanchana Buri**

Highway 323 west of Bangkok. Trains run daily at 08.00hrs and 13.50hrs from Bangkok (Noi station)
Kanchana Buri Province offers grand scenery, with waterfalls, caves and rugged hills accessible within an hour or two of Bangkok. The train journey from Bangkok, which takes three hours, is a real pleasure, passing lush wetlands, forests and paddies; the same train continues to Nam Tok (see panel).

Kanchana Buri Town, 130km west of Bangkok, has strong associations with World War II, but today the ghosts of the town's grim past seem exorcised, and it is a pleasure resort popular with residents of Bangkok, who at weekends frequent the food stalls by the river and party all night on fancifully designed rafts.

Beyond a bland town centre (bus station and TAT office), older streets towards the river retain characterful wooden shophouses with balconies, and the city gate still stands. A number of waterside guesthouses are relaxing and attractive, although the all-night weekend discos on the river can be irritating.

The Bridge on the River Kwae Three kilometres from the town centre is a grotesque remnant, symbolic of the traumas of the Death Railway, built by POWs in World War II (see pages 132–3). Only the two central pairs of girders – the straight-topped ones – are original. The others are post-war replacements. Today trains make special stops at this macabre tourist attraction, and souvenir stalls sell plastic models of the bridge. It is possible to walk across between the rails, but there are unguarded drops. Two original locomotives are preserved here, and boat trips leave for the Floating Nun (see below), JEATH museum and the Chung Kai cemetery. In early December, a strange weekend sound and light spectacular takes place here, culminating in a mock-up of the Allied bombardment on the Death Railway in 1945, complete with flashes and explosions.

Close by are the **Japanese War Memorial** and the **Museum of War, Gems, Stamps and Watches**. The

latter was in the preparation stage at the time of writing; its bizarre exterior is adorned with life-sized statues of historic warriors and figures from World War II. Count Winston Cherchill (*sic*) bears a remarkable resemblance to Mussolini!

Chung Kai War Cemetery This is located on the west bank and most easily reached by long-tailed boat from the bridge or from the pier near the old city gate; 1,750 prisoners are buried here.

The War Cemetery at Kanchana Buri

Excursions are offered by River and PS guesthouses and by RSP Travel (tel: (034) 512280). Sunya Rux Raft Trip (Pak Praek Road, tel (034) 513868), which makes overnight river trips, with swimming and sunset dinner, as well as shorter outings.

Kanchana Buri War Cemetery Opposite the town's railway station are the gates to these well-tended burial grounds, where 6,982 POWs are interred. An alphabetical register pinpointing locations of graves is kept in the office on the far left-hand side of the site.

JEATH War Museum JEATH is an acronym for the main nations involved: Japan, England, America, Australia, Thailand and Holland.
The museum is at the far south end of town and is reached by boat from the bridge, or by *samlor*. It consists of a reconstruction of a POW *atap* hut and houses a modest but sobering display – objects from the camps, photographs, press cuttings and a series of paintings based on prisoners' sketches that resemble medieval depictions of hell.
Open: daily, 08.30hrs–18.00hrs.

Kanchana Buri Province
Wat Tham Monkorn Thong *6km west of Kanchana Buri town on Highway 3429.* This cave temple is of minor interest – consisting of a staircase leading to a meditation cave – but is celebrated for the Floating Nun who sometimes meditates afloat in a pool and blesses the audience by blowing candle smoke over them.

Prasat Muang Singh Historical Park *Follow Highway 323 westwards, turning left on to Highway 3229, then right on to 3455 as signposted.* On the way you pass the turning for Bankao Museum, devoted to the archaeology of the area.
Prasat Muang was a Khmer outpost sited on a scenic loop of the Kwae Noi river. The major shrine dates back 800 years, its form pierced by four gateways. A shelter

Dawn ferry on the River Kwae

Lawa Cave, in Sai Yok National Park, is one of 21 such cave sites in Kanchana Buri Province which is home to the kitti, or hog-nosed bat, *Craseonycteris thonglongyai.* This is the world's smallest mammal. Looking no larger than a butterfly, it weighs just 2g. Only 2,000 have been recorded and the bat is one of the world's 12 most endangered species.

by the river houses 2,000-year-old skeletons, discovered in 1979; clay pots, bronze, shell and bone bracelets are still *in situ.*

Highway 323 to Three Pagodas Pass A road notorious for its smuggling, this pass leads into Burma through scenery characterised by sugar cane fields and curiously shaped limestone hills. This is an unstable and unpredictable area – there have been border skirmishes in the past – and you would be wise to seek local advice before travelling there.

A bus from Kanchana Buri to Sangkhla Buri takes five hours; there are morning *songthaews* from there to Three Pagodas Pass. The main sights on the highway are:

The Hellfire Pass Memorial, *signposted at the 66km stone.* This is a short circular trail incorporating a section of abandoned track from the Death Railway. Begun by Australian POWs in April 1943, the pass was completed in 12 weeks and earned its nickname from their night-time campfires. The trail opened in 1987 and some rails have been relaid.

Sai Yok National Park, *at the 82km stone, 4km off the highway.* (There is no bus.) Best known for its bat cave (see panel), which can be reached by boat from the pier here, and Sai Yok Noi waterfall.

Hin Dat Hot Spring, *a right turning at the 108km stone.* This spring is a pleasant 40°C – a little above normal body temperature – and can be combined with a cool dip in the adjacent stream.

Sangkla Buri, *beside the vast Khao Laem Reservoir.* Here the forest has been submerged, but eerie tree-stumps can still be seen above water-level. A spectacular matchstick-like wooden bridge straddles the water and leads into the adjacent Mon settlement. Above this there is a hilltop *wat,* which offers a good view of the lake.

Three Pagodas Pass. Along the dirt road to Phra Sam Ong, the route heads past three modest pagodas at the border. It is often possible to walk into the Burmese village of Payathonzu, but cameras must be left behind at the border post. Across the border it is strikingly primitive, in contrast to Thailand. This is a remote and often dangerous area: only the very intrepid tend to travel here.

Tham Lot Cave North of Kanchana Buri, this is one of the province's finest caves (electrically lit) with a waterfall near by. There is no bus.

Erawan Waterfalls These are to be found on Highway 3199 and can be reached by hourly buses and additional excursion buses.
The splendid falls have seven stages; a wet, enjoyable walk to the top takes between three and four hours to do the sight justice. There are pools for swimming, limestone encrustations, tufa and petrified logs. Overnight accommodation is available near by.
Further north, **Huay Khamin Waterfall**, remote but majestic, is reached by boat across Sri Nakharin Dam from Takadan pier.

Erawan Waterfalls

The Death Railway

■ **The railway made famous by David Lean's movie *The Bridge on the River Kwai* commemorates one of the most appalling episodes of World War II. In the midst of the war in southeast Asia, the Japanese saw the need for a rapid land route to get troops and supplies into Burma; the voyage by sea across the Straits of Malacca, followed by a cross-country journey from Rangoon to Moulmein, was slow and hazardous. In January 1942 they decided to build a 400km railway over some of Asia's most inhospitable terrain. .....■**

Forced labour Allied Prisoners of War captured in Malaya, Borneo, Singapore and Indonesia were brought here to build the railway; 16,000 died. Asian labourers were also enlisted, some from foreign companies in Malaya that had closed because of bombing; others came from India, Thailand, Indonesia and Burma. Many were press-ganged into service. They were regarded by the Japanese as totally expendable and were treated even more badly than the POWs; the death toll among them was in the region of 100,000 – roughly one dead for every sleeper laid.

<< David Lean's famous Hollywood film was a fictionalisation of these events, based on Pierre Boulle's novel. Among the cinematic inventions were the blowing up of the bridge by Allied commandos (when in fact it was bombed by the RAF), the use of British engineering skills to construct the bridge (the Japanese knew perfectly well what to do) and the efforts of the Allies in building as quickly and well as possible (they botched it wherever they could). >>

The initial task for POWs was to construct camps at Kanchai and Ban Pong (near Nam Tok). Priority was given to completing the Japanese guards' accommodation, then workhouses and working parties' huts, and lastly the buildings for sick prisoners.

Work began at Thanbyuzayat in Burma on 1 October 1942 and a little later at Ban Pong in Thailand. The two parties met at Nieke in November 1943 and the 423km line was completed in December. Reconnaissance flights by Allied Forces began in 1943 and bombing followed; POWs were now working on patching up and maintenance, cutting fuel for the locomotives, handling stores and building roads. By the end of October, Japanese troops and supplies were getting through to Burma and bombing intensified. Conditions for the prisoners temporarily improved in spring 1944 as the Japanese began to worry about world reaction to the heavy POW casualties, but things got worse from May until the end of the war.

Appalling conditions Malnutrition, disease and torture were the main causes of the high mortality rate. Food deliveries were erratic and what got through was often rotten or infested. Many prisoners came to regard maggots as a vital protein source, and some even went to the length of washing the contents of Japanese officers' latrines to retrieve beans that had passed through their captors' digestive systems. Red Cross parcels were occasional godsends, but were often held up by the Japanese, who sometimes deliberately let new food consignments rot.

Malaria, dysentery, vitamin deficiency and cholera were rife. POW camp doctors had to make do with what few medical supplies they had brought with them. Equipment was ingeniously improvised; drips were made from bamboo. Only the sick could tend to the sick; even some of these were forced to work. Prisoners became walking skeletons. Tropical ulcers gnawed them to the bone; rotten flesh was 'cleaned out' by fish, which ate away the loose material.

Hours were long and bamboo lashings frequent. Japanese and Korean guards devised sadistic tortures for those who were in breach of discipline or not working hard enough. Offenders were suspended by the thumbs from a branch with their feet only just touching the ground, or they were tied to trees with barbed wire. They were forced to hold heavy stones above their heads, or made to kneel on sharp sticks while bearing weights.

The shadow of death was always close and despair crept into many prisoners' minds. Many died in Allied bombing raids, as they were forbidden to build a white triangle on a blue base, the international recognition symbol for a POW camp.

After the war American corpses were repatriated but those of other nationalities were transferred from the camp burial ground to three war cemeteries – one in Burma and two in Kanchana Buri. Mass graves are still discovered from time to time in the jungle.

In 1945 the British dismantled 4km of track at the border and two years later gave the remaining 300km to Thailand. Thai authorities dismantled the line from Nam Tok westwards and upgraded the rest. The line reopened in full in 1958.

133

Memorial to the victims of the Death Railway at Kanchana Buri (above) and (below) the line itself

IN HONOURED REMEMBRANCE OF THE FORTITUDE AND SACRIFICE OF THAT VALIANT COMPANY WHO PERISHED WHILE BUILDING THE RAILWAY FROM THAILAND TO BURMA DURING THEIR LONG CAPTIVITY
THOSE WHO HAVE NO KNOWN GRAVE ARE COMMEMORATED BY NAME AT RANGOON SINGAPORE AND HONG KONG AND THEIR COMRADES REST IN THE THREE WAR CEMETERIES OF KANCHANABURI CHUNGKAI AND THANBYUZAYAT
I will make you a name and a praise among all people of the earth when I turn back your captivity before your eyes, saith the LORD

▶ ▶ Khao Chamao National Park

Off Sukhumvit Road (Highway 3) at km 274 and a further 17km up to Ban Nong Nam Sai

Located in the Klaeng district of Rayong province, Khao Chamao's 83 sq km were declared a National Park in 1975. Waterfalls are plentiful; on the list to see are Khao Chamao, Nam Pen, Khlong Paa Kan, Khlong Hin Phloeng and Khlong Phra Jao. Khao Chamao, also known as Khlong Nam Sai, has very beautiful rock formations. Look out for the big fish in the rock pools, especially the Pla Phluang at Wang Matcha.

Many of the caves at **Khao Wong** have extensive systems of caverns, some of which are very deep. Waai li Lo, Thong Phra Rong, Phra and Sa Song have plenty of stalagtites and stalagmites, and some caves shelter pools of water (complete with fish). Khao Wong can be reached by turning off Sukhumvit Road at km 286 and continuing for 12km. It is a laterite road: tough going in the rainy season.

▶ ▶ ▶ Khao Sam Roi Yot National Park

Reach by private transport or by tour. South of Pran Buri on Highway 4, the turning to this National Park is found at Kuiburi, by the 286km post, but it is quite difficult to spot. About 40km south of Hua Hin

This is a most impressive, desolate moonscape over flooded paddies, with the mountains clearly visible.

The park office has refreshments and very helpful staff. Park beds are available for about 100 baht, and groups can rent a dormitory house for around 500 baht.

A canal behind the office can be explored in a long-tail boat. Between the office and Khao Daeng summit, birds and monkeys abound on all sides. The park is also home to the *serow*, an endangered goat-like animal.

Modest Samphraya beach, 6km north of the park headquarters, has tents for hire. The more remote and beautiful **Laem Sala beach** (17km) is accessible either by boat or by vehicle. Here, King Rama V built a glittering little pavilion at Phraya Nakhon Cave to catch the sun.

▶ ▶ ▶ Khao Yai National Park

Highway 1 to Saraburi, then Highway 2. A bus leaves from Bangkok Northern Bus Terminal at 09.00hrs, returning at 15.00hrs

Thailand's richest National Park for wildlife lies just over 200km to the north of the capital, and extends across 2,168 sq km, straddling four provinces and rising to 1,351m. The road up to the top (Highway 3182) has a signposted viewpoint looking across the park.

Park wildlife The park encompasses a diversity of habitat – tropical rainforest, hill evergreen, dry evergreen, dry deciduous forest and grassland – that gives rise to over 2,000 plant and 300 bird species. Bird check-lists and trail maps are on sale at the park headquarters. It is easy to get lost here, and you would be well advised to hire a guide.

Each evening at 20.00hrs, trucks leave on night safari from the park headquarters and restaurant. As they beam spotlights over the adjacent jungle there is a fair

Khao Yai missed out on gaining World Heritage Site status because of illegal encroachment around its peripheries, a highway slicing through its very heart and a recurring threat of a major dam construction on a site partly covered with virgin forest and inhabited by elephants. In 1992 talk was of demolishing the Motor Lodge hotel accommodation and turning Khao Yai golf course into a field – in the interests of conservation. The park bungalows may well go too, although it seems likely that the campsite and dormitory accommodation will remain. For up-to-date information telephone the Forestry Department (02) 579 0529.

134

Khao Yai National Park

chance of spotting one of the park's 100 elephants which frequent salt-licks near the road. Samba deer are the largest deer species, and display magnificent antlers. Porcupines, palm civets (small, spotted cats), gaurs (wild black cattle) and slow loris are commonly seen and a watchtower in the grassland is well placed for a rare view of Khao Yai's 50 tigers.

Park trails Khao Yai has 12 waymarked trails through tropical forest, thick with winding creeper and luxuriant ferns. Look out for gibbons, civets and monkeys. Exotic birdsong haunts the forest; the birds themselves often remaining tantalisingly out of sight, but with patience you should get the odd sighting, maybe of the great hornbill, the park's largest bird.

Haew Suwat is the most accessible and popular of the park's many waterfalls, and has a beautiful pool where you can swim behind the curtain of water.
The **Million Bats Cave** is off the Pak Chong road (outside the park at the 21km stone, by a *wat* and a sign to Forest Hill; fork right after 2km to reach a parking area). A steep path leads up to a small cave where a dark swirl of countless wrinkled-lipped bats leaves at dusk. They hunt for eight to 10 hours and trap 6,000 mosquitoes each night. Their guano is collected for fertilising fruit trees and for use in gunpowder manufacture.

Park accommodation This is in a state of flux (see panel on page 134). Bungalow accommodation gets heavily booked at weekends and starts at 600 baht per bungalow. Dormitory accommodation is basic in the extreme (just floorboards to sleep on) but much cheaper – bring a mat and sleeping bag, as it can get very cold. There is also a campsite. Guides should be arranged in advance through the Forestry Department. Numerous up-market resort hotels and golf courses are found on the road to Pak Chong, just outside the park.

Walk   **10km circular walk in Khao Yai: trails 1, 3 & 4.**

Getting there Khao Yai is about three hours by road from Bangkok. Two-day tours from nearby Pak Chong are offered by **Khao Yai Wildlife Tour** (tel: (044) – 3130545) and **Jungle Adventure** at 752/11 Kongvaksin Road Soi 3, Pak Chong. Both leave daily and no booking is required. Additionally, many travel agencies in Bangkok can arrange trips. There are four buses an hour from Bangkok to Pak Chong.

Start at Pha Kluai Mai (Orchid) Campsite.
Allow five hours; tread quietly to enhance your chances of spotting wildlife. The walk leads through dense jungle but the way is shown with paintmarks.

Turn right out of the campsite, along the road. After 350m take the trail on the left signed Gong Gheo Waterfall (7km) and follow Trail 3 (red and yellow paintmarks).
The paths are generally well trodden although at times overgrown.

After one and a quarter hours turn right at path junction (Trail 1; orange paintmarks). The left path is signed to Visitor Centre. Ignore another left turn for Visitor Centre 10 minutes later.
In the rainy season, cover yourself with insect repellent to guard against leeches. Inspect yourself for ticks, pin-head sized brown insects that fall from plants and burrow into the skin. If you get one, don't pull it out; cover the area with nail varnish or glue.

After another hour's walking continue on to Haew Suwat at the junction, ignoring the left turn to Haew Praton.
The final section has fine waterfalls and there is a well-sited restaurant.

Fifteen minutes later, Haew Sai waterfall can be reached by a short, steep path to the left, or by continuing along the main path. Both routes unite near the foot of Haew Suwat waterfall, from which it is an easy one-and-a-half–hour riverside stroll on Trail 4 to the campsite.

Take precautions against mosquitos at Ko Samet: they are malarial. Netting, cream and spray would be advisable for a stay here.

King Norai: a statue in Lop Buri

▶ ▶ ▶   Ko Samet

Off the eastern coast of Rayong Province, in the Gulf of Thailand

It is easy to drive or get a direct bus to Ban Phe, the supply port, then take one of the regular boats. On being dropped at Samet harbour, the walk round to the beaches is not arduous, but a pick-up service is available. There are also tour buses.

Also known as Ko Kaew Phitsadan, 'the enchanted crystal island', Ko Samet inspired some of the writings of the classical Thai poet Sunthorn Phu. Its beauty, however, has been under threat, and this is another park (like Khao Yai) where the authorities have felt compelled to reinforce the National Park status in the wake of massive surreptitious development. Towards the end of 1990 the island was officially closed in a tense stand-off between the government and bungalow operators. The bungalows were allowed to stay, but an unrepentant government refused to rescind the ban. Maybe the operators realise the insecurity of their investment and are unwilling to increase it. Cynics doubt the government's sincerity, suspecting them of wanting shares of a bigger pie.

None of these political considerations seems to affect Ko Samet's popularity as an island retreat for Bangkokians. Despite the fact that boats stop running in the evening, despite limited well-water and unreliable electricity, the weekends in particular see hundreds of Thais coming to 'hang out in the air' or *tak agat*. It gets very busy in August and from December to January.

Paying the National Park fee first, it is an easy matter to walk down to the sea at Hat Sai Kaew. This first beach is popular with Thais who have built restaurants and bungalows here. At Ao Phai beach, Sea Breeze and Naga bungalows are recommended. Beyond a charming little cove is Ao Wongdeuan and some up-market developments. Forest trails run west from the track, linking this string of beaches to another beach and coves, where there are splendid sunset views.

▶ ▷ ▷   Lop Buri

Highway 1 north from Bangkok. Buses and trains (Chiang Mai line) from Bangkok

There are frequent buses to Lop Buri from Bangkok and trains run on the Bangkok–Chiang Mai line. Note that buses take you to New Lop Buri, which is of no intrinsic interest; take a *samlor* from here, as it is much too far to walk. The railway station is within a few minutes' walk of all the historic sights.

The town of Lop Buri lies 155km to the north of the capital. Lop Buri has considerable appeal for its compactness and modest demands, although it hasn't the wealth of historical remains found in Ayutthaya or Sukothai. Sites of interest can be walked around comfortably in a half day.

During the Dvaravati period of the 6th to 11th centuries, Lop Buri was named *Lavo* and was a major centre. In the 10th century it became part of the Khmer empire, but its heyday was as the second capital after Ayutthaya, during the reign of King Narai in the 17th century.

Narai Rajaniwet Palace The walled palace dominates the town centre. It was built between 1665 and 1677 for King Narai, who died here in 1688. French architects assisted in its design, which shows European as well as Khmer influences. Numerous European emissaries stayed here. The palace stands partly ruined in a pleasant park setting of shady lawns.

Entering through the main gateway, the path leads past a former reservoir, on the left, which once supplied the city and which was fed by terracotta pipes from a source 20km away. The long red-brick building behind is the old treasure house. Over the path ahead, a pointed arch shows clear Islamic influences.

Beyond, a complex of three pavilions house the **Lop Buri National Museum**, a substantial collection, with objects from the Dvaravati period onwards, including fine Lop Buri-style religious artefacts found locally.

Behind this is the roofless audience hall, where Narai received the ambassador of Louis XIV, the Chevalier de Chaumont. Arch-shaped doors and windows hint at the European connection, although others are traditionally Thai tapering oblongs.

Open: Wednesday to Sunday except national holidays, 08.30–12.00, 13.00–16.30hrs. Admission fee.

The ruins of Sam Yot, near Lop Buri

Wat Phra Sri Mahathat Opposite the railway station, this impressive site dates from the 12th century. Its central *prang* is Khmer in style; later additions include *chedis* in the Ayutthaya and Sukotai styles. There is an admission fee.

Phra Prang Sam Yot By the railway line 200m north of the station, these three giant laterite and sandstone *prangs* show both Hindu and Buddhist influences and represent the quintessence of Lop Buri style. They denote Brahmin, Siva and Vishnu, the Hindu trinity. Across the railway, San Phra Kan is a modern Hindu shrine abutting an ancient laterite mound. Well-fattened monkeys and docile goats frequent the compound, feeding on temple offerings. The 'monkey feast' held at the end of November is a big media event here.

Vichayen House This was built for the Chevalier de Chaumont, and was later the residence of Constantin Phaulkon, Narai's chief minister from Greece; he was the only *farang* to hold such a post in the Siamese court and was killed in a *coup* by Phra Phetracha, who subsequently moved the court to Ayutthaya. Remains of a chapel and hall of residence are visible. There is an entry fee.

King Narai's city wall fortification still encloses the old city, although it is little more than a rough bank. A town gate survives on the south side.

'Newsmen, young ladies, senior citizens – why be slow? Happiness awaits in Nakhon Nayok. Cast off your sadness into Wang Takhrai falls. Boost your morale at Sarika – where can compare with our house?' – Thai promotional leaflet.

▶ **Nakhon Nayok**
North from Bangkok along Highway 1, then Highway 305. Buses from Bangkok (northern/northeastern terminal)
About 140km from the capital, Nakhon Nayok is only an hour or two's drive from Rangsit, situated to the northwest of the airport, along Highway 305. The road crosses a series of parallel canals. Follow Route 3049 across the main intersection in town to get up the mountain to Wang Takhrai.

The Chumphot-Phanthip botanical gardens These were founded in 1952 and named after the lemon grass which grows here in abundance.

Sarika waterfall is a 3km turn-off to the left on Highway 3049. This popular beauty spot is close to a number of prettily designed bungalow resorts such as Chor Mamuang Cottage, Sut Jai and Po Daeng Wang. These will serve the faint-hearted, while the energetic will find, above the headwaters of Sarika, the **Mae Plong waterfall**, which must be trekked to and camped at.

Takhrai Resort was probably the first ever bungalow resort built in Thailand. The **Sidari Resort** offers accommodation at Nang Long waterfall, towards the road's end.

Dong Lakhorn To the south of the city are the ruins of this settlement, which dates from the Dvaravati period until the time that the Ayutthayan influence made Nakhon Nayok pre-eminent. It was abandoned to the forest 100 years ago.
Ironically, today the surrounding forest is all rice paddies and Dong Lakhorn itself is now a last refuge for many forest species. Of special interest among the artefacts uncovered are glass beads and small earthenware pots.

Nakhon Pathom

*West along Highway 4 about 54km west of Bangkok.
Buses(southern terminal) and trains from Bangkok*
Believed to be the oldest city in Thailand, Nakhon
Pathom's name is derived from the Pali expression
Nagara Pathama, 'First City'.

Phra Pathom Chedi The whole city is dominated by this
huge tower, which can be seen for miles around. At
127m, it is the highest Buddhist monument in the world.
The original *chedi* was a much more modest affair, built
during the Mon empire and the oldest Buddhist
monument in the country. Nakhon Pathom was then one
of a loose collection of city states that flourished
between the 6th and 11th centuries. When the town
was beseiged by King Anawrahta of Burma in the 11th
century, the *chedi* was destroyed and the town left in
ruins. Restoration was begun by King Mongkut in the
mid-19th century, but eventually these attempts had to
be abandoned as the fabric of the building proved to be
so unstable. Instead, a new one was built over the
original site. This new temple fell victim to a particularly
bad period of rain and storms and was finally completed
by King Chulalongkorn as the magnificent structure seen
today. It commands an appropriately large park setting
and is surrounded by trees. Dance drama is sometimes
performed next to the outer walls and a fair is held in the
temple grounds each November.
A nearby museum contains some interesting sculpture.
Open: Daily. Museum open Wednesday to Sunday,
09.00hrs–12.00hrs, 13.00hrs–16.00hrs.

141

Nakhon Sawan

*North off Highway 117. By bus and train (Chiang Mai
line) from Bangkok*
Nakhon Sawan town is situated at a major river
confluence, where the rivers Nan, Ping, Wang and Yom
unite to form the great Chao Phraya. A meeting of
Central and North Thailand adds significance to this large
town, whose sights include Wat Chom Kiri Nak Phrot,
towering over the plain and offering a huge view.
At the Chinese New Year a lively dragon procession
draws the crowds from far around.

*Wat Phra Pathom
Chedi, Nakhon Pathok*

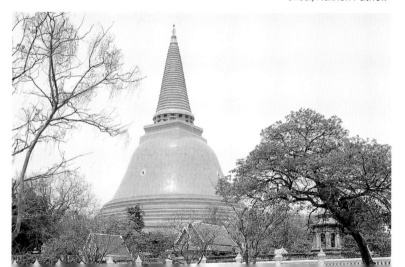

▶ ▮▮▮▮ **Pattaya**

Off Highway 3 on the eastern coast of the Gulf of Thailand. Buses from Bangkok (eastern terminal)

The legend of Pattaya is well known. From a few GIs sleeping on the beach grew a city to rival its political master, Chon Buri. Starting out with attractions aimed at the young single military man, the settlement soon added other items for family clients, as the new tourist resort turned to the Deutschmark, as the main incoming foreign currency. The days of 'R 'n' R' are still far from over. The US Navy rewarded their Gulf War personnel with an extended binge in a town that might be likened to a latter-day Sodom or Gomorrah.

Urban decadence: Pattaya

Rapid growth Development has been fast, furious and mainly unplanned, to the extent that the 'Pattaya syndrome' has been specifically avoided by everywhere else, even Phuket. As at Patong in Phuket, some visitors may feel uneasy in a place that is almost no longer 'Thai', but for jaded urban decadence, Pattaya is heaven. The foreign-food restaurants are a prime example, offering a Babel of menus that easily rivals Bangkok's.

Night-time entertainment, besides the 'bar-beer', includes night clubs and discos, of which the Palladium is the largest.

Building sites litter the place, and this is a town where seediness is endemic. The disadvantages of carelessly disposed waste are painfully apparent, as swimming becomes an unpleasant obstacle course. However, wide publicity of Pattaya's unsavoury aspects has not discouraged the visitors, and, to be fair, it is a lot more appealing than some cold and wet places in Europe.

The beaches There are two beaches: **Pattaya**, named after a sea breeze, and the larger **Jomtien** to its south. The former area, a 'ladder' of parallel *sois*, is where the night action takes place in noisy bars. Jomtien is a more pleasant venue for just enjoying the beach, although it is not clean, and sitting in the wrong place can mean onstant harassment by a stream of vendors.

The package tourists generated Pattaya's second splurge of growth. Water sports by day are of most kinds – parasailing, water-skiing, windsurfing and gamefishing. It scores over Phuket, with dinghy sailing encouraged by the King, whose Royal Varuna Yacht Club is in nearby Jomtien, and has the single-handed Laser dinghy for hire.

Leaving early in the morning are tours to **Ko Lan** with the glass-bottomed boat excursion. Less than an hour away, there is a regular ferry, although most people book a tour. Further out, and for divers only, are **Ko Sak**, **Ko Lin** and **Ko Pai**, the latter having an old shipwreck. Charters are pricey.

For the children Pattaya Park, at the Pattaya Park Beach Hotel, is the perfect water palace with huge slides. A death-defying Bungy Jump has been installed, and now a new version will propel you up into the air. Kids may love a little zap on a water scooter, or, away from the beaches, the elephant show at Nong Nooch garden may appeal to them, as might the scale-model **Mini Siam**.

143

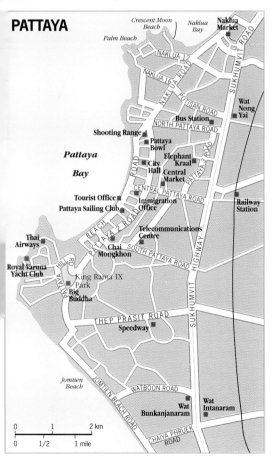

Katoeis
Thailand's transvestites are transsexuals who use hormones and are so convincing that it is a challenge to spot them. The *katoei* is generally understood to be a passive homosexual who has long had a role in the traditional village burlesque or *Likay*. In Pattaya they make serious money by titillating coachloads of package tourists with lip-synch cabaret routines. The phenomenon has spread from there to Bangkok, and recently to Patong beach in Phuket. The shows are genuinely entertaining, with an eclectic menu of Chinese, Thai and Western songs. Pattaya's pioneering shows, still going strong, are called Tiffany's and Alcazar.

Wat Mahathat at Phetcha Buri

Mareukha Thaai Wan Palace was moved by Rama VI from Jao Samran to a little way off Cha-am. The three double-decker buildings are known as 'the palace of love and hope'.

▶ ▶ Phetcha Buri (Phetburi) Province
165km south of Bangkok, on Highway 5. Buses from Bangkok (southern terminal)
The provincial capital of Phetcha Buri is within comfortable driving distance of Bangkok. Phet's proximity to the capital makes it very popular with Thai weekenders; it is worth a visit with a stopover, to take in the many worthwhile sights in and around the capital. The town itself is haphazardly and quaintly laid out. Rivers and canals abound and the march of the concrete shophouse is at least partially arrested.

Wats In town, **Wat Mahathat** is an ancient *wat* of Mahayanist inspiration, with a sister temple in Nakhorn Si Thammarat. The large white *prang* (rounded spire) can be seen from quite a distance away. This important temple is always a hive of activity.
Wat Yai Suwannaram has weird murals in a windowless chapel associated with Phra Jao Seua, 'the tiger king'.
E-Ko mountain, to the north of Khao Yoi district, has an important *chedi* and customary 'merit walk'.
Well worth a visit is **Wat Kamphaeng Laeng**, a complex of temples which as a whole is in good condition. Indicative of a Khmer presence a millenium ago, there are four red sandstone *prangs* from the reign of Woraman VII in Bayon style. In 1956 a statue of Umadevi was found inside a broken *prang*. On Kamphaeng Laeng Road in town, the walls remain.

Beaches Once a favourite haunt of 16th-century King Naresuan, **Jao Samran beach** has now been well developed with hotels and eateries. The wide choice of places to stay includes Jao Hut bungalow (in the budget range), Wong Jan bungalow (moderate to expensive) and Hat Jao Samran hotel.

Hat Beuk Tian is another clean, wide beach 7km to the south of Jao Samran. The broad white sands are reached by the Phetkasem highway, turning left at Thaa Yaang. Accomodation at Beuk Tian Villa (tel: 428-299) ranges from budget to expensive.

Out of town To the west is the major landmark of **Khao Wang**. It is the site of King Mongkhut's palace and hilltop settlement known collectively as **Phra Nakhon Khiri** (Holy City Hill). A cobbled path leads up the hill and there are good views to be had, particulary at sunset. The vista spans the city, the surrounding river and rice fields and even the border with Burma to the west. The walk up is harder than it looks, and is usually completed with monkeys looking on from their vantage points in the trees and surrounding walls. An alternative is provided by the electric tram.

The site is now a National Historical Park, and there is an entrance fee. There is also a national museum on the site.

Open: Wednesday to Sunday, 09.00hrs–16.00hrs.

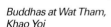

Caves 3km out of town, **Khao Luang** is a famed Buddhist shrine, where a big cave has a tree-lined entrance secured by a door. In the illuminated caverns locals have installed images and a footprint. Opposite the entrance is **Wat Bun Thawee** with striking designs by its former artisan abbot. The legend of nearby **Tham Klaep** caves tells of a secret door leading to a mysterious land which is populated only by young maidens.

Khao Bandai-it is to the west. Vehicles have easy access to the mouth of this pretty Phetcha Buri cave system with its Ayutthaya-period religious accoutrements.

Khao Yoi, another cave system, in the isolated mountain area, is 22km out of town but on the railway line and boasts a reclining Buddha, 10m in length. This was a favoured meditation spot of Rama IV when he was a monk.

Buddhas at Wat Tham, Khao Yoi

The beach at Wa Kor, 14km south of Prachuap Kiri Khan, has been chosen for an ambitious government 'science park' scheme. Still a long way from completion, it promises to be a major tourist attraction. Its construction is in honour of King Rama IV, who viewed a total solar eclipse here. Unfortunately he caught malaria and died soon afterwards.

▶ ▶ ▷   **Prachuap Khiri Khan**
Off Highway 4; 90km south of Hua Hin. Buses from Bangkok (southern terminal) and Hua Hin
Thailand is only 10km wide at the narrowest part of this slender lifeline linking Bangkok with the south. Attractive beaches are dotted down the coastline, which makes up a large part of this province.
Hua Hin is a favourite with Thais (see page 125) and **Pran Buri** is a small town just over 23km to the south which is trying to emulate its northern neighbour.
Prachuap Khiri Khan town has an attractive waterfront, a glittering panorama of harbour and mountain. Conveniently close is the walkway up **Khao Chong Krajok** ('mirror mountain') to a *chedi* and pleasant viewpoint, taking in nearby Burmese mountains and the town laid out below. The 'mirror mountain' earns its name from a hole in its side which seems to reflect the sky. Halfway up, look out for the guardian monkeys. Apart from this Prachuap is a typical quiet provincial centre with several budget /moderate bungalows.
Suan Son ('casuarina garden'), is a sandy beach in the north of the province, and nearby Khao Tao is good for swimming. Just off Suan Son is Ko Singto, from where boats can be hired for diving and fishing.
Wana kon is a long casuarina-lined beach with clear and shallow water, fine for swimming. Kasetsat University Forestry Department have a bungalow which they hire out (tel: 579-0520).
A few kilometres from here is **Huai Yang Waterfall National Park**, refreshing and fish-filled. South again from this is **Thap Sakae**. The moderate/expensive Chanruen Hotel, right on the end of Thap Sakae beach (tel: 032-671890), has spotlessly clean bungalow units but the overall atmosphere is a bit bleak. The budget Chavalit is a small hotel on a right turn off Highway 4. The beach is not very suitable for swimming.

Offshore islands seen from Khao Chong Krajok

The last district before Chumphon is Bang Saphan Noi, where **Pa Klang Ao** is a preserved forest campsite only 2km out.
The port at Ban Pak Khlong services **Ko Thalu**, which has fine shallow beaches: a great camping spot. Near the end is **Ao Bor Thong Lang**, a pretty, crescent-shaped rocky bay.

147

North of Bangkok on Highway 1
Saraburi is an unremarkable central province with three main attractions.
Thailand's most famous Buddha footprint, **Phra Buddhabat**, 27km north of Saraburi town on the road to Lop Buri, is housed in a most impressive pagoda.
Muak Lek waterfall is fine for swimming and is easy to find in Muak Lek district on the road and railway to Khorat (Nakhon Ratchasima).
The remarkable **Wat Tham Krabawk** is a Buddhist answer to drug addiction. At the Krabawk cave monastery, addicts undergo an intensive course of herbal emetics to clean out their systems. The success rate is higher with Thais, because of their respect for the monkhood. Reformed addicts put on displays to warn schoolchildren and herbal products are on sale.

Si Racha

Southeast of Bangkok on Highway 3. Buses from Bangkok (eastern terminal)
Exactly 100km along the recently built Bangna-Trad highway from Bangkok, Si Racha is in the middle of government efforts to develop the Gulf of Thailand's eastern seaboard as a manufacturing base. This is not really a destination for tourists; more a fishing port which is passed through *en route* for the island of Ko Si Chang.
South of the provincial centre of Chon Buri is **Ang Sila** and its distinctive *wat*. Many Thai tourists head for the beach resort at **Bang Saen**. Serious efforts have been made to clean up this beach, which at times is clogged

Squid fishing boats, Si Racha

148

Ko Sichang has recently been the centre of an embarrassing scandal, in which over-zealous quarrying caused half the island to collapse.

up with plastic bags and bits of rope. On the plus side there are deck chairs, food stalls and swimming showers.

Si Racha may not be a swimming centre, although there are two small beaches. The town has a 'seaside' appeal all the same, unlike the rushed, modern Pattaya. Prime spot of the market/fishing town is pretty **Ko Loi**, a small island with a fetching Thai-Chinese temple on it. Sitting at the end of a long causeway, it cuts a pretty silhouette at sunset.

About halfway between here and Si Racha are clear signposts to **Khao Khio open zoo**, an 18km detour to the left. A variety of species roam over a wide area. Perhaps this is the best place to appreciate gibbons; elsewhere, domesticated animals are kept on chains and in the wild mothers are shot for their babies.

Ko Sichang This is one of the closest islands to Bangkok. The boat there takes 45 minutes and costs about 20 baht. It leaves from Tha Jalin, left of the intersection coming in from the main road to Si Racha.

The island has one town, where the boats arrive, and a hilltop temple overlooking it. The system of roads is toylike and not suitable for cars; however there are motorbike taxis available. The island is small enough to walk round and a stroll to the far side will take you to several beaches.

Khao Khaat (Hin Klom) beach, on the other side of the mountains from the port area, is amazingly clean for this area, powdery grey sand and shallow waters making it ideal for swimming. It is somewhat inaccessible by road and involves a climb down the rocks. There is another beach at Laem Nguu, but not as good.

Other attractions on the little island include the **summer palace**, whose site is still atmospheric even though the best of it was moved to create Wimanmek in Bangkok. The hilltop *wat* looks out over the developed, low-lying side of the island, at its base an impressive Chinese arch. The **Chakraphong caves** here hold Buddha images.

Besides beaches, the hilly western coast has Tham Phang (cave), Hin Tukata (rock formations), and the garden of Kratok Rok. Pick-up services are available. The oldest established bungalows on the island are 1km from the boat jetty.

Si Racha is good for sea food, and also home to the spicy sauce that graces many Thai dining tables – *nam phrik si racha.*

Staying at Ko Sichang At Thiw Phai the manager, Toom, speaks impressive English. They party all night here, but it is a long way from the beach. Prices range from 90 to 450 baht, which includes accommodation, TV, short-wave radio and fridge. There are also telephones to the outside world (see **Directory**, page 279). Toom also organises a day trip to nearby Ko Khang Khao from 10.00–17.00hrs. The cost per group is in the region of 780 baht. Activities include fishing, snorkelling, swimming and nude sunbathing.

Benz Bungalow is another bungalow accommodation site near the dirt-track which leads up to the beach (see page 279). Alternatively there are a couple of guesthouses in the town.

▷▷▷ Suphan Buri

Northwest of Bangkok and about 70km northeast of Kanchana Buri on Highway 340. Buses from Bangkok (northern terminal)

Suphan Buri town is at the apex of a triangle with Bangkok and Kanchana Buri. A moderately sized, prosperous centre, it is fairly typical of others in central Thailand, although it is not high on the list of tourist venues.

It does have its attractions, not least of which is its long history, dating back to the Dvaravati Period between the 6th and 10th centuries. However, the town today is modern and dull, and probably only worth seeing if you are changing buses here.

On the outskirts of town is **Wat Palalai**, the town's most notable and biggest attraction – biggest because of the tall whitewashed walls around the *bot*. Their height was necessary to accommodate a huge 15m seated Buddha image, which draws hundreds of believers daily to pay their respects and to worship. Many of the surrounding buildings are very old, having been built originally in the U Thong Period. To complete the scene, goats wander round outside the temple.

Nearer the Suphan Buri river and the centre of town, is **Wat Phra Si Mahathat**, set a little way back off Malimaen Road. Most impressive is the Khmer *prang* which contains a chamber at the top of a staircase, housing a replica of another *prang*.

To the west of Suphan Buri is the war memorial and famous battle site of Don Chedi. It was built to commemorate the defeat of the Prince of Burma and the freeing of Ayutthaya by Prince Naresuan and his forces, riding on elephants.

The site fell into disrepair and was eventually lost and forgotten. It was rediscovered in 1913, after Rama V had tried and failed to find it, but was not restored until the 1950s.

During fair week (see panel), buses run from Suphan Buri and, at other times, from the Northern Bus Terminal in Bangkok. Transport can also be arranged via travel agents in the capital.

Don Chedi Monument Fair is held annually during the week which includes Armed Forces Day, 25 January. As part of the celebrations there is a re-enactment of the battle of the princes and their elephants.

149

A taste of Thai food: chilli fish sauce

CENTRAL THAILAND

► ▶ ▷▷ **Trat**
Southeast from Bangkok down Highway 3. Buses from Bangkok (eastern terminal)
Trat province is on the border of Cambodia, 400km southeast from Bangkok. Its strange shape dates from Siam's most serious tussle with France, when Rama V gave up swathes of the north to remove French troops from this strategic shoreline.
Malaria still plagues the province, so take good precautions as you go east. To prevent mosquito bites, it is as well to use several methods of protection (eg screens, net, repellant, coil) simultaneously.
Perhaps in part owing to Cambodia's troubles, and also because of its remoteness, some unpleasant incidents have given rural Trat a poor reputation for safety. Travelling alone is not to be recommended. No doubt security will improve; the tourist influence is regarded beneficial to this area as a whole.

Coconut boats offloading near Trat

The gem markets Northern Trat, like Chanta Buri, is a famous ruby-mining area. The province's most important gem market is in Bo Rai district, found by taking one of the many roads about 50km north towards the Cambodian border. It takes a trained eye to tell the value of a raw stone. Use the afternoon market on the road to Khlong Yor for small souvenirs, bearing in mind that it is possible to be taken in by some of the wares. An added attraction at Bo Rai is the nearby **Khao Salak Dai waterfall**.

Trat town is best used as a starting point for trips to the offshore islands. Its large market is well suited for stocking up with equipment and provisions. All the boats to Ko Chang leave from Laem Ngop district, 19km to the southwest of the town of Trat.

Incurable sightseers will want to see the 300-year old Wat Bupharam off the road to Bangkok. In the older quarter, too, are some reminders of the brief French occupation. Several beaches on the coast along from Trat town are excellent for swimming, such as Mai Rut, where purple shellfish litter the beach. On the western side of the Trat estuary is remote but beautiful Ao Tan Khuu, found by carrying on west from Laem Ngop.

Staying over If Trat is a stopover before heading for the hills or exploring its offshore islands, there are one or two hotels to choose from.

In the moderate to expensive bracket is **Muang Trat**; moving down-market, in the budget to moderate range there is the **Thai Roong Roj**, which is nice and clean.

The offshore islands Trat's islands are becoming increasingly well known; this whole area is a Marine National Park. **Ko Chang** is the country's third largest island and, together with other coconut- and fishing-based paradises like its neighbours **Ko Mak** and **Ko Kut**, it is now receiving tentative development. It is a dry area, where water is scarce; even the park accommodations have shared washing facilities.

Ko Chang Here on the Khlong Mayom, whose beauty attracted kings, there are some beautiful waterfalls. The park office is at the *khlong* mouth and a passable road links settlements on the northern coast. The **Thanmayom** waterfall is a rewarding sight, as is **Nonsee** waterfall, opposite Tha Dan Mai jetty.

Three super-budget resorts are sited next to beaches. Spots to head for are **Hat Sai Khao**, an easy 2km stroll from the jetty at Ao Khlong Son, and **Chaichet**, nestling inside a headland about 5km further on. On the south side, the atmosphere at **Bang Bao** comes recommended. This place marks the end of the trail some 20 km further south, where a beach stretches over the mouth of a stream.

Ko Kut This, the second biggest island, has been mooted as the next victim of predatory development. The trip takes six hours if you can talk your way onto a coconut- or fishing-boat in town. The boats leave several times a month. More surefire, perhaps, is a trip east down the province's thin tail (Highway 318) to get a (quite expensive) long-tail boat at Ban Ta Neuk, from where the trip will only take an hour.

Once on the island, there is only the very tiny and basic **First** bungalow – on **Haat Taphao** ('turtle beach'), a short distance by dirt track from where the boats pull in.

Ko Mak is an example of Bangkok business exclusivity with an expensive resort, which could be fun if you can afford it.

Border country
Carrying on further south from Ban Neuk, Khlong Yai is the last district before the Thai border melts into the sea, surrounded by Cambodia. A border market is conducted near here, and there are some budget/moderate hotels. Not so far away on the Khmer side is Pailin, whose underdeveloped ruby mines are some of the best left. Exports from Cambodia are mostly handicrafts exchanged for everyday Thai consumer goods. Khlong Yai is just one of many markets on the Thai–Cambodian border now thriving in a tentative post civil- war atmosphere.

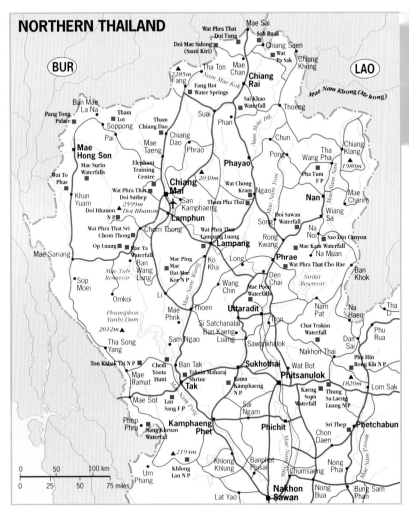

The green, intricate folds of Thailand's northern mountains merge into the wilds of Burma and Laos. Teak forests and patchworks of slash-and-burn agriculture dominate the highlands above the pancake-flat rice plains and prosperous-looking cities. High up, hill tribes subsist in villages of bamboo huts, roofed with palm thatch or corrugated iron. Waterfalls, hot springs and bat-inhabited caves exist in profusion.

Northern Thailand is still culturally distinct. It retains its own dialects, cuisine and architecture. Temples in particular show legacies of ancient Lanna and Burmese styles. Much of the best of the region lies in unsignposted obscurity. Fortunately the north is well endowed with tour agencies and trekking companies that get to places that an individual would never find. Tortuous dirt tracks winding up into remote jungle make exciting but demanding driving. Given the very real dangers of the notorious Golden Triangle, one of the world's foremost drugs-producing regions, it is best to go with a guide.

Chiang Mai is likely to be most visitors' first stop in the north. Thailand's second city makes a good starting point: accommodation is plentiful, eating out wonderfully varied and the range of Thailand's famous souvenir shopping comprehensive. It is well placed for Doi Inthanon, the roof of Thailand, and for organised trips to see waterfalls and elephant shows. Yet there are indications that the city has gone too commercial; many tourists find that for all its packaged convenience it has lost its innocence; the real rewards for exploratory travel lie elsewhere.

Mae Hong Son and Chiang Rai provinces offer fine scenery and hill-tribe culture (although the main towns are nothing special) and are gaining popularity. Seekers of the real back of beyond should also sample the Mekong River east of the Golden Triangle, or the highlands of Nan province.

The lower north has a trio of historic ruined cities, of which Sukothai is the undisputed pearl. Westwards, Mae Sot is on the edge of some of the grandest mountains in the country.

Harvesting rice in Northern Thailand

Map labels: Ban Huai Pung, Pang Tong Palace, Ban Mae La Na, Tham Lot, Ban Piang Luang, Ban Tham Tab Tao, BUR, Mae Aw, Soppong, 1794m, Wiang Haeng, Ban Ping Khong, 1521m, Wiang Ko Sai National Park, 2042m, Pai, Tham Chiang Dao, Chiang Dao, Phrao, Ban Nai Soi, 1962m, 1718m, Ban Tha Prong Daeng, Mae Hong Son, Pa-Pae Hot Spring, Hill Tribe Centre, Elephant Training Centre, Nam Tok Mae Surin National Park, 1731m, Muang Paeng Hot Spring, 107, Mae Taeng, Ban Balaan, Ban Wat Chan, Ban Huai Pang, 1910m, Mae Surin Waterfalls, Mae Sa Valley and Waterfalls, Mae Rim, Doi Saket, Ban Se Pe, Elephants at Work, 1096, Doi Suthep, Ban Mae Ngao, Khun Yuan, Samoeng, Phu Phing Palace, San Sai, Wat To Phae, Ban Mae Sa, Wat Phra That Doi Suthep, CHIANG MAI, Nong Haeng Hot Spring, Ban Hua Pon, Ban Mae Win, San Kamphaeng, Ban Pa Thaw, 1818m, Ban Mae Win, Hang Dong, San Pa Tong, Lamphun, Doi Ithanon 2599m, Doi Ithanon National Park, 1192, 1009, 108, Pa Sang, 11, 1715m, Mae Klang Waterfall, Chom Thong, Mae Tha, Tham Mae Hu, Mae Chaem, Wat Phra That Sri Chom Thong, Ban San Hang Sua, Mae La Noi, 1741m, Ban Hong, Ban Mae Ha Tai, 1088, 106, Ban Mae Lob, 1634m, Op Luang, Ban Op Luang, Mae Sariang, Ban Kong Loy, Ban Kiew Lom, Ban Wang Lung, 0 10 20 30 40 km, 0 10 20 miles

154

Drive — A circular route starting at Chiang Mai

Allow four to seven days for the circuit, including a few side trips. Take warm clothes in the cool season; unsurfaced side roads are prone to flooding in the rainy season.

Start at Chiang Mai. From Chiang Mai, Highway 108 heads southwest through straggly villages. Just before Chom Thong turn off up Highway 1009 to see the natural wonders of Doi Ithanon National Park.
The wild northwest is an area of complex mountain ridges, thickly cloaked in forest and laced with waterfalls, caves and hot springs. *Either continue on Highway 1192 to*

Mae Chaem then take Highway 1088, or carry on along Highway 108. Just east of the junction of Highways 1088 and 108 **Op Luang National Park Office** is visible, with a pretty gorge crossed by a wooden footbridge just behind. Carpets of wild flowers interrupt the green monotony – the most diverse blooms appear before the rainy season, while in winter bright orange swathes of sunflowers make a fine show. In the section of road between Chom Thong and Mae Sariang the Chaem river is a prominent feature. **Mae Sariang** is of little interest but makes a pleasant enough stopover.

Continue northwards on Highway 108.

Northwards the scenery is unvaried; a hot sulphur spring (emphatically not for bathing) near the 256km post can be spotted by the lawn and restaurant. Slash-and-burn agriculture has denuded some hills, which are being reafforested with teak and pine. Dirt roads head off into the jungle to remote hill-tribe villages. Soon the road makes a dramatic plunge into **Mae Hong Son**, a noted centre for organised centres and treks. The province of Mae Hong Son is peopled by an ethnic mix of Shan, Tha Yai, Karen, Hmong, Lisu, Lahu and others; only about 2 per cent of the population is Thai.

Continue along the main road to Soppong, forking left up a dirt track to visit Tham Lot, one of Thailand's finest caves. Back on the main road , carry on southeast to Pai, another good trekking centre.

The road , proceeding now in roller-coaster fashion, is a scenic treat. Between Mae Hong Son and Pai, there are some magnificent views.

Continue back towards Chiang Mai. Highway 109 bypasses the city to the west and has a number of specially made tourist attractions.

Those not starting from Chiang Mai would do well to omit the city as the busy roads leading from it are devoid of interest.

Loop round from Mae Rim along Highway 1096 and turn south at Samoeng to join Highway 108.

Recommended overnight stops
Doi Ithanon National Park is worth an extended stay and there are park bungalows available there for stopovers.
Mae Sariang provides a basic hotel and a few guesthouses.
Mae Hong Son has a wide range of accommodation available while **Soppong**, **Tham Lot** and **Pai** each have guesthouses to let .
There are also resorts along Highway 1096.

Public Transport *Buses from Chiang Mai to Mae Hong Son take about 9–10 hours, but the journey can be split up by overnighting at Mae Sariang, Soppong and Pai. There are no buses along Highway 1096. Songthaews to Doi Ithanon leave only intermittently from Chom Thong on weekdays (the service is better at weekends) and it is necessary to return to Chom Thong for buses along Highway 108.*

Wat Phra Doi Suthep, near Chiang Mai

▶ ▶ ▶   Chiang Mai

From Bangkok: by bus, journey time of 9 to 12 hours; by train, 12 to 14 hours; domestic flights, 1hour.
Thailand's second largest city, dubbed the 'Rose of the North', is about a fortieth the size of Bangkok. Without the suffocating heat and quite the same volume of traffic it is undoubtedly easier to live in.

History In 1296, the city superseded Chiang Rai as the capital of King Mengrai's Lanna kingdom, following the capture of the Mon city of Haripunchai (Lamphun) four years earlier. It prospered as a cultural and commercial centre, initially with its southern and eastern boundaries secure thanks to alliances with the kings of Sukothai and Phayao. However, it suffered centuries of hostilities with Ayutthaya.
In 1556 it became a vassal state after it was invaded by Burma, and was ruled by Burmese overlords for 200 years. Despite liberation by King Taksin in 1775, the centuries of warfare had sapped its spirit and its citizens deserted to Lampang. Twenty years later the population started to return to the abandoned city, which gradually became the major northern outpost of the newly formed kingdom of Siam.
The old city used to contain the palace and nobles' quarters but now the most visible reminders in its past are the temples. There are dozens of them, many exhibiting signs of Burmese and Lanna influences. A particularly distinct piece of evidence of the past is the neat square of the old moat which nicely frames the

In the 1920s, visitors to Chiang Mai had a hard time getting there, encountering bridgeless river-crossings, tigers and other jungle hindrances *en route* by elephant or boat.

Chiang Mai's old city walls

area of the old city. Five gateways exist on this fortification, but on closer inspection it can be seen that they are all reconstructions.

Times have changed The old-world Shangri-La found by visitors in the earlier part of this century has altered beyond recognition. Far from being fossilised in exotic charms, Chiang Mai is now developing faster than any other provincial centre.

The first phase of egg-box architecture occurred in the 1950s and 60s, and today high-rise condominiums are a 1990s addition to the increasingly prosperous-looking skyline. Residents complain that the traffic, worse every year, is developing a Bangkok-like intensity, and the city has obtained a Los Angeles-style smog.

Chiang Mai's popularity with both visitors and Thais stems from its manageability and unsticky climate. The city is now sophisticated, commercially geared and visibly prosperous. A cultural mix is diluting the cultures of the hill tribes – a feature which is probably accelerated by the numbers of tourists.

In the city, the number of *farangs* is immediately noticeable. The choice thrown up by this cultural mix is almost bewildering; this is most noticeable in the eating places in particular.

There is an extraordinary choice of souvenir shopping, ready-made opportunities for hill-tribe treks (not the cheapest in the north), a vast amount of accommodation from top-class hotels to world-travellers' guesthouses and a bustling streetlife and nightlife.

Getting about Chiang Mai's simple geography, aided by the prominence of the river and moated area, make it an easy place in which to find your bearings. The huge form of Doi Suthep looms over the city, a reminder of its proximity to the country's upland region.

It used to be a city to walk around, but the increasing traffic is making it tough going. However, cycling and motorcycling are feasible, though a bit frightening; hire shops proliferate along Mun Muang Road.

The city's bus system only operates up to 19.00hrs; fares are cheap. Slightly more expensive are the *songthaews* or pick-ups, and it's pot luck whether one is going your way. Easiest by far are the *tuk tuks*, whose drivers have been migrating from Bangkok since 1987. Most rides are about 20 baht or 30–40 baht for more distant destinations. Finally, pedalled *samlors* are fine for short journeys.

There are city tours organised by dozens of agencies and hotels.

The downtown area This stretches between Mun Muang Road on the east side of the moat to the Mae Nam Ping river. Mun Muang Road itself is much given over to the *farang* industry. There is a great concentration of trekking-tour operators for which the city is famous, guesthouses, Western-food restaurants where travellers swap stories over milk-shakes, and ethnic fabric shops. The many nightclubs add to its reputation as something of a red-light area.

The Thai love of *sanuk* (fun) is much in evidence in the exuberant spirit in which festivals are celebrated here. During the three-day flower festival in early February and the boisterous festivities of Songkran Day on 13 April (Thai New Year) not many people escape a comprehensive dousing in water by hoses, water-pistols or even water-filled condoms; the elderly get a gentler treatment, with a sprinkling of jasmine-scented water – but be prepared – *farangs* are prime targets.

A visit to Samphet market makes a good early-morning or early-evening stroll. A whole new world opens up here: there are exotic fruits and lady-stallholders serenely skinning frogs or hacking up live fish. Further to the east there are several ugly and noisy main roads linked by quieter sois. This is the area of the Night Bazaar and Warorot Market.

Better safe than sorry
One sure way to have a holiday ruined is to have something stolen. It goes without saying that constant vigilance is needed, but beware: even supposedly secure places are not always so. There have been reports of items going missing even from guesthouse safes, so obtain an itemised receipt whenever possible.

Thai Boxing (see page 110)
This is a sport where anything seems to go in a free-for-all. The atmosphere is one of frantic excitement and terrific energy. The Thais take this very seriously and many baht are won and lost at an evening spent watching this explosive sport. Contests take place on Friday and Saturday nights at the boxing stadium on Khong Sai Road near the railway station.

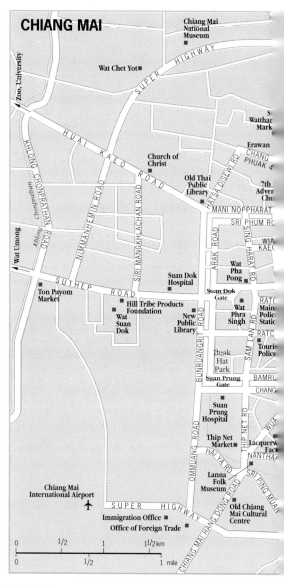

City Sights

Chiang Mai National Museum

Super Highway (Highway 11, north of the centre)
A notable collection of religious art, dominated by an enormous Lanna head. Upstairs there is an entertaining miscellany, including hill-tribe gear, musical instruments, domestic equipment, looms and some spectacular elephant howdahs, as well as a mosquito-proof bed, which was built for a 19th-century king of Chiang Mai.
Open: Wednesday to Saturday, except national holidays, 09.00hrs–16.00hrs. Admission charge.

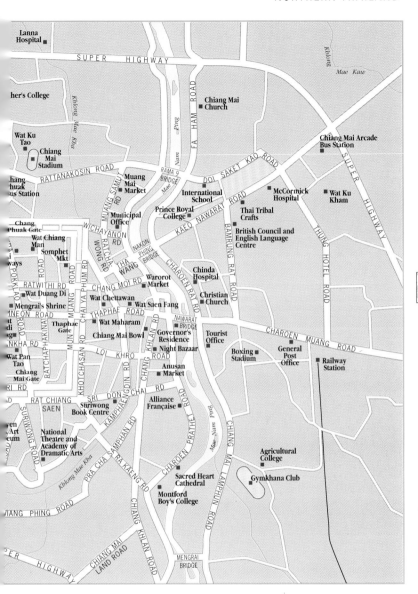

Lanna Hospital

SUPER HIGHWAY

Khlong Mae Kaw

her's College

Chiang Mai Church

Wat Ku Tao

Chiang Mai Arcade Bus Station

Chiang Mai Stadium

Khlong Mae Kha

Mae Nam Ping

FA HAM ROAD

RATTANAKOSIN ROAD

RAMA 9 BRIDGE

DOI SAKET KAO ROAD

SUPER HIGHWAY

hang huak us Station

Muang Mai Market

International School

McCormick Hospital

Wat Ku Kham

Chang Phuak Gate

MUANG SAMUT RD

Municipal Office

Prince Royal College

Thai Tribal Crafts

KAEO NAWARAT ROAD

BAMRUNG RAT ROAD

THUNG HOTEL ROAD

Wat Chiang Man

WICHAYANON RD

Somphet Mkt

British Council and English Language Centre

ways

RATCHA RD

NAKON PHING BRIDGE

THA WANG

CHAROEN RAT RD

Chinda Hospital

159

RATWITHI RD

CHANG MOI RD

CHAIYA PHUM RD

Wat Duang Di

Wat Chettawan

Warorot Market

Christian Church

Mengrai's Shrine

NEON ROAD

MUANG RD

THAPHAE ROAD

Wat Saen Fang

di

THAPHAKINA

Thaphae Gate

Wat Maharam

NAWARAT BRIDGE

Chiang Mai Bowl

Governor's Residence

Tourist Office

NKHA RD

RATCHAPHAKINA

KHOTCHASAN RD

CHIANG KHLAN RD

LOI KHRO ROAD

Night Bazaar

CHAROEN MUANG ROAD

Wat Pan Tao

Anusan Market

Boxing Stadium

General Post Office

Railway Station

Chiang Mai Gate

RI RD

RAT CHIANG SAEN

SRI DON CHAI

KAMPHAENGDIN RD

CHIANG KHLAN RD

Suriwong Book Centre

Alliance Française

SURIWONG ROAD

National Theatre and Academy of Dramatic Arts

CHAROEN PRATHET ROAD

PRA CHA SAMPHAN RD

RA KAENG RD

Mae Nam Ping

CHIANG MAI LAMPHUN ROAD

Agricultural College

Khlong Mae Kha

en Art cum

Sacred Heart Cathedral

Gymkhana Club

IANG PHING ROAD

CHIANG MAI LAND ROAD

Montford Boy's College

CHIANG KHLAN ROAD

ER HIGHWAY

MENGRAI BRIDGE

Chiang Mai Zoo

Huri Kaeo Road

Thailand's best zoo has a semi-jungle setting and adjoins a large arboretum. Minibuses for Doi Suthep pass by entrance.

Open: daily, 08.00hrs–17.00hrs. Admission charge.

Lanna Folk Museum

185/3 Wualai Road

Opened by the Siam Society, this modest display gives a rare glimpse of the interior of a traditional Lanna house built in the latter part of the 19th century. Note the

The celebrated Chiang Mai flower festival takes place on the first weekend in February, with a parade of flower-laden floats and a host of beauty contests drawing big crowds to the city.

The city pillar close by Wat Chedi Luang commemorates the spot where King Mengrai was supposedly struck by lightning – his memorial is on the opposite corner of the Ratchadamnoen /Phra Pokklao intersection.

The Buddha Phra Singh in Wat Phra Singh is regarded as the original despite the fact that two identical ones exist at Nakhon Si Thammarat and Bangkok. The head of this one was stolen in 1922 and a replacement was made.

octagonal stilts on which it is built, and the walls sloping inwards as they rise – both typical features. The guide prepares crushed betel leaf in the time-honoured manner for visitors to try out.
Open: daily, except Thursday, 10.00hrs–16.00hrs. Admission charge.

Tribal Research Centre
Chiang Mai University Campus (5km west of the city)
Part of the interest here is finding the place, poorly signposted on the large campus. Perseverance is rewarded by a small but informative museum on hill-tribes, explaining the life styles of the major tribes.
Open: Monday to Friday, 08.30hrs–16.30hrs. Admission charge.

Wat Chedi Luang
Phra Poklao Road
Apart from the splendid *naga* (dragon-headed serpents) flanking the steps to the *wiharn* the main interest here is a vast *chedi* built in the 15th century and later enlarged by King Tilokaraja. The restored structure is an impressive sight. Legend has it that the city will stand as long as the gum tree in the grounds does.

Wat Chet Yot
Off the super highway (Highway 11) just southwest of the National Museum; look for the sign for the Rajamangala Institute of Technology
Built in 1455 to house the relics of the monk Phra Mahathera Uttamapanya, the *chedi* retains outstanding stucco reliefs of cross-legged figures giving a *wai*. Wat Chet Yot is a copy of Buddha Gaya in India, where the Buddha attained enlightenment under a bo tree; the seven spires referred to in its name represent the seven weeks he spent there.

Wat Chiang Man
Ratchaphakinai Road
Built by King Mengrai in 1296 this is thought to be the city's oldest *wat*, known for two small but much venerated Buddha images: the 8th-century marble Phra Sila, thought to be from India or Sri Lanka, and the Crystal Buddha, supposedly presented to the Queen of Haripunchai in the 7th century.

Wat Pan Tao
Phra Pokklao Road (next to Wat Chedi Luang)
A fine, untampered example of a Lanna *wiharn*, retaining its original panelled walls.

Wat Phra Singh
Sing Harat Road
This absorbing temple in the old city was founded in 1345 to house the ashes of King Kham Fu. It has a new *wiharn* dating from 1925, a wooden *bot* behind and a late Lanna *wiharn* (c 1806–11) which contains the celebrated Buddha Phra Singh. The walls are decorated with murals depicting legends and scenes of old city life. Look for the textiles and tattoos popular at the time.

Wat Suan Dok
Suthep Road
Virtually next-door to the Hill Tribe Products Foundation, this contains the burial ground for many of the Chiang Mai royalty. The wedding-cake stucco on the *chedis* housing the remains presents a dazzling show. A central *chedi* contains a Buddha relic that was brought by a white elephant, so the story goes, hence the White Elephant Gate – Pratu Chang Puak – in the city wall. Herbal massage is on offer here.

Wat Umong
Off Suthep Road (signposted)
Located on an obscure *soi* (lane) in the extreme west of the city, this forest *wat* dates from 1296 and is perhaps the city's most quirky temple. A multitude of signs moralise from every tree: 'Time unused is the longest time'; 'Love is a flower garden to be watered by tears'; you can hardly see the woods for the wisdom.
Monks' bungalows are scattered around the forest, which gives on to a lake fringed with banana palms. At the top of the site, an emaciated Buddha image sits contemplatively close to a *chedi*, his ribcage sunken inwards as the result of fasting. Immediately below is a labyrinth of subterranean meditation chambers: sermons in English on meditation are given. They begin at 15.00hrs on Sundays and go on until about 18.00hrs.

Environs
Doi Suthep
The much-visited temple of Wat Phra Doi Suthep stands on the sacred mountain that towers over Chiang Mai. The white elephant that carried a Buddha relic to Wat Suan Dok (see above) is said to have fallen and died on this spot. From the road where jade and ivory factory showrooms do a roaring trade, a 300-step staircase flanked by a pair of huge *nagas* (dragon-headed serpents) leads to the top. A cable-car glides up in seconds and very cheaply.
Doi Suthep was founded by King Ku Na in 1383 and contains an exquisite courtyard with a gold *chedi* housing a Buddha relic, and intricate gold parasols. Signs announce 'Don't shake the bells' and 'Dress impolite, can't enter this temple'. The view on a clear winter's day extends over a seemingly infinite plain making Chiang Mai look surprisingly compact.

continued on page 164

Songthaews are one of the usual ways of getting to Doi Suthep. They depart from the northwest side of Chang Puak Gate and the fares are posted on the bus-stop. You can also be taken to the temple, palace gardens and Meo village.

Traditional Thai massage (see page 47).
This is offered throughout the city. Ask for 'ancient massage' to distinguish it from the sexual variety, and try to set aside three hours for a 'full body' treatment. Eleven-day courses on practical massage are offered by the Foundation of Moh Shivagakomarpaj at the old Chiang Mai Traditional Hospital, tel: (053) 275085.

161

Wat Phra Doi Suthep

Chiang Mai Shopping

■ There are dozens of shops between the NIght Bazaar and Moonmuang Road selling ethnic clothes and crafts. Of the hill tribe products, everyone has a personal favourite. The many designs are made into anything that will sell: oven mitts, jackets, cushion covers, rucksacks, bumbags and even baseball caps. Other ethnic goods include attractive Lanna-style cotton and silk fabrics, and Burmese-style souvenirs, many of which are actually made in Thailand. .....■

Hill tribe products Of the many different styles, Yao textiles are characterised by intricate cross-stitch embroidery, those of the Hmong by larger, coarser stitchwork, Akha fabrics by long stitches – bright diamonds and triangles on black with silver bangles and medallions, Lahu by bright colours and sequins, while Lisu work ismade of colourful bands and squares. There is an assortment of highly idiosyncratic souvenirs including opium pipes, Karen *sung* banjos, Akha bamboo musical blow-pipes, double-sided drums, laquered buffalo horns, Yao dolls and so on.

Burmese-style souvenirs The wall-hangings are spectacular. There are cushion-covers, typically with embroidered elephants, peacocks and scenes from Burmese folk tales sewn on to velvet. The better ones use silver for the sequins and quartz for the beads.

Silk Thai silk is justly famous for its quality and is sold as plain coloured, check patterns or printed with designs. It is still manufactured using wooden hand-looms.

Woodcarving An age-old tradition, as a glimpse at virtually any temple in the city will tell. Ban Thwai, southwest of the city, is a major centre.

Basketry Straw, rattan and bamboo basket products of all kinds are made at Hang Dong, 13km southwest of Chiang Mai on Highway 108.

Umbrellas These are made of cotton, rice-paper and bamboo, and are hand-painted in bright colours.

Ceramics Celadon, a high-biscuit finish with a pale green glaze, is much prized by collectors and comes in plain light green or middle blue; beware of imitations. Benjarong, which means 'five colours', is a low-biscuit finish which lends itself to richer decoration, including 12-carat gold.

Silverware Hand-hammered before being given its final lustre by an application of tamarind. Beware of base-metal substitutes.

Chiang Mai Shopping

Lacquerware A three-month process of repeated coatings of clay and lacquer sap is the traditional method; this is followed by careful painting or the addition of a gold-leaf design. Burmese lacquer tends to be made on a bamboo base (as opposed to a teak one), which is less brittle.

Where to buy There are two excellent non-profit making shops selling hill-tribe products, where all the money goes directly back to the craftspeople making the goods: the government-run Hill Tribe Products Foundation, 21/17 Suthep Road and Thai Tribal Crafts, 208 Bamrung Rat Road (not to be confused with Northern Tribal Crafts a few doors along).

The Night Bazaar Situated in Chang Khlan Road, this is one of the great markets of Asia, both for its range and its atmosphere – indeed, part of the attraction is the people-watching. Virtually nothing carries a price tag and haggling is the order of the day.
Fake designer-label clothes, pirated cassette tapes, while-you-wait artist portraits, wooden toys, hill-tribe gear and inexpensive jewellery are good buys for those who bargain hard enough. Beware of fake silver, jade and gems, and don't expect those 800-baht 'Rolex' watches to last more than a few months.

Home industries (factory tour) Straggling along Highway 1006 on the eastern outskirts, the 'villages' of Bo Sang and San Kamphaeng are really a huge industrial zone, where workshops produce handmade crafts in great quantity – notably leather, umbrellas, lacquer, silverware, silk and ceramics. A 20-baht tuk tuk tour (the driver picks up commissions regardless of whether you buy anything) lasts three to four hours and you can stop off wherever you like.
Prices are often fixed and there is no hard sell beyond the occasional hovering attendant, and someone always appears to explain the production process. Mailing services are provided for large items. It is great entertainment, even if you don't buy a thing.

163

Hand-carved wooden ornaments at a Chiang Mai factory

continued from page161

Phu Phing Palace The King's northern palace, 4km further along the road from Doi Suthep, can be viewed from outside. Although it is nothing remarkable architecturally, its temperate rose garden and neat lawns seem evocatively English (so too does the winter air – bring a sweater). The gardens are open to the public on weekends and holidays.

The roadside verges hereabouts are full of wild sunflowers.

Open: 08.30hrs–11.45hrs; 13.00hrs–16.15hrs when the king is not in residence.

Meo village At the end of the same road and reached by a very bumpy track is this spectacular example of a tourist trap (see panel), with stalls stacked up with imported souvenirs and villagers dressed in Meo tribal costume posing for cameras for a few baht. The half-hearted Hill Tribe Museum does not even merit the 5 baht entry.

If this is regarded merely as a sociological insight into the decline of the hill-tribe culture, or as a shopping trip, then the village might be worth a visit. At least the wood-smoke smell, free-running chickens and dirt roads are authentic, and the view from the waterfall is a good one.

Mae Sa Valley

Take Highway 107 north from the city, turn west at Mae Rim (16km) on to Highway 1096

Highway 1096 has been developed for the tourist industry and is a popular half-day visit from Chiang Mai. The road is quite scenic and there are a number of attractive bungalow resorts, such as Mae Sa and Erawan resorts, with beautifully maintained gardens and views of the hills; these places tend to get booked up at weekends.

Mae Sa Snake Farm About 25 types of snake native to Thailand are kept here; dare-devil antics with them are performed daily at 11.30hrs, 14.15hrs and 15.30hrs. The performance lasts about 30 minutes. Admission charge.

Mae Sa Waterfall *Six km along Highway 1096; 300m access road*. Entry fee for cars, less for pedestrians. A mountain stream tumbles down a ravine over a series of ten waterfalls which provide delightful shady pools for swimming. The trail along then gets rockier and noticeably quieter on the 1km trek to the top.

Other places accessible from Chiang Mai include:

Butterfly and orchid farms There are four of these, each charging a small admission fee to see commercial orchid nurseries, where hybrid and native types are cultivated. Butterflies flit around the indoor tropical gardens and end up as framed souvenirs which are sold in the entrance shops and in Chiang Mai's bazaar.

Open: daily, 08.30hrs–17.00hrs.

The down side of tourism is seen in the effect it has had on the people of this Meo village. Their lives today are geared to the tourist industry and this has given them a keen eye for profit. Their knowledge of English extends to phrases such as 'you buy' and 'no profit'. These once nomadic people used to depend on opium as a cash crop until the government tried to steer them into less harmful ways of subsistence.

164

Elephants at Work Ten miles along Highway 1096 on the Fang road there is one of three elephant shows around Chiang Mai (the others are near Chiang Dao and Lampang). Elephants bathe, perform logging skills and obey commands. Shows take place in the morning, but in order to see the elephants' bath time, get there as early as possible. Although contrived and commercialised, it is an impressive spectacle, full of photo opportunities. *Open*: shows daily, 09.30hrs–11.00hrs. Admission charged.

Most of the handicraft shops in Chiang Mai sell wooden elephants, ranging from half-life-size to those that could fit into a matchbox (many made of teak).

Working elephants having their daily bath: get there early to see this part of their routine in the shows near Chiang Mai

Chiang Dao *On the bus route from Chiang Mai to Fang* **Elephants at work** south of Chiang Dao, is a show which is virtually identical to the one at Mae Sa (see above).
Open: shows daily, 09.30hrs–11.00hrs.
Tham Chiang Dao (*songthaew* from Chiang Dao) is a popular cave which contains much Shan statuary; at the entrance to the cave, *chedis* and an ornamental royal barge in a pool serve to enhance the mystical atmosphere.

Lamphun *Frequent buses from Chang Puak bus station in Chiang Mai.* Located 26km south of Chiang Mai, the area around Lamphun is famed for the beauty of its women, for its *lamyai* (longan) orchards and for its silk products.
The main road from Chiang Mai passes along a fine avenue of *yang* trees; pegs are placed on the trunks to facilitate regular pruning.
Lamphun was founded in AD660 as Haripunchai, the centre of Mon culture. It was ruled by the Mons until the 13th century when infiltration by King Mengrai led to its downfall: the king sent Ai Fa, an officer, to undermine the enemy's defence minister and viceroy, deliberately wasting the city's resources and whittling its defences, thus paving the way for rebellion and takeover by Mengrai's forces.

After five years of training, elephants work for 50 years; reaching peak efficiency around their 40s. Thai law dictates a retirement age of 61, after which they typically live another 20 years. Elephants make excellent loggers because of their night vision, their near-perfect memory of jungle trails and their ability to carry loads of up to 300kg. Teak logging now faces a government ban and it seems likely that the elephants' future role will be as tourist attractions.

National Museum Just across the road from Wat Phra That Haripunchai (see below) is this briefly interesting museum in a building that looks as if it was designed for something more comprehensive. There are good specimens of Lanna art, figures and silverware, and inscribed stones mostly of the 15th and 16th centuries. *Open*: Wednesday to Sunday, except national holidays, 09.00hrs–12.00hrs; 13.00hrs–16.00hrs. Admission charge.

Wat Chama Thevi (Wat Ku Kut) Follow the minor road to the left of the museum, cross the main road and continue for 1km until the wat is reached on the left; the walk is rather dull, so it is a better idea to take a samlor to the *wat*.
Known for its late Dvaravati-style *chedi*, which stands 21m high and rises five tiers with trios of Buddha images (not the originals) in niches on each level.

Wat Phra That Haripunchai Located in the town centre, this is one of the most interesting temples in the region, and dates from 1044. It is dominated by a dazzling gold *chedi* (the model for the infinitely more visited Doi Suthep), surmounted by an umbrella made of 6.5kg of solid gold. The library is a fetching example of early 19th-century Lanna style, and a *sala* shelters an elaborate Buddha footprint (four prints, one inside the other). Also to be seen here is northern Thailand's largest temple gong, cast in 1860.

► ▬▬ **Chiang Rai**
Buses from neighbouring cities; domestic flights; boat daily and from Tha Ton at 12.00hrs (Tha Ton is a four-hour bus trip from Chiang Mai) .
Chiang Rai was founded in 1262 as the capital of the Lanna kingdom, but despite its history and the mushrooming growth of new hotels and guesthouses, there is little to see. Much of the city's recent boom is a result of the upgrading of the highway north of Mae Sai and through Burma which will make a major land route into China. As a base for exploring the surrounding countryside it serves well enough.

Hill Tribe Museum and Handicrafts Shop *Population and Community Development Association, 620/25 Thanalai Road*. The association gives practical aid to local people in matters as diverse as water supply and family planning. The Chiang Rai branch helps tribespeople in particular, and has set up a small museum of tribal artifacts and a craft shop (proceeds go directly to fund its projects). An English-language slide show gives an excellent introduction to hill-tribe culture.
Open: Monday to Friday, 08.30hrs–17.00hrs.

Boat trip from Tha Ton to Chiang Rai The boat makes a five-hour journey along the Mae Kok river, which is so shallow that it often runs aground and the passengers have to get out and push it free. An isolated attack by bandits a few years ago has fuelled interest in the journey as an adventure outing.

Khantoke dinners are a Lanna-Thai speciality, formerly given only on ceremonial occasions. You sit down at low tables and are served five dishes by waiters or waitresses attired in traditional costume; Lanna dancing, with orchestra, accompanies your meal and diners are invited to join the dance at the end. The most popular places are the Old Chiang Mai Cultural Centre and the Diamond Hotel.

The trip winds past hill-tribe villages set beneath angular mountains. Possible stop-overs include a Lahu village, a hot spring and a cave, although accommodation is best organised through a trek offered at one of the guesthouses at Tha Ton village.

Tha Ton itself is a peaceful village sited on the river bank. Steps to the left of the bridge lead up to a hilltop *wat*, which gives fine views of the river.

Fang *Bus from Chiang Mai, minibus to Tha Ton.* For most visitors this is just a bus change *en route* for the boat trip to Chiang Rai. At Ban Muang, 10km to the west, a hot sulphur spring gushes out of the ground at temperatures close to boiling point.

▶ ▶ **Doi Ithanon National Park**
Head southwest on Highway 108; turn off north near the 57km post. Buses from Chiang Mai and Mae Sariang to Chom Thong. A songthaew *service makes a tour of the main attractions. The service is sporadic in the week but frequent at weekends.*

The park takes its name from the highest peak in Thailand. This statistic is just one of many exceptional features. Attractions are signed in English and listed in the order they are passed. Some 30 Hmong and Karen villages are dotted around the area.

The scenery varies from unspoilt lowlands to rugged, partly wooded highlands which are being afforested by the government, and a number of fine waterfalls.

Mae Ya Falls Signposted on the left almost immediately after leaving Highway 108, the 15-minute drive affords magnificent views over rice fields set beneath the backdrop of the mountain range. The falls, a short walk from the car park, plummet dramatically a full 250m.

Mae Klang Falls Close to the road, easy access has been made to these, the most visited feature in the park. A battery of souvenir and food stalls has inevitably grown up as a result. Close by, the Visitor Centre sells a useful map of the park and a booklet detailing the bird species found here.

Varchiratharn Falls Signed by the road, this majestically graceful single fall involves a steep 10-minute walk down to its base. The effort is amply rewarded.

Park headquarters Enquire here for accommodation (eleven bungalows, starting from 500 baht for four people). Just before the headquarters, a right turn (signposted Tribal Silverware) leads via a left turn to the 1km path to **Siriphum Falls**. On the way the route leads through a Hmong village which is commercialised. American Express is accepted at the silverware stalls and the women hard-sell everlasting flowers and chrysanthemums. The latter are grown in greenhouses visible below – part of the government scheme to introduce cash-crop farming among the tribes in an attempt to safeguard conservation interests.

Rafting can be arranged at Tha Ton village and ten-seater boats can be chartered from Chiang Rai pier for exploring the river (about 1,700 baht for a day).

167

Mae Kok Elephant Camp
Reached by boat or bus from Chiang Rai, the camp operates elephant treks; for details contact the office near the Wangcome Hotel in Chiang Rai (tel: 053-711897).

Drive to the summit of Doi Ithanon A good road winds up to the very top of Thailand's highest mountain (2,595m). As the road ascends views open out over distant ridges extending far to the southwest and east.

A modern octagonal pagoda, Napamaytanidol Chedi enjoys the most enthralling panorama of all, best on a clear winter's day, but unfortunately all too often obscured by mist.

The summit itself, chilly in the extreme in winter, is an anticlimax, with trees almost completely obscuring the view and a huge airforce radar installation dominating the scene. A sign gives the mountain's height to the nearest millimetre!

Walk back down the road a few paces and turn right on a path signed in Thai leading to the only site in Thailand of *Rhododendron delavayi*. This thrives in the temperate climate and produces red blooms from November to February.

Environs
Chom Thong *Chiang Mai–Mae Sarang bus passes by.* This is a small town on Highway 108, 58km from Chiang Mai. On Saturday mornings, the cattle market presents an animated scene.

On the left side of the main street approaching from Chiang Mai, **Wat Phra That Sri Chom Thong** dates from 1451 and displays Thai and Burmese features. The *wiharn* dates from 1817 and has wood-carvings characteristic of the period. Carved tusks surround the central reliquary, which contains a Buddha relic. The *bot*, built in 1516, is a charming example of the Burmese style.

► **Kamphaeng Phet**
Junctions of Highways 1, 101 & 111
Built by King Ki Thai in the 14th century, Kamphaeng Phet city was a replacement for Chakangrao, the garrison town for Sukhothai, sited on the west bank of the nearby Ping River.

Signposts from the city centre point to the museum and Historical Park, which covers a large area, both inside and outside the ancient moated fortification.

Buses from Sukhothai and Phitsanulok pass the Historical Park, sited 1km to the northeast of the modern city. Ask to be dropped off at the *muang kao* (old city) at Lak Muang Shrine. Cars can go into the Historical Park.

Marking the summit is a shrine to Inthawichayanon, after whom the mountain was renamed in a shortened form. In the 19th century he prophesied the dangers of loss of tree cover in this great watershed area and requested his remains to be placed here.

A view at sunset from the summit of Doi Ithanon

National Museum This features art styles from the Dvaravati period onwards and numerous terracotta fragments found in the old city.
Open: Wednesday to Sunday, except public holidays, 09.00hrs–12.00hrs and 13.00hrs–16.00hrs. Admission charge.

Wat Phra Khaew *Opposite the museum.* Entry fee covers all sites; free map from the entry booth. The old royal temple for the (largely vanished) palace retains its elephant-buttressed base and three Buddha images.

Wat Phra Si Iriyabot *From the modern Lak Muang Shrine, follow the main road east through the ramparts and branch off left as signposted.* The signs explain the sites hereabouts; few are more than piles of laterite rubble. This one has four much-weathered Buddha images in different postures.

Wat Chang Rob *Further along the same road.* This is flanked at its base by 68 stone elephants; steep steps give access to a fine viewing platform over the surrounding countryside.

▶▶▶ **Lampang**
Junction of Highways 1 & 11 Reached by bus, train and domestic flights.
Lampang will never be a major tourist attraction, but it is of interest for its Lanna and Burmese style temples.
The North's second-largest city, it has a distinctly prosperous air; rich Thais come here to retire. The river that forms the geographical middle is leafy and unspoilt, and the old part of town clustered on the south bank is characterised by wooden shophouses and well-kept teak residences set in lush gardens.

Doi Ithanon is outstanding for birds. A species list of 362 has been recorded for the park, including the local ashy-throated warbler and the green-tailed sunbird.

169

Wat Chang Rob

Unique to Lampang are the horse carriages that take visitors and residents for pleasure trips around town. These appeared in Lampang in 1915, having been in use as VIP transport in Bangkok until cars were imported from Europe for the purpose. The whole operation – carriages, drivers and horses – was transported by the newly opened railway. Many of the carriages are original, although the colours are not!

Wat Prakeo Don Tao

Ban Sao Nak *Radwattana Road.* Built on 116 pillars, this dark teak mansion is worth a short visit for those wanting to see inside a typical wealthy home built in the northern Thai/Burmese style. The two main rooms are filled with a briefly absorbing collection of antiques.
Open: daily, 09.30– 17.30hrs. Admission charge.

Wat Pongsanuk *Pongsanuk Road.* A modern *wat* encloses the raised platform which retains an excellent example of a *mondhrop* built in Lanna style; a tiered roof shelters four Buddha images gathered around the sacred bo tree.

Wat Prakeo Don Tao *Prakeo Road.* The city's first major temple is known mostly for two Buddha images which are now elsewhere. The Emerald Buddha is now in Wat Phra Keo in Bangkok's Grand Palace (see page 79), and Don Tao is now at Wat Phra Luang. The temple possesses a square *mondhrop* of 1909 in Burmese style, with a typical multi-tiered roof. An adjacent museum displays mostly Lanna-style wood-carvings.

Wat Sri Chum *Sri Chum Road.* A glimpse into Burma: six of the eight monks here are Burmese and the temple is full of eye-catching cameos. Notice the wooden dancing figures above the steps, the gorgeous mirror-studded ceiling and the lacquer murals depicting life in Lampang in the early 1900s – complete with outings into the forest by car and a stop-off at a roadside food stall.

Wat Phra That Lampang Luang *Reached by* songthaew *as far as Kho Kha, followed by a 3km walk or a change to another* songthaew. *It is possible to charter one at a cost of about 150baht for the round trip.*
Sited 18km south of Lampang, this is the sole survivor of one of four fortified satellite settlements built in the Haripunchai period to serve Lampang. A triple rampart with moats still encloses a farming village clustered round the *wat*, itself a supreme example of the Lanna style and in an excellent state of preservation. The main *wiharn* dates from 1496 and contains early 19th-century murals of nobles in Burmese costume. Another *wiharn* displays intricate mosaic-inlaid gables. An open-sided *wiharn* dating from the early 16th century is thought to be the oldest timber building in Thailand.

Young Elephants Training Centre *36km west on Highway 11, on the Lampang– Chiang Mai bus route.* An elephant show similar to the Elephants at Work near Chiang Mai (see pages 164–5), except that these are from Thailand's only baby elephant training centre, located near Ngao, itself no longer open to the public.
Open: daily shows in the morning, closed on Buddhist holidays.

▶ ▶ **Mae Hong Son Province**
End of Highway 108. Buses from Bangkok, Chiang Mai, Mae Sariang, Soppong and Pai; domestic flights.
Lying in a valley amid densely wooded mountains and tucked away in Thailand's northwest corner, Mae Hong

Son has recently changed face from a remote small town to a booming resort full of guesthouses and trekking agencies.

A thick morning mist shrouds Mae Hong Son, adding drama to the town's pretty **Chong Khum Lake**, fringed by neat lawns and shrubberies. Two adjacent Burmese-style temples make a splendid backdrop to the water; both look best from the outside, although **Wat Chong Klang** is worth a quick look for its wooden figurines and painted glass panels brought from Burma in 1857.

Perched on a steep hill, **Wat Doi Kong** presides over the town and is the place to make for at sunset. The 15-minute walk up can be started near the Mai Tee Hotel (take the road opposite Singhanat Bumrum Road, fork left and continue until the temple steps appear to your right). Back in town, there is a lively morning market (06.00–08.00hrs); hill tribe people come to buy and sell.

The best guesthouse locations are by the lake or in Phachachon Uthit Road.

Environs

Motorbikes, mountain bikes and jeeps can all be rented in town. Enquire locally before making independent trips – border fighting, treacherous roads and lack of signposting are major hazards.

Tour agencies offer trips to hot springs, caves, waterfalls and tribal villages. One excursion heads east to **Tham Pla** ('fish cave', inhabited by cat fish) and climbs the rough road to Mae Aw (a KMT/ Hmong village now on the Burmese border), passing the king's summer palace (Pang Tong). Trekking, elephant riding and rafting are also on offer. Trips to see the long-necked Pa Dong tribeswomen are much-touted and overpriced. The women wear rings around their necks to attain a swan-like beauty. Most of the money ends up in the pockets of their quasi-captors.

Tham Lot (Lot Cave) Reached by taking a bus to Soppong, where it is possible to get a *songthaew* or make the hour-and-a-half walk. A fork at Soppong leads

continued on page 175

Ban Thung Kwian Market, on the Lampang–Chiang Mai bus route 25km west on Highway 11, provides an opportunity for the camera rather than the purse. Most of the items on sale here are poached from the Ban Thung Kwian Forest Park near by. Snakes, turtles and monitor lizards are served up as 'jungle food', while rabbits, civets, squirrels, monkeys and wolves are sold as pets. Although many species are legally protected, no one pays much attention; the stallholders simply flee when officials approach.

171

The entrance to Tham Lot, where swifts and bats enter and exit respectively at dusk

Hill Tribes

■ The rugged, forested limestone hills of northern Thailand are home to a *mélange* of some of the most colourful tribal peoples in the world. The Lao, Karen, Hmong, Mien, Lahu, Akha and Lisu minorities are a fascinating survival of a vibrant pre-industrial way of life. They originated in south China, and live on the migration route which the Thai people themselves travelled 1,000 years ago. Indeed the Lao are sometimes referred to in Thailand as 'the Thai that have not yet come south' and their culture is unlike that of the hill tribes. .....■

Roots The Lahu and Akha came via eastern Burma and northern Laos, beginning to cross over into Thailand in the early decades of the 20th century. The Lisu migrated from the headwaters of the Salween river in China via Kang Tung state in Burma. To this day only a minority of these peoples live in Thailand, the majority remaining in Burma and China's Yunnan province. The Hmong (or Meo) and Mien came across the Mekong river from Laos after siding with the royalists in their vain attempt to prevent the Communist takeover of Laos in 1975. They were settled at first in refugee camps on

Long-necked Pa Dong woman: a sobering example of the exploitation of tribal customs for the tourist trade (see page 171)

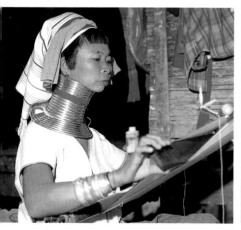

the border, and have since moved into Thailand's northern forests. The Karen are the biggest tribal grouping of them all, numbering by some counts over four million. Their precise origins are shrouded in mystery but their culture contains Burmese, Mon and Thai elements.

Separate tribal identities Karen culture centres on a sophisticated fallow agricultural system, and its feasts and rituals celebrate harmony with the natural environment – extended to human society with an unquestioning submission to acknowledged leaders.
The Hmong are fiercely independent. In Laos they expressed this by fighting Communism which threatened to engulf their way of life. Mien culture stresses propriety, etiquette and avoidance of open conflict.
The Akhas' rituals are based upon keeping alive links with ancestors, whom they revere as awesome guardian spirits protecting the continuity of tribal history.
The Lisu are the most competitive in seeking to provide the best singers, weavers – or opium growers.

A typical day in a hill tribe village begins early as the roosters herald dawn. The women and girls are first to rise; they roll up their sleeping mats to begin pounding the rice to be eaten that day. Children usually collect water, sometimes – if they are lucky – from bamboo aqueducts

which carry the water right into the village. Breakfast consists of rice and vegetables from the garden, cooked with roots and jungle spices, served with salt and chilli peppers.

The workers returning from the fields at sunset bring with them firewood and food for the pigs. Families living long distances from their fields often camp out in the fields for days on end. After the evening meal the women congregate in groups around smoky kerosene lamps or pitch pine torches to sew, while the men gather to smoke pipes, drink tea and discuss the day's happenings.

In the dry season the air is choked with dust and smoke from the burning fields. During the monsoon the dust turns to sticky mud. Women and children must trudge ever increasing distances to find firewood.

Crafts Each tribe has its own craft tradition, making jewellery, musical instruments, baskets, tools, utensils, weapons and traps. Some villagers become artisans specialising in musical instruments, weapons or traps. The highest status is given to the blacksmith on whom the villagers depend for making and mending their tools and weapons. In recent years Thai crafts which were previously practised only for domestic use have become much in demand from tourists. That demand has bred a whole new breed of skilled entrepreneur tribesman who

purchases handicrafts from the villages and sells them at the colourful night bazaars of Chiang Mai, Chiang Rai or Bangkok.

Society The extended family is the most important social unit. Most tribes are patrilocal, including the families of married sons in the household, with the exception of the Karen and the Lahu where it is common for daughters also to set up families in their parents' household. Marriage is usually monogamous but polygamy is also acceptable in all the tribes except the Karen.

The religions of the hill tribes are sometimes described as 'animist' but this is an oversimplification. The Lisu and Akha beliefs show extensive Chinese influence while the Mien practice a form of Taoism. Most villages have two types of religious specialist – a priest for ritual and a shaman for communicating with the spirit world. There is a village headman who must have an understanding of the mythology and rituals of the tribe but also represent the village effectively in its dealings with the provincial and central governments of Thailand. Conflict arises, for example, when officials try to get a fluent Thai speaker appointed as village headman when he may not have the confidence of the villagers in other respects.

King Bhumiphol first became interested in the plight of the hill tribes in the 1960s when he was hiking in the forests around his hill palace of Phuping. He came across a desperately poor Hmong village with pathetically scraggy pigs. He patiently demonstrated to them how to raise a better breed of pig – and then became drawn into combatting their 'bad habit' of growing opium poppies

Realising that the successful eradication of opium could not just be imposed legalistically, King Bhumiphol initiated a programme of research into alternative crops which could be profitably grown to replace opium. He set up an experimental orchard at Kasetsart University, which showed that apples, peaches, strawberries, roses, lilies, chrysanthemums, Brussels sprouts, mushrooms, coffee, turnips and cabbages could be satisfactorily grown in these areas. For a time the tribes took to these new crops, but there has been a degree of reversion to opium.

<< The hill tribes people wear beautiful and elaborate clothing. The showiest garments are worn by young people of marriageable age. The styles worn by each tribe are not unchanging but rather a result of constant innovation. Teenage girls spend hours weaving, sewing and beading, in the effort to produce the prettiest costume in the village. >>

For the marketing of opium villagers rely on heavily armed convoys of Yunnanese traders. Because of the illegality of the trade tribespeople are powerless to avoid exploitation and intimidation by these middlemen.

The main crops are rice and maize, supplemented by melons, squash, cucumbers, tomatoes, onions, beans and cabbages. The most common livestock is chicken and pigs. Cattle and water buffalo are highly prized, partly as a status symbol and also as a real asset which can be sold in hard times. The buffalo are used for ploughing and harrowing.

Bartering is still common. A blacksmith may often be paid in rice or maize and a family might provide labour in a neighbour's field in return for some pork. When the villagers travel to the nearest market to stock up on supplies, they take handicrafts, vegetables, charcoal, broom grass and bamboo shoots to sell. Health care is primitive and caring for opium

<< The main tradition of tribe communication is an oral one. This is entering a new era with the introduction of radio. Radio stations broadcasting to the tribes now transmit from Chiang Mai and Mae Chan. >>

addicts creates an even greater burden. Illiteracy is widespread and the hill tribes suffer the indignity of being laughed at by townspeople and gawked at by tourists. The building of new roads confers great benefits but also produces tension when villagers' interests are overlooked and the pressures of modernisation come too fast and insistently along the road from the town.

Conflict and dilemma Even more serious is the destruction of the environment in the hill tribe areas. This is due to the tribal practice of slash-and-burn cultivation, where one patch of forest is cut down for cultivation for a few years until the soil becomes drained of nutrients – when a new field must be cleared.

With increasing population, the pressure on the land has tightened, reducing the period of fallow from 10 to five and sometimes as little as two years. The resulting soil erosion causes bigger floods on lowland rivers. The long-term solution is reafforestation of watershed areas, but this has become a major source of conflict between uplanders and the government.

Restrictions on forest clearing threaten the very livelihood of some hill tribespeople, even if they survive the exposure to tourists and city merchants. Their culture is on the edge of extinction.

continued from p171

through the village and 9km up to a Shan village, where this superb cave is signposted. Guides (about 100 baht per party) and lanterns can be hired at the entrance. The limestone formations and sheer size are impressive, but insist on seeing the third chamber (this involves some wading) where at dusk there is the breathtaking spectacle of huge numbers of swifts and bats entering and leaving the cave mouth.

Near by, Cave Lodge offers simple accommodation and cave treks.

Pai *Buses run from Mae Hong Son, Soppong and Chiang Mai.* An aimiably dozy small town, with inexpensive trekking and guesthouses, it is good for gentle excursions. East, over the river bridge, a dirt track leads past a hilltop *wat* 15km to a signposted hot spring. Thick-skinned visitors claim the water is not too hot for swimming.

 Mae Sai
Highway 110. Buses from Bangkok, Chiang Mai and Chiang Rai

The town Thailand's northernmost point is a classic border post, where a bridge spans the Mae Kok river and leads into the adjacent Burmese town of Tha Khi Lek. A constant procession of Burmese and Thais cross over for the markets on either side. People of other nationalities are not allowed into Burma at present, but it is possible to stand on the bridge and be technically across the border, which is the middle of the river.

Mae Sai excels as a place for people-watching; hill-tribe children, some of them just Thais dressed for the part, pose for tourists' cameras, a blind beggar holds out a metal tankard, while a wizened brown-skinned woman puffs a fat cheroot.

On Buddhist holidays a fascinating market takes place on the bridge itself. At other times Burmese crafts (string puppets, wall-hangings, wooden musician figures and lacquerware) and jade are on offer – much of it brought in from Chiang Mai.

Mae Sai's modern main street is wide and drab, but a string of bungalow-style guesthouses by the river entice a few days' stay.

Opposite and to the left from the Top North Hotel, 207 steps lead up to Wat Doi Wao, which faces into Burma.

Mai Sai lies in a district known for its cultivated strawberries, sold from stalls along the main road in the winter months.

Motorcycles can be hired from Mae Sai for exploring the area.

Environs
Sob Ruak (The 'Golden Triangle') *Hourly minibuses from Mae Sai, morning only, and all day from Chiang Saen, from where boats can be chartered for the trip.*

A huge new luxury hotel and a plethora of souvenir stalls pander to the needs of the hordes of tourists who come here to be photographed in front of a hideous concrete sign announcing this to be the Golden Triangle. Except on postcard racks, there isn't an opium poppy in sight; the growers of the illicit plant discreetly carry on elsewhere and the altitude is too low anyway. But despite the tackiness of the place, this is a view to remember – the confluence of the Mekong and the Mae Ruak rivers at the meeting of Thailand, Burma and Laos, with mysterious mountain ranges stretching into the distance. **Wat Prat That Phu Khao**, perched on a hill, gives the best panorama.

Unfortunately, the Burmese have recently constructed a casino in the middle of the river to lure Thais to gamble their baht and prop up an ailing Burmese economy (casinos are banned in Thailand).

Chiang Saen *Buses from Chiang Rai.* Nicely situated on the Mae Nam Khong, this sleepy small town lies to the east of Sob Ruak. Around the neat grid-pattern of streets are dotted a number of ancient ruins from the old town, which was founded in the 13th century and retains its 14th-century fortifications. The Burmese briefly controlled it in the 16th century, and Rama I later destroyed the town, fearing a repeat capture. Chiang Saen remained unoccupied until the time of King Rama V.

The National Museum is in the main street, which leads away from the river. This contains hill-tribe artefacts, inscribed stones, ceramics and Lanna objects. Close by is the 58m-high octagonal *chedi* of Wat Chedi Luang, built in 1290.

Open: Wednesday to Sunday, 09.00hrs– 16.00hrs.

Wat Pa Sak Keep along the main street and turn right as you cross the town wall for a ruined forest *wat* among the trees that retains some fine stucco decoration; Wat Pa Sak is the most impressive monument in Chiang Saen.

Continuing along the road for 1km, with the moat on the right, brings you to Wat Chom Kitti, which is approached by a long staircase and provides a good view across to Laos.

Chiang Khong This is reached by buses from Chiang Rai; a *songthaew* to Chiang Saen via a dirt road daily at 11.30hrs returns at 07.30hrs. Also on the Mekong river, which is the sole feature of interest. Riverside guesthouses and bungalows make the most of the view (more than in Chiang Saen where the accommodation is nothing special).

Doi Mae Salong/Santi Kiri *Frequent buses run between Chiang Rai and Mae Sai; alight at Basang for a songthaew. There is a sporadic service; the last one back leaves Santi Kiri at 15.30hrs.*

Perched high on the Mae Salong mountain, 36km from the main road, Santi Kiri is an extraordinary place, inhabited by Yunnanese and completely Chinese in character. Yunnan is spoken; the shops sell strange herbal liquors, lychee and prune wines and locally grown tea. Stalls along the street sell noodles for 5 baht a time; at daybreak Akha women conduct a lively produce

Little China in Thailand
Formerly known as Mae Salong, Santi Kiri ('hill of peace') has existed since 1961 as a refugee village for the soldiers and their families following the 1949 Chinese Cultural Revolution. After settling in Thailand they engaged themselves in smuggling and in the opium trade. The Thai government has launched a re-education programme and persuaded them to switch to growing tea, coffee, herbs, fruit and corn. Thai language classes are given and a loudspeaker broadcasts information on taxation matters and health education.

market. A *wat*, a mosque and a Haw Chinese shrine serve the community.
Stay overnight and experience the early morning life: there are medium-priced resort bungalows above the village and two fairly basic guesthouses.

Doi Tung *Frequent buses from Chiang Rai to Mae Sai; alight at Highway 1149 for a songthaew for Doi Tung.* The paved road winds up past Shan, Akha and Lahu villages to the 1,700m summit 17.5km from the main road, where Wat Phra That Doi Tung and its vast assemblage of bells of varying pitches look far into the hills. Halfway up, the simple bungalows at Akha Guesthouse are only one step up from camping, but for views and rural atmosphere it can hardly be bettered. You would be wise only to trek in this area if you have a guide.

Wat Doi Wao, Mae Sai

177

Burma

This former British colony has suffered brutal repression from dictatorships since 1962 when General Ne Win wrested power in a coup. In 1988, students demonstrations against the government were met with atrocities and many fled to Thailand, settling around Mae Sot. Despite a crushing electoral defeat by the National League of Democracy in May 1990, General Sauw Maung refused to cede power. In recognition of Burma's struggle for democracy, Suu Kyi, the democracy leader, was awarded the Nobel Peace Prize while under house arrest.

Mae Sot

Off Highway 105. Frequent buses from Tak

The westernmost town in Tak province lies close to the Burmese border and is a smuggling post for teak and jade. The streets throng with Chinese, hill-tribe people smoking cheroots, Burmese in sarongs and dark-skinned Muslims in lace skullcaps. The town centre is punctuated with Burmese-style *wats* whose golden *chedis* glint in the hard sunlight.

Mae Sot is a good base for exploring hill-tribe villages, Burmese refugee camps and the mountainous border areas in the vicinity. Among several tour companies which organise trekking tours is SP Tour (tel: (055) 31670).

Environs

Songthaews leave frequently from various locations around town to these and other destinations.

Rim Moei Market *Ten minutes' drive west on Highway 105.* This border market town is on the Mae Nam Mae, where locals take the ferry or swim across to the Burmese bank now that the road bridge has been destroyed.

The market is full of Burmese wares – lacquer products, jade, rubies, embroidered waistcoats, Burmese currency and even school slates.

'Death Highway' to Um Phang

Hourly songthaews *in the morning only; journey time about five hours.* Highway 1090, south from Mae Sot, earned its nickname in the 1960s and 70s when Communists held the area and attacked road builders.

Today it is safe (there is a police checkpoint, so bring your passport) and the magnificent road looks over huge areas of scarcely inhabited terrain, including Thailand's second highest mountain, Khao Kha Khaeng (2,400m).

Um Phang, 165km from Mae Sot, is one of Thailand's remotest villages within reach by good road. Several guesthouses offer simple accommodation and organise one-day raft trips and three-day treks (dry season only) to **Hee Lor Sue**, Thailand's largest and mightiest waterfall.

Closer to Um Phang, guides will take you to **Tham Mae Klong Cave**, a 5km-long cave with limestone formations, a bat colony and a hermit monk; and **Doi Hua Mod** ('bald mountain') which has a spectacular sunrise view.

Forty-one kilometres from Mae Sot on this road, a signposted track leads 700m to **Pha Charoen** waterfall, which tumbles down a 93-step natural staircase.

Nan

End of Highway 101. Frequent buses from Bangkok, Chiang Mai, Lamphang and Phrae. Daily bus from Chiang Rai; domestic flights

The town Relatively remote and considered a dangerous area until recent years, Nan is far from being the most visited part of the north. However, many visitors stay on longer than they intended, captivated by the town's laid-back, atmosphere. The most exciting bus-route approach is on Highway 1148 from Chiang Rai, along a tortuous single track for five and a half hours, past mountains, Hmong villages and opium fields.

The National Museum *Pha Kong Road.* Erected in 1903 as a palace for the feudal lord, this houses one of the best provincial museums.
Open: Wednesday to Sunday, 09.00hrs–12.00hrs; 13.00hrs–16.00hrs.

Wat Phumin Opposite the museum, this 18th-century *wat* is memorable for its Lanna-style woodcarvings and superb murals.

Environs
Nan province is relatively undiscovered, with time-warp villages, mountain scenery and good views. Guesthouses and the Youth Hostel (tel: (054) 710322) organise trekking and tours. Motorcycles and bicycles can be rented from shops near the Devaraj hotel.

Doi Phukha National Park *Highway 1256 northeast of Phua (north of Nan), signposted in English.* The highest point in the province (1,980m), the Park abounds with waterfalls, views and caves. The world's only known Chompu Phuka tree, which produces pink flowers, is here. Non-Thai speakers will need a guide. A day trip could take in salt mines at Bor Klua and weaving and silver-making villages.

Wat Manee Pasi Son in Mae Sot

The Lanna Boat Race at Nan
Nan's major event of the year takes place in late October or early November, when gaily decorated boats made out of hollowed-out trees, are used for an exuberant rowing race, the scene accompanied by singing, drumming and the usual commotion associated with northern festivals. The race dates back over 100 years, when it was introduced as part of the competitive games played on Songkran Day, but is now associated with a robe-giving ceremony at Wat Phra That Chae Haeng.

Pak Nai *Bus from Nan, changing at Na Noi and Na Muan.* A few hours' drive south from Nan is this peaceful fishing village, built on stilts over Sirikit Reservoir, a huge water bounded by hills. Simple, inexpensive rafthouse accommodation and boat hire are available. Some 10km south of Na Noi, a turn leads to Sao Din, a curious area of pinnacles and pillars formed by water erosion.

Wat Khao Noi *Just south of Nan, signposted off Highway 101.* A minor road leads to the hilltop *wat*; the statuary is garish in the extreme but the view over the rice-paddies of the Nan valley and surrounding hills is satisfying enough.

▶ ▶ ▶ Phitsanulok
Junction of Highways 12 and 117. Buses from Chiang Mai, Bangkok and neighbouring towns, trains and domestic flights
Most tourists visiting this friendly city are passing through *en route* for Sukothai but there is enough here for a leisurely half-day exploration. The tourist office at Borom Trailokanat Road has helpful hand-outs, including maps of the area and a recommended town walk.
Phitsanulok looks at its best by night along the Nan river – venue for annual boat races in October or November (see panel). Houseboats with rusting tin roofs and tottering TV antennae line the banks; amid them are a number of floating restaurants, one of which even has a boat attached for evening dinner cruises. A precarious-looking cable car, running 06.00hrs– 22.00hrs, crosses the river for a mere 2 baht. On land, the night bazaar brings after-dark animation, with cheap food and clothes stalls.

Wat Yai (Wat Mahathat) *Phuttabucha Road.* This contains Thailand's most beautiful image, Phra Buddha Chinnarat, much copied (see panel on page 181).

Folk Museum *Wisuthikasartri Road.* Unprominently signposted in a sleepy backstreet, this two-storey house is crammed with the personal collection of retired Sergeant Major Tawee Booranakate. All kinds of bygones are here, mementoes of a life style that Thailand is fast shedding. Among them are utensils, ploughs, home-made toys and vicious-looking traps.
Open: daily, 08.30hrs–12.00hrs; 13.00hrs–16.30hrs; donations welcome.

Buddha Foundry Roughly opposite the folk museum and even less prominent (it's the door to the left of the Music School), this is run by the same person. Visitors are welcome to look around and watch the production process, where wax images are coated in clay and sand prior to casting, then the cast image is covered with lacquer and gold leaf.

Environs
Kaeng Sopa Waterfall *Highway 12, 72km east of Phitsanulok (signposted in English); 3km access road from main road.* The *Phitsanulok to Lom Sak bus passes*

along the main road; Kaeng Sopa is about 3km from here.

A waterfall rushing down three steps strewn with massive boulders, Kaeng Sopa is the best-known feature of **Thung Sa-Laeng Luang National Park**, a large area of forest and wilderness, five per cent of which has been illegally depleted.

House boats on the Nan River, Phitsanulok

At the night bazaar in Phitsanulok you can see the city's most eccentric claim to fame, *pak boong loi fah* (the 'flying vegetable'), where morning glory is tossed high from the wok to be caught across the street by the waiter.

Cast in bronze in 1357, Phra Buddha Chinnarat is a magnificent example of the late Sukothai style. In 1631 King Ekathotsarot of Ayutthaya melted down some of his gold and personally coated the image. In 1756 King Boromkot donated the doors inlaid with mother of pearl. Murals of the Buddha's life and a Jataka tale were added at this time. The image is the most important in Thailand after the Emerald Buddha in Wat Phra Keo in the Grand Palace.

■ **The opium poppy was introduced to the Orient by Arab traders during the Mongol invasions of the 13th century. Minority hill tribes in southern China grew it as a cash crop to pay their taxes to the Chinese Emperor. They took it with them when they migrated south to Thailand and Burma. .....■**

The Golden Triangle The commercialisation of opium and its more lethal refined form, heroin, in Southeast Asia is a direct result of the tangled recent politics and warfare of the region. Its widespread use by American GIs during the Vietnam War dramatically increased the demand for it, while also providing outlets to the world market. The illegal trade bolstered the power of opium warlords. The whole inaccessible area between Thailand, Burma and Laos became known as the 'Golden Triangle'.

Drug barons and cash flows The 'king' of the opium warlords was the colourful and shady Khun Sa. In the 1950s, with US backing, he used opium to finance the futile rearguard battles of the Chinese Nationalists or Kuomintang against Mao Zedong. By the late 1960s, however, he was in fierce competition with his erstwhile comrades. The battle for the opium trade eventually escalated into a full-scale war in 1967 in which one of his convoys carrying 16 tons of opium was actually napalmed. He survived this and a score of other clashes with the Thai and Burmese armies until his death in 1991.

Counter-measures Nowadays the government prefers to wean hill tribes away from opium to produce other cash crops – such as coffee, flowers and cabbages – instead. This is part of the broader hill-tribe development programme launched by King Bhumiphol. There has been some success; checks are made and large opium fields destroyed, although villagers still grow opium on a small scale for their own use, as many are addicts. However,

Thailand now accounts for less than 2 per cent of world opium production.

Thailand is also inventing imaginative solutions to heroin addiction. Addicts are increasingly being sent to treatment centres rather than jailed. One such detoxification programme is in a Buddhist monastery run by Phra Chamroon Parnchand (see page 147), who administers an emetic to addicts which induces spectacular ritual vomiting. He claims to have cured more than 60,000 addicts since 1959.

A Lahu woman smoking opium

<< The victims of opium include the hill tribes who cultivate the poppies as well as Thailand's 500,000 heroin addicts. There are no millionaires living in the hills. Few families average more than US$300 or US$400 a year. The profits are all cornered by warlords, middlemen and international heroin syndicates. >>

Border Problems

■ **Continual battling with neighbouring tribes and peoples has played a significant part in forming the identity of the Thai people. The Shans of northeastern Burma and the Laotian people are ethnically related to the Thais while the Cambodians and Malays have both experienced some degree of Thai rule. .....■**

Border history Colonialism in the 19th century revealed the need for strictly defined geographical boundaries. Although Thailand was never colonised, its present boundaries reflect its role as a buffer state between the British in Burma and the French Indochinese empire.

Burma The Golden Triangle, along the border with Burma (or Myanmar as it now calls itself), is notorious for its rebels, bandits and opium trade. Neither government has full control over the border area.
Because of the practice of slash-and-burn cultivation many of the hill tribes who live in Thailand frequently move over into Burmese territory and vice versa.

Laos Problems along the Laotian border mounted when the Vietnamese-backed Pathet Lao came to power in the 1970s. Many anti-Communist royalist factions resisted from bases within Thailand, while refugees flooded across the border to be housed in camps (they are now being repatriated).
Much of the border is the Mekong river, which is also the main transport artery of Laos. Now increasing trade is reflected in plans to build a bridge across the Mekong.

Cambodia Thai fears over the border with Cambodia reached a high point after the Vietnamese invasion of Cambodia in the late 1970s.
Tensions eased following the 1991 peace settlement in Cambodia. But the potential for trouble remains. Thais have in the past claimed the Cambodian provinces of Battambang and Siem Reap.

Malaysia Even the short border with Malaysia is ill defined. Until recently one bus journey between two Malaysian towns used to pass through Thai territory. Nine Malaysian forestry officials were arrested recently, accused of logging inside the Thai border.

In 1989 the Burmese government tried to cut off the finance to the Karen rebels by selling teak concessions to the Thai army. The Burmese junta were quite happy to see Burma's rainforests destroyed if it reduced cover and hiding places for the rebels. The infamous 'opium king' Khun Sa used to be active in this area, commanding 4,000 armed guerrillas at the time of his death in 1991.

Border checkpoint, Mae Sot

Seldom seen even by local people, Thailand's most primitive tribe, the Mrabri – known also as the Phithong Luan – pursue a nomadic lifestyle on the borders of Phrae and Nan provinces. These humble and gentle people wear loincloths and have no use for money, using instead a bartering system. Now numbering about 100, they face extinction as deforestation continues apace. Their corpses are not buried, but placed on trees to be pecked to pieces by birds. They are excluded from the Thai social system but have become a tourist attraction in the worst zoo tradition with special enclosures for visitors to stand and gawp.

Buddha at Phrae

Phrae
Highway 101. Buses from surrounding cities, domestic flights

Phrae city has little to offer the tourist except as a base for exploring the surrounding uplands. The name of Phrae is associated with the indigo work-shirts *seua maw hawn*, much worn by farmers, *samlor* drivers and even local schoolchildren and teachers – it becomes the Phrae school uniform on Fridays. Made at Ban Thung Ong north of the city, these hard-wearing garments are on sale throughout town; a shirt will cost you about 80 baht, and you can get jackets and trousers made of the same material.

Downtown Phrae is blandly modern, but the adjoining old part of the city retains traces of its moated fortifications and has a maze of peaceful streets of old-style wooden houses.

Wat Chom Sawan, on the northeast side of the city, is a Burmese-style temple, with multi-tiered tin roofs and a good deal of creaky, old-world charm.

Environs
Phae Muang Phi *18km to the northeast; take Highway 101 towards Nan, branch off right as signposted in English after 12km. There are no buses.* This translates as 'ghost land': soil erosion has left a surreal moonscape of earth pillars, best seen in the early morning when the shadows create some strange effects.

Tham Pha Nanloi *30km to the northeast, on Highway 101 towards Nan. On the Nan–Phrae bus route.* An electrically lit cave with limestone formations, used as a Buddhist shrine and extending 200m into the hillside.
This is the setting for an ancient and famous legend of a king's daughter, who is saved by a soldier from drowning. She elopes with her saviour and has his child. The king, furious at their behaviour, sends men after them to ambush the soldier as he leaves the cave. Unaware of his death, the princess waits eternally for his return; a rock in the cave is said to represent the princess and her child.

▶ ▶ **Phu Hin Rong Kla National Park**

Off Highway 12 east of Phitsanulok. Hourly buses between Phitsanulok and Lom Sai; change at Ban Yeang for frequent bus to Nakhon Thai; change for minibus to the Park at 17.00hrs only

Approached by a road that rises through rugged highlands and passes remote Hmong villages, Phu Hin Rong Kla has a magnificent setting – best appreciated from the knobbly rock pavement known as **Lan Hin Boom**, perched on a cliff above a hair-raising drop. Deep rock fissures harbour ferns, lichen speckles the boulders and orchids and white rhododendrons are among the diverse flora.

Today the park is visited for its solitude and quiet beauty, yet from 1968 to 1982 it was the stronghold of the Communist Party of Thailand (CPT). Remnants of that era survive today (there are probably unexploded shells about, so keep to the trails).

Following the road westward from the park headquarters (towards Nakhon Thai) for 300 metres, a left turn near the park sign leads on to a trail across the rock plateau. The memorial on the right near the road commemorates those who died in a major KMT (Kuomintang) conflict.

Eastwards from the park headquarters on the main road, a cluster of signs in English points to three KMT relics. The air-raid shelter is a deep natural rock crevice, explored by a short circular trail that leads up and down ladders. Close by, a waterwheel survives; fed by a wooden chute. This was constructed for the purpose of grinding rice for CPT consumption. Further along, on the other side of the road, are the remaining huts of the **Political and Military School**, the camp training centre.

Adequate bungalow accommodation, starting from 100 baht per person (book in advance: 579 0529), and tents at around 40baht for one or two people, are provided. Of the two restaurants, Dungjai's is better; the proprietor's *som tum* (spicy carrot salad) has won her TV appearances. The park headquarters gives away free but basic maps,and maintains a small KMT museum.

Huts, air-raid shelters, bunkers, an abandoned digging machine, a flagpole, some rapidly overgrowing graves and a simple memorial are humble reminders of a period when the Communist Party of Thailand fortified itself in one of the country's most impenetrable areas. From the 1940s, Hmong tribes settled in this virtually unpopulated region. They planted opium and many were arrested over the next decade. As their relationship with central government deteriorated, the CPT took up their cause. In 1982 the government weakend the grip of the CPT until they gave in. The park was established in 1984.

185

Phu Hin Rong Kla

Si Satchanalai Historical Park

Junction of Highways 101 and 102, 2km to the south of the new town of Si Satchanalai and 1km off the Sukhothai to Phrae bus route

Cars are not allowed in the Park itself, but elephant rides are available from the entrance and bicycles can be rented from the pink entrance gate to Wat Phra Si Rathana Mahathat, 2km from the park. There is a small entrance fee.

The old city of Si Satchanalai coexisted with Sukhothai and was ruled by Sukothai princes. It flourished as a centre for Sawankhalok celadon ware, first produced by Chinese potters; old kilns dot the area and the industry has been revived, with stalls operating near the old city.

Walk A walk in Phu Hin Rong Kla.

Allow one-and-a-half to two hours for this 3.5km walk.

Start at the car park signed 'Communist Headquarters' from the main road, 2 miles east of the national park headquarters. Take the path at the bottom of the car park. Fork left at the Thai signpost after 200m. Ignore a small path joining from the left and cross a rock pavement. Notice the pock marks in the rock caused by shelling.(You will return to this point; to the right is your eventual continuation.) Keep to the left of the abandoned gun and take the right-hand of two paths signposted in Thai.

The left-hand path leads to the former huts of the Political and Military School, where it is a short walk left along the road for signed turnings to the waterwheel and air-raid shelter.

Immediately fork left again and reach a hut on your right, formerly used for pounding rice.

Just ahead lie the former CPT headquarters and wooden-barred jail.

Take the path by the hut. It leads through another air-raid shelter (a natural rock crevice). Walk on and rejoin the main path, keeping left on it to return to the rock pavement and the abandoned gun. Turn left.

The path soon leads to Pa Chu Thong, or Flagpole Cliff edge

(passing to the right of the Flagpole Cliff itself) to the rock pavement of Lan Hin Boom. This is the most famous land form in the park.

Retrace steps to a fork; bear left. Later, Flagpole Cliff comes into view and you pass mushroom-shaped rock formations. At a wooden gateway on the left, a short path leads past the site of a CMT burial ground, where a few overgrown humps can be discerned.

Keep left on rejoining the main path and return to the car park.

Wat Chedi Chet, Si Satchanalai

Over 140 ruins cover an otherwise largely deserted 300-hectare area, the centre of which is enclosed by fortifications and contains the Park. In its extent, it is almost as striking as Sukhothai itself. Sites are numbered and a map is available at the entrance.

Wat Chang Lom (Site 1)
A Singhalese style *chedi* with 39 elephant buttresses; similar to its Sukhothai namesake but much better preserved.

Wat Chedi Jet Thaeo (Site 2)
This has 30 monuments in various styles, including a Sukhothai-style lotus bud *chedi*, and it is thought to enshrine the three princes of Sukhothai.

Wat Nang Phya (Site 4)
Early Ayutthaya style; still embellished with intricate stucco on a column and on the *wiharn* wall.

Wat Chedi Jet Thaeo

Wat Khao Phanom Phloeng (Site 8)
Reached by a flight of laterite steps, the ruin is unremarkable but it commands a large view, partly obscured by the trees.

Wat Si Rathana Mahathat (2km south)
Approached from the main road by a rickety wooden suspension bridge, this working temple stands inside a loop in the Yom river and retains a Sukhothai-style seated Buddha image

▶ ▶ ▶ Sukhothai
Junction of Highways 12 and 101, west of Phitsanulok. Buses from Chiang Mai, Phitsanulok, Bangkok and neighbouring towns

Three Sukhothai temples: Wat Chetupon...

If you only have time to visit one ancient site in Thailand, it must be the old city of Sukhothai. New Sukhothai, 12km east, is a quite separate town, only of interest as a place to stay and eat. There are no inhabited buildings within the old city.

From the new city, cross the main road bridge over the Yom river, and take a minibus from just behind the police box on the right. Cars are not allowed in the old city ruins; buses tour the main sites from the museum and bicycles can be rented from the shop by the bus stop for about 20 baht. Distances are too great to cover on foot. There are admission charges for each of the city's five zones; the historic park is open daily until dusk.

History Established in 1238, when the central plains were inhabited by Mons and Khmers, Sukhothai was the capital of the first large Thai kingdom in Siam and became a vassal state of Ayutthaya in 1365. It was a cosmopolitan kingdom, host to a variety of cultures from Borneo, Ceylon and China, all of which contributed to the diversity of its monuments. King Ramkhamnaeng extended the kingdom with his warrior skills and was responsible for much of the flowering of Sukhothai culture. He brought in Chinese ceramic skills, introducing the Sankhalok celadon industry to the region. Sukothai-style Buddha images are unmistakable for their oval heads bearing crowns, their plain torsos and their serene, mystical smiles.

Of the 193 historic sites, a third are within the walls, which are still visible and are pierced by four gateways. The city is walled and threaded by beautiful canals and lakes carpeted with lotus flowers. These waters were supplied by a reservoir built to the southwest of the city and were both functional and ornamental.

The National Museum An excellent introduction to the historic city, including much in the Sukothai style. Look too for the chart showing the evolution of the Thai alphabet, thought to have been invented by King Ramkhamnaeng; a set of photographs showing the overgrown ruins before restoration in 1953; and a copy of a Khmer stone which has told scholars much about the history of the site.

...Wat Mahathat...

Open: Wednesday to Sunday, except national holidays, 09.00hrs–12.00hrs; 13.00hrs–16.00hrs. Admission charge.

Royal Palace and Wat Mahathat Only the base of the palace survives, but the royal temple ruins contain 200 structures.The main *chedi* bears a Sukhothai lotus-bud motif and its base bears a frieze of 111 Buddhas.

Wat Trapang Thong and Wat Trapang Ngoen 'The temples of the gold and silver ponds' adjoin the waterside, with a *bot* built on an island. This is the original site of the Loi Krathong festival.

Wat Si Chum The tallest and most famous Buddha image in the city stands 11m high and has eyes of inlaid mother of pearl. A passage on the left, bearing Jataka inscriptions, is locked off because it enables one to climb above the Buddha's head.

Information Centre A beautiful modern pavilion overlooking a lake; inside are a pleasant coffee shop and a fine scale model of the city(*open*: 09.00hrs–16.00hrs).

Wat Phra Pai Luang An atmospheric ruin, with partly restored Khmer *prangs*; rather overgrown. It is thought to be at the heart of the original city which was restricted from growth by the canals.

Wat Saphan Hin Turn off just past the sign for a scout camp and you will reach this hilltop *wat*, from where the kings could survey their city and kingdom.

Rama Khamhaeng National Park *Off Highway 101 towards Kamphaeng Phet at the 414km post*. A bumpy 15km access road finally leads to the National Park office and bungalows (which can be rented). People come here to climb Khao Luang mountain (1,185m). Views are often misty but can be huge, and tents (40 baht) near the summit offer sunset and sunrise views.

...and Wat Sra Sri

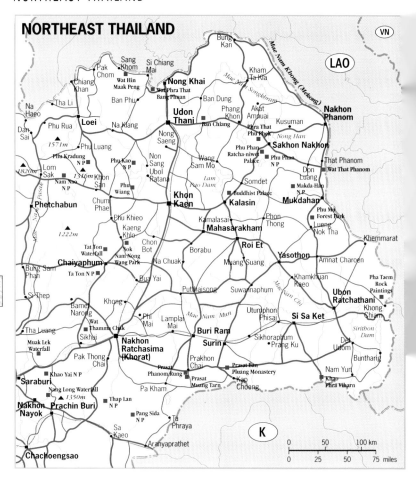

NORTHEAST THAILAND

This region is known as 'Isan' by the Thais, and natives of Isan's 18 or so provinces are justly proud of their region's distinct identity. Khorat and Khon Kaen have been earmarked for industrial development but agriculture is still the basic occupation of the majority of people. Nature here is a harsh master, with yearly droughts or flooding.

With the Mekong river and the Laotian Peoples' Democratic Republic to their north and east, many Isan folk identify themselves culturally as Laotian although their political allegiance to the Thai crown is still very strong.

Isan is famous for its food – the sticky rice staple, papaya salad and barbecued meat. Its folk music tradition, *mor lam*, is also special.

In a recent chapter of the region's history thousands of American troops fought in the second Indochinese war. Later upheavals have come in the wake of the Cambodian civil war.

Poverty here is such that the peasants who scratch a living from the soil supplement their diet with frogs and insects. The per capita income is still the lowest in the country, a paltry few thousand baht per year. Government attempts at development have been partially successful. The birth-rate is falling and increasing numbers of buffaloes are replaced by the *E-taen*, a low-slung vehicle that can serve a multitude of purposes which include ploughing, pumping, threshing and ferrying people about.

For the visitors There are plenty of attractions for the visitor. Be prepared for a trip through a land which although barren at times, has much to amaze – both natural and cultural. The northerly provinces of Loei and Nong Khai have stunning scenery along the Mekong, Loei being particulary mountainous; southern Isan, with its strong Khmer (Cambodian) flavour, has a wealth of remains from the days of Angkor's glory; and Surin is famous for its elephants.

Warm welcome One thing immediately noticeable in the more obscure provinces is the open curiosity and generosity of the people. If you drive around, you will find yourself constantly waving and smiling to roadside greetings. The famous Thai welcome to strangers is possibly warmer here than anywhere else.

Temple ruins at Suwannaphum

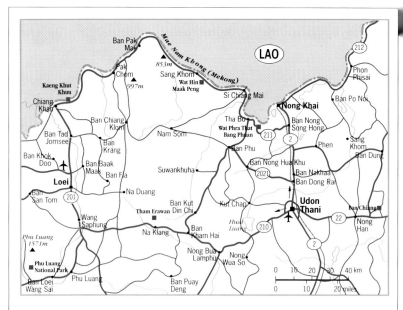

Drive **A tour around Udon Thani, Loei and Nong Khai.**

This tour is best spaced over five days.
Suggested schedule
(book national park accommodation in advance).
Day 1: Early morning, leave Udon Thani. Optional detour to Ban Phu. Arrive in Phu Luang National Park around twilight. Stay overnight in reserved accommodation.
Day 2: Leisurely drive to Chiang Khan. Stay in guesthouse.
Day 3: Leisurely drive to Sang Khom. Stay in guesthouse.
Day 4: Leisurely drive to Nong Khai. Stay in hotel or guesthouse.
Day 5: Short drive to Udon Thani. Day excursion to Ban Chiang.

Start in Udon Thani with its extensive handicraft markets. To arrive in Loei before sunset take the main Highway 210 west. Alternatively, take Highway 2 (The Friendship Highway) north.
A diversion to **Ban Phu** at the well-signposted Highway 2021 will mean arriving at dusk, especially if time is taken to explore the rock garden and cave systems of **Phra Putthabat Bua Bok**. This is not signposted in Ban Phu district.
On arrival at the crossroads go straight across by the market and look for Highway 2348.
The road down to Highway 210 and Loei from Ban Phu is not remarkable; there are a few interesting *wats* back from the road.
Mountains of awe-inspiring scale start at the border of Loei Province as the road climbs gently upwards.

Highway 210 swings a sharp 90 degrees right at Wang Saphung district to become Highway 201; keep an eye out for the turn-off to avoid plunging into the paddies.
Jeep drivers may have time for the very well-signposted 20km trip south from Wang Saphung to **Phu Luang National Park**, where there is accommodation. Phu Luang can be seen from the road here, a grey stone leviathan dominating smaller neighbours.
The short approach to Loei in the other direction is no less scenic. Loei town may not amount to much but it has a ring of mountains and all the amenities of civilisation such as guesthouses and hotels.

Alternatively, go on to Chiang Khan district 50km due north.
This is an excellent spot to rest before contemplating the 200km drive along Highway 211 into Nong Khai, where guesthouses taking advantage of the riverside ambience are plentiful.

Sang Khom is a modest target from Chiang Khan; Highway 211 sticks to the Mekong river for very long stretches. Khut Khuu Rapids is a short and reasonably signed left-hand detour just out of Chiang Khan. The scenery is formed by the meandering middle-aged river. The water level can go down so far in the dry season that it is unclear where the border actually lies. Shoals of rocks and extensive bogs dominate the view.

The 60km to Sang Khom ('Society') are more of the same marvellous Mekong moonscape. The road scales a series of cliffs passing some viewpoints in order to cross the well-marked provincial boundary. Shortly afterwards **Than To** waterfall is prominently signposted with the blue tourist signs as seen on the road to Phu Luang. **Sang Khom** provides a leisurely stopover to relax peaceably by the now broad and clearly defined river. There are budget guesthouses here. Near by is Wat Hin Mak Peng, an atmospheric spot enhanced by an interest in meditation.

Alternatively travellers may press on a further 40km into Si Chiang Mai. Shortly after Si Chiang Mai the road swings away from the river and you are back into dusty, featureless Isan. The road becomes wider as one approaches Tha Bo.

Highway 211 cuts across the flat fields past Wat Bang Phuan to link up with Highway 2, a full 10km short of Nong Khai. Note that following the white signs all the way will lead into Nong Khai.
A dirt track turning left about 5km out of Tha Bo returns to the river all the way into **Nong Khai** railway station, but the turning is difficult to locate. It will be easy to find a room in Nong Khai, although Highway 2 back into Udon is very fast. From Udon Thani it is a 50km drive (Highway 22) to Ban Chiang, where excavations have revealed bronze and clay artefacts thousands of years old (see page 194)

A Bronze Age skeleton from the Ban Chiang burial pits

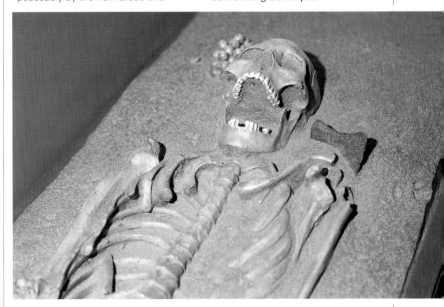

▶ ▶ ▶   **Ban Chiang**

Off Highway 22. Buses from Udon

The otherwise fairly nondescript province of Udon Thani made the headlines when pottery and bronze artefacts discovered in Ban Chiang were dated to the 3rd millennium BC, contemporary with Sumer, suggesting that metalworking was discovered independently in Southeast Asia.

Village crafts are largely reproductions of ancient Ban Chiang ware in all shapes and sizes. The native Thai Lao weaves and embroideries are also on display in the museum.

Archaeological finds Little is known of the early Ban Chiang people's language and ethnic origins, but the large and beautiful pots besides the metal tools and weapons are a rich testament to their technical sophistication. We also know that they farmed rice, domesticated animals, wove their own clothes and eventually progressed to working iron. The find stimulated research in geographical history, which showed a decrease in water sources.

Pottery The ancient pottery-making techniques are essentially the same as those used by modern villagers selling cheap reproductions. The patterns show an evolution through the period of the culture (*c*3600BC–AD300), the primeval inhabitants favouring the distinctive whorl. From about 2,000 years ago the potters incorporated figures of animals and people into their designs, and by the later period they had developed a process of printing patterns on to the pot with the aid of wooden discs.

When an American anthropology student came to Ban Chiang in 1966 he chanced upon one of the major archaeological sites of Southeast Asia. Dusting himself down after tripping over a tree root, he noticed pot rims protruding from the ground. He collected a sample and alerted the Unive4sity of Pennsylvania, and the antiquity of his discovery was established.

194

Reproduced 'Bronze Age' pottery, Ban Chiang

Metalwork The metallurgy, too, shows a progression through a long period of experimentation. The search for minerals, the control of temperature, the greater admixture of tin for a shinier finish and a 'lost-wax' moulding process were all well-developed. It appears that bronze was first cast from around 2000BC onwards. Axe-heads, spear tips and arrow tips bear this out. The people of Ban Chiang had discovered techniques of smelting iron by 800BC and the stronger metal came to be used for heavier implements. Bronze came to be used for mainly decorative purposes, such as arm bangles and household objects like ladles.

Modern Ban Chiang The area was settled by an inward migration of the Thai Lao about 200 years ago. Like their forebears here who were subsistence rice farmers, they built Wat Po Si Nai which is one of the excavation sites.

The National Museum Finds from the site are displayed in the modern National Museum. A *songthaew* drops passengers here from the main bus station in Udon for about 13 baht. Visitors are greeted on the stairs up by a skeleton disinterred from a long sleep. As with ancient cultures everywhere, burials supplied the greatest amount of cultural information. Bones reveal that life expectancy was as low as the early 30s, while the relative scale of the burials indicates a social structure. The main Princess Mother building, which opened in 1987, houses an exhibition which once toured the world and has also been on display for a lengthy period at the National Museum in Bangkok. There are the fascinating details of the discovery, which was authenticated by a team from Pennsylvania University led by the late Chester F Gorman. The other smaller building contains more artefacts.
Open: daily, except Mondays, Tuesdays and public holidays.

Swirling patterns, favoured in Bronze Age pottery

195

Locals soon cashed in on the Ban Chiang booty, collecting the pots by the car load for worldwide distribution, and by 1973, when an organised archaeological dig at last got under way, the site had been sadly depleted of its treasures. But some artefacts were still to be found, most importantly the bronze which was to change archaeologists' understanding of the development of metal-making. Fortunately, the looting ceased, and much archaeological work on the site was carried out by Thai volunteers.

Hor Nang Usa, partly weathered, partly man-made stone 'cave' near Ban Phu

▶ ▶ ▢ Ban Phu
Junction Highways 2021 & 2098. Songthaew from Udon or Nong Khai

This obscure corner of Udon is great for bushwalkers. Bring some water for the arduous tramp. Getting there is relatively straightforward, and it is a feasible day-trip from Udon Thani, Nong Khai or Sang Khom. While the final route is a bush-track, metalled roads and buses run into Ban Phu where there are motorbikes for hire, making it feasible to go another 10km to **Nam Som**.

The maze-like rock gardens have cave paintings dating back approximately 4,000 years. It is fascinating to trace the rise and fall of civilisations and cultures through their sculpture.

This is one of Thailand's minor 'stone forests'. Local legends grew around some of the stranger formations such as *Hor Nang Usa*, 'Usa's bedchamber', Usa being a woman who followed her lover here. Humans have arranged circles of stones, and there are curious formations caused by natural erosion. An imitation of That Phanom stands at the top of the hill. Wat Phra That Phra Putthabat Bua Bok, with relic and footprint, points the way along a path to the cave paintings and the mushroom-like sandstone 'bedchamber'.

Rock painting of early Buddhists

▶ ▢ ▢ Chon Bot
Off Highway 2

This district of Khon Kaen is reached by a turn-off at 399km, Ban Phai. Follow the road for another 12km.

Chon Bot is famous for the locally tie-dyed *mudmee* silks. The silk is cheap and there is a good selection available. There are plenty of factories, busily serving markets in Chiang Mai and Bangkok. They are small, informally run and welcoming to visitors.

▶ ▷▷ ### Khon Kaen

Junction of Highways 2 & 12. Buses from Bangkok (north terminal), Phitsanulok and Khorat; trains from Bangkok and Khorat; domestic flights

Officially a 'development centre', Khon Kaen is the undisputed chief city of the northeast. Rapid industrial growth has been fostered by Khon Kaen University, the biggest in the region. The city's name came from Phra That Kham Kaen in Wat Jetiaphum, 30km north of town. According to legend it was here that a tamarind log (*kham kaen*) began sprouting new shoots.

Attractions start with two large lakes, **Beung Kaen Nakhorn,** and the larger **Beung Kaen Sang**. The cool atmosphere makes these popular picnic spots, even if the views are nothing out of the ordinary. Stalls sell Isan food such as *som tam* salad and barbecued chicken.

The Khon Kaen National Museum (*open*: Wednesday to Sunday; admission charge) has Dvaravati artefacts from Muang Fa Daet in Kalasin.

Environs

For palaeontologists, **Phu Wiang** is a detour worth making off Highway 2038 to see the bones of a Cretaceous-period dinosaur.

197

Tham Pha Phuang forestry reserve, Chum Phae district is a 4km turn-off some way along the road to Chum Phae. The huge cave here is an indirect walk from the car park. There is a terrific view from the cave mouth, but it is probably better to drive on to Phu Kradung just over the boundary in Loei Province, where there is a National Park.

Pha Nok Khao (Owl Cliff) on the border refers to the strange shapes that can be seen on the Pong river. They can also be seen from Mount Phu Kradung, which is visible in the distance from here.

Pong Neep (Ubol Ratana Dam), 26km out of town, is the biggest multi-purpose dam in the northeast. Completed in 1966, it created a reservoir of 410sq km and makes electricity for eight provinces.

Processing silk worms in Khon Kaen

►►► Loei

Highway 201; a border province with Laos. Regular buses from Udon; buses from Bangkok (northern terminal)

Temperatures can plummet below zero in this mountainous province, which is the coldest in the country. Have warm clothing to hand.

Loei town is a cotton centre and goods are on sale in town at reasonable prices. There are many hotels here, of which **King's Hotel** is the most luxurious while still remaining in the moderate price range. **Muang Loei** guesthouse is typical of the budget accommodation on offer.

Northwest of Loei town an ancient city waits for discovery at **Ban Khok Doo**, while **Wang Saphung** district a short way south out of town has a few spots worthy of a visit amid a ring of mountains. On the Udon Thani road are the **Erawan caves**, where a long tunnel through a mountain is full of stalactites.

National parks Loei's mountain national parks – Phu Kradung, Phu Luang and Phu Rua – are breathtaking in their scope and are centred around the mountains that lie to the town's south and west.

Heavily visited by tourists, **Phu Kradung** (which may be closed during the rainy season) is best appreciated on weekdays. It is a long way to the south of Loei town on Highway 201. There are 50km of well-marked trails to explore across the forested plateau. The southern trail runs along a precipitous edge where gibbons can be heard calling from below. The park HQ is on the summit. Climb a trail up the table mountain past fields of colourful wild flowers and carnivorous pitcher plants hidden in the grass. Wildlife includes wild boars, wild dogs, giant black squirrels, langurs, macaques and herds of elephants.

It is a tiring 9km to Sri Than park station, but once there such civilised amenities as restaurants and bungalows are on hand to help you get your strength back.

Beds can be booked on tel: (02) 579 0529 or tel: (02) 579 4842 (Bangkok nos). Stalls selling soft drinks are set up along the trail but are closed during weekdays in the off-season.

Driving north back into Loei, **Phu Luang** can be seen towering behind Wang Sapung district, from where it is signposted. It is worth the trek up to the plateau for waterfalls, stone gardens and forests of flowers.

Accommodation can be booked locally at the provincial office on tel: (042) 811776 or on the Bangkok numbers given for Phu Kradung.

Phu Rua lies 48km to the northwest, but drivers must skirt the thickly forested mountains after leaving Loei, turning right on Highway 203. *Phu Rua* means 'boat mountain' and is so named because of its unusual prow-like summit.

It is possible to drive all the way up Phu Rua, assuming your vehicle can manage it. The progression of vegetation from lush tropical to the more barren temperate varieties is as well defined as in a geography textbook. Early morning mist makes a breathtaking

spectacle around the mountain. If you want to stay, the park bungalows are about halfway up the mountain.

The border with Laos Driving on from Phu Rua, you reach Dan Sai district and Na Haeo behind it. Turn right off Highway 203 as it swings down towards Petchabun. Passing Dan Sai, follow an unprepossessing sign right to **Ban Muang Phrae.** This village is where it is possible, technically, to cross into Laos. There is a large sign bearing the inscription 'The end of Siam', and a little wooden bridge with the legend, 'Lao-Thai friendship will endure'. See the Lao town hall and rickety little mudpile of a temple, dark inside with guttered wax. Walking further is not recommended as the area is still sensitive, and there are military checkpoints on the border road.
The important *wat* in Dan Sai cemented a Thai–Lao pact in 1560, with *chedi* Phra That Sri Song Rak. Around May and June, there is dancing for the rain god in *papier mâché* masks that have a striking resemblance to African art, the dancers becoming fearsome *Phi Takone* ghosts.

Chiang Khan district, in the north, is an excellent starting point for a long scenic drive along the Mekong river. Chiang Khan town is on the Laotian border where Highway 201 becomes 2186. The road goes to the east past narrow rapids at Khut Khu and carries on to Pak Chom.
For accommodation, the **Nong Ball** has *farang*-friendly services and an English-speaking owner, its restaurant having a fine Mekong-side ambience.

199

A village near Loei

The Mekong River

■ **The Mekong, which forms the border between Thailand and Laos for more than 600km, is one of Asia's great rivers. It springs in the high Tibetan plateau, and then stretches more than 4,000km to the South China Sea to become the world's 12th longest river. ....■**

See how it runs The Mekong first pursues a turbulent course through the high Chinese mountains of Tibet and Yunnan, then flows parallel to the Yangtze and the Salween through Yunnan province. The river forms the border between Burma and Laos, and then between Laos and Thailand. Even in its upper stretches it is, in some places, more than 2km wide.

Passing Vientiane and Phnom Penh, an eventual 475 billion cubic metres of water per year burst into the sea in a Vietnamese delta. When it is in flood, the water can rise by 15m and yet in the dry season the flow is reduced to a trickle, and the people of northeastern Thailand can walk across the riverbed into Laos.

The river's banks are heavily forested except in the drier areas of northeastern Thailand. Thick bamboo grows, as well as kapok and banana trees. Crocodiles are rare these days, but monkeys, pythons and the ubiquitous mosquitoes abound.

<< The people on both banks of the upper Mekong speak the same 'northern language'; there are eight times as many Lao-speakers in Thailand as there are in Laos itself. >>

<< The river has given its name to a fierce rice liquor, Mekhong whisky. When it is drunk on the river a measure is sometimes poured into the stream for the water spirits. >>

Embarking to cross the Mekong

Hydroelectric power Laos uses the Mekong for hydropower; a dam at Nam Ngum generates 150MW. Half of the electricity generated can be exported to Thailand, whose booming economy is hungry for power, but deforestation and resultant erosion is making the reservoirs silt up.

Four dams have been built across Mekong tributaries and others are under construction or being planned.

<< On the Mekong River you will see the extremely simple Lao boat called 'three planks', which translates into Lao as *sampan*. >>

For the people The river is a source of food – fish, shrimps, crabs and frogs – to supplement the staple diet of *kao niew* or sticky rice

200

Poverty

■ **When the World Bank annual meeting and the Miss Universe Pageant were held in the sparkling new US$90 million Queen Sirikit Convention Centre in Bangkok, the Thai government moved to another area some 7,000 slum dwellers thought to be too visible to all those foreign eyes. ...■**

Rich and poor With one of the fastest growing economies in the world, Thailand is tipped as the next Asian country to achieve Newly Industrialised Economy (NIE) status. Indeed, overall wealth just in Bangkok is close to the level of some of the poorer European countries such as Portugal. But in the kingdom as a whole there is an enormous gap between rich and poor, and extreme poverty still exists. A good quarter of the population falls below the poverty line defined by the World Bank. The rapid growth of the late 1980s has actually widened the gap between rich and poor.

Isan in the northeast, where 40 per cent of the Thais live, is one of the most poverty-stricken regions of the country. Across the large, arid plateau stretching from Nakhon Ratchasima all the way to the Laotian border, millions scratch a living growing rice and tapioca. Almost all but old people and children move away from home to search for work in the central plains region or in Bangkok itself. Some travel further afield to the rubber plantations of the south or to man Thailand's fishing fleet. They return to the villages only for the planting and harvesting seasons.

Isan still suffers from malnutrition, landlessness and poor infrastructure. Children are still forced to cut short education to go to work. Many of the poor and landless end up in one of Bangkok's numerous slums, where they lack the support of a village community.

Solutions There are many new schemes to help the very poor, from land-sharing to commercialised agro-industry, village adoption to co-operatives. In the past five years hundreds of millions of baht have been poured into the northeast by the government and some improvement is noted. But the overall phenomenon of poverty in Thailand remains.

Making a living from the sale of water melons in the poverty-stricken northeast of Thailand

A viewpoint at Phu Pha Terp, near Mukdahan

 Mukdahan

Highway 212, on the eastern border with Laos. Buses from Nakhon Phanom and Ubon Ratchathani

This newest of Thailand's provinces has one chief tourist attraction – views along the Mekong. In Mukdahan town a laid-out riverside walkway extends from the customs checkpoint and car ferries work their way back and forth over the river. Across the river on the opposite side is the important Lao centre of **Savannaket**. A little further upriver is Kaeng Kabao, a dry-river islet.

The southern road is mountainous. Not far out of Mukdahan is **Phu Manorom**, a brisk climb up ending in a *chedi* and a pavilion. A good diversion off Highway 212 in this direction is **Phu Muu Forest Park**, near Nikhom Kham Soi. Rich in forestry, wildlife and water, the area has rest shelters on the mountain-top with good views of the plain below. Near town, on Jom Nang mountain, are 'red-handprint' caves which are similar to those at Pha Taem.

The area boasts a jumble of colourful Thai sub-tribes such as Phu Thai, Saek, So, Khaa, Yor, Kalerng and Kula. January 9–15 is when the local people stage The Thai Tribes of Mukdahan festival. The end of Buddhist Lent is marked by a boat race.

▶ ▶ ▶ **Nakhon Phanom**

Off Highway 22, near the Laos border. Buses from Nong Khai; possible to travel by bus from Udon (journey time over seven hours)

The main attraction in Nakhon Phanom province is **That Phanom**, a striking *chedi* of great antiquity, located 76km south of town. There is a museum containing relics on the site, and a festival is held there every year, in April.

Renu Nakhon, near the provincial capital, is a similar structure on a more modest scale.

For accommodation try the **Charoen Sook** (budget) hotel. A guesthouse may be opening too.

▶ ▷▷▷   **Nakhon Ratchasima (Khorat)**

Highway 2, 250km northeast of Bangkok. Regular buses from Bangkok (northern terminal); trains from Bangkok; domestic flights

Khorat is a day's drive by car from Bangkok on Highway 2. The town is a railway junction for Nong Khai and Ubon Ratchathani.

The moated city has long been a Siamese redoubt against aggressive Lao and Khmer. It is often described as 'the gateway to the northeast', and indeed, traffic to most Isan provinces must pass through Khorat. The scenic Lam Ta Khong reservoir is on the left entering the city.

The city owes its present plan to King Narai who hired a French architect in the 17th century. A worthwhile sight on the outskirts is **Wat Salaloi**, representing a ship beating against the waves. Ceramic tiles used to roof this innovative modern *wat* were made in **Dan Kwian**, a stopover easy to spot on the southwestern road to Phanom Rung. Special black clay characteristic of Dan Kwian pottery gives the distinctive 'latticework' patterns a bright metallic sheen.

No visitor to modern Khorat can fail to notice **Khunying Mo**, one of Thailand's martial heroines. This scourge of the Lao is immortalised in front of the city's main gates, and a parade in her honour is held every March. Near her effigy is **Maha Weerawong** museum containing a hotchpotch of exhibits.

Another museum near the Khmer temple of Phi Mai has artefacts going back to the area's earliest cultures. Opened in 1991, the prehistoric site museum (on the left just before the Phi Mai turn-off) is a find second only in importance to Ban Chiang (see pages 194–5). **Ban Than Prasat** has been continually settled for 2,500–3,000 years. Skeletons have been found here of people who are believed to have worked bronze and patterned red pots.

Just before Ban Than Prasat is the left-hand turning for another Khmer sanctuary, **Prasat Hin Phanom Wan**, some 1,000 years old. A century older, the Dvaravati (Mon) culture is still preserved in **Muang Sema** and its twin **Khorakhapura**, but these are way back along Highway 2 in the Bangkok direction. Only the oval walls remain of a site rich in finds.

The **Silver Lake Park** is an artificial lake just outside Khorat, off Mitraphap Road, with an aviary, flower garden and swimming pool.

Staying over   In a fine spot by the moat in Khorat, in an atmospheric green, wooden building, is the rather basic budget **Muang Thong Hotel. Faah Sang** is a budget alternative way out past the station. There are plenty of moderate and expensive hotels, of which the central **Anajak** is moderate with good service and takes VISA cards.

Pak Thong Chai is a silk-weaving centre due south on Highway 304 – a day trip from Khorat. Once famous for the silken men's lower garment *pha jong kraben*, decline set in as trousers gained wide popularity. The area has since revived and the royally promoted *mudmee* patterns are woven here. Plenty of workshops reveal the secret of this temperamental fibre.

203

Silver Lake Park

Wat Phochai, at Nong Khai town's eastern end, is the focus for festivals. The complex has a tall bell-tower and the main image is solid gold.

Street market in Nong Khai

▶ ▶ ▶   Nong Khai

Highway 2, near Vientiane on the Laotian border. Buses from Bangkok (northern terminal: journey time nine hours); trains from Bangkok

Like the province, the town of Nong Khai is long and thin, clinging to the river. The town preserves its old wooden houses by the river bank and along Meechai, the 'main drag'.

After an independent Vientiane had been crushed, King Rama I established controlling lordships, one of whom was based here in Nong Khai. The currents of history swept Marxism to power in Laos and until recently Nong Khai has been the most Communist-influenced of Thailand's provinces, with many Russian goods available, such as watches, cameras and fur hats.

An enduring legacy of the earlier French presence in Laos is freshly baked baguettes. Once these were imported, but prohibitive taxes forced the Thais to bake them for themselves.

Orange robes are prominent in Nong Khai: there are many novices studying in colleges here. The classic spot for visitors, **Tha Sadet** (the jetty), is on Rim Khong Road. There are some quaint shops here selling filigree silver jewellery and Lao weaves. Locals are secretive about the market where Lao traders dispose of their goods.

Near here is a co-operative called the **Village Weavers**, a handicraft centre that weaves indigo-dyed *mudmee* cotton. The co-operative was set up in response to the lack of off-season opportunities causing many locals to go off to find new work in Bangkok.

Take a pleasant stroll among the *wats* and houses, looking across at Laos and the river views. Here, more than anywhere, Laos seems poised to open up to the outside world. By 1994, it is hoped that the bridge linking Nong Khai and Vientiane (pronounced 'Wiang Jan') will be complete. Thai–Lao trade will boom, but the status of Western tourists is unsure. The Lao authorities are still very grudging with visas and group tours are favoured. The situation changes rapidly; check at the Lao embassy in Bangkok. Australians might have special rights as their government is funding the bridge!

Nong Khai is now rather overwhelmed by civil works. The rising water table led to the loss of a few houses recently, and a concrete bank is now under construction. Just west of the jetty are some riverside restaurants with a very pleasant ambience. From here you can see a sunken *chedi* – under water for 150 years – but only in the dry season.

Nearer the town's centre of gravity, about halfway to the railway station, there is a monument to a failed rebellion of Haw Chinese outside the town hall.

In town, the spread-out and informal **Mut Mee** guesthouse is a mine of local information. There are now many moderate hotels for those unwilling to 'rough it'.

Provincial Nong Khai is very pleasant, with the Mekong saving the province from the fate of its more barren southern neighbours.

Take Highway 211 west of Nong Khai to pass the *chedi* at **Wat Phra That Bang Phuan**, said to contain the Buddha's excrement. The spectacular scenery starts around Sri Chiang Mai on the river, where Vietnamese make spring rolls; there are budget bungalows here.

Further on in Sangkhom district is Than Thong, a waterfall-cum-river feeder and popular stopping point. Among budget bungalows in Sangkhom town is the **TXK Guesthouse.** Its bamboo balcony is pure relaxed tranquillity and the atmosphere is engagingly informal, if the place is short on modern facilities.

Wat Hin Mak Pheng, near Sang Khom, specialises in *Thudong*, a voluntary ultra-asceticism. Its teachers and fine riverside setting attract visitors.

Along the border nearly 200km to the east along Highway 212, **Wat Phu Tork** is reached by a spiral walkway around a strangely shaped mountain. There are budget hotels in **Bung Kan**, 185km from Nong Khai.

No-one should miss Wat Khaek, just a short way out of Nong Khai town and a good stop for children. The eccentric Luang Puu in charge has built a garden of extraordinary statuary, loosely based on Buddhist and Hindu iconography. It often slides into the bizarre: dogs driving a car, or the latest addition, a seven headed snake. All the town *tuk tuks* will urge you there.

205

A Nong Khai tuk tuk

▶ ▶ ▶   Phanom Rung

Accessible in a day from Khorat, Buri Ram or Surin; turnings off route 24 at Prakhonchai district to the east and Ta-ko to the west

Set a long way out in dusty Buri Ram, this temple dedicated to Shiva has a remarkable setting on an inactive volcano rearing up from bare, scrubby plain. Seven-headed serpents flank a long avenue which leads to the main *prangs*, in a series of terraces rising out of the crater.

The earliest inscriptions are 9th century; the story given in the stones tells of Biranya, a religious leader who was ordained here and enlarged the sanctuary. One of the inscriptions in Sanskrit expounds the phallic dogmas of the Hindu Pasupat sect.

Aspects of Khmer belief can be seen in the cruciform main *prang* – such as the monstrous Kala head, representing Eclipse, the most fearsome planet god. A lintel of Vishnu, recently returned here from the US, attracts many Thais, who lobbied for its return. A small entry fee is charged to see the temple.

Before leaving it is worth taking a look at the smaller **Prasat Hin Muang Tam**, 8km away.

Khmer ruins at Phanom Rung...

▶ ▶ Pha Taem (Rock Paintings)

100km east of Ubon Ratchathani on the Laos border. Reach by private transport or tour

Take Highway 217 from Ubon east along the river (Mae Nam Mool), cross the rapids along Route 222 into Khong Chiam at the confluence of the Mool and the Mekong rivers. Turn right at Route 2112 through a strange rock garden to arrive at Pha Taem.

This is a magical place. Layers of different civilisations are represented – Thai, Khmer, Mon, Ban Chiang – going back 4,000 years to when people first inhabited this lonely cliff overhanging Laos. Was it their art gallery, or temple? Pha Taem is the largest of many sites all over Isan where 'hand' motifs appear on the cave wall, made by spraying paint over the hands from the mouth. There are also representations of people pouring water into long-necked pots, fish, and elephants swimming.

▶ ▶ ▶ Phi Mai

60km from Nakhon Ratchasima province; off the Friendship Highway (route 2). Buses from Khorat

This sanctuary in the small district town of Phi Mai is set in a luscious garden of red sandstone with pools of water. Evidence points to construction in the reign of King Jayavarman VI (1082–1107), and its dominant religion is presumed to have been Mahayana Buddhism. Four intricately carved porches surround a tall central *prasad* (tower). Being so convenient to visit, the sanctuary is often used as a set for dancing troupes. Recently restored, it is Thailand's best known Khmer shrine, and attracts a never-ending stream of visitors.

...and at Phi Mai

► ▷▷ Roi Et

Highways 23, 214, 215, southeast of Khon Kaen. Buses from Ubon Ratchathani

Roi Et town has a name which is also a number (*Roi Et*=101). It has modest ancient remains, and the barren land has seen successive waves of depopulation. Nowadays farmers commute to cities to work in the dry season.

Rice is life, and some may revere her spirit. *Thung Kula Rong Hai* ('where crops die and people cry') is the object of irrigation efforts. The town has a lake, which is cool and refreshing, with plenty of fish to feed, and the reservoir is popular.

At **Wat Burapha** in town there is a huge Buddha up on a hill; the view there is panoramic. Climb up inside the statue and look over his right hand. At **Wat Neua** there is an old *chedi,* and the city shrine is unmistakably phallic.

The best place for souvenirs is the non-profit making Community Development Centre at the back of City Hall. Not least among local crafts is the *kaen,* a kind of bamboo mouth organ. All over Isan its reedy, jumping wail accompanies the *mor lam* singers. Also on sale are cushions, silks and basketry in the excellent market on Padung Panit road, near the *wat.*

Roi Et celebrates the **Bun Pha Wate festival** in March, including a parade with flags and 101 floats.

▷▷▷ Sakhon Nakhon

Highways 22 , 213, 223, east of Udon Thani. Buses from Udon, Nakhon Phanom, Khorat, and from Bangkok (northeast terminal)

This province in the northeast of the Isan region is home to the sacred Phra That Choeng Chum and Phu Thai sub-tribe who build castles of wax.There were two meditation masters, both named Achan Man, who passed through the cycle of existence in Sakhon Nakhon. Their remains are at **Wat Pa Sutthavat** and **Wat Pa Udom Somphon** respectively.

Giant **Nong Han** lake has islands such as Don Sawan, reachable by boat. Worthy of visit is **Phu Phan Racha-niwet**, a palace still used by the royal family and open to visitors when their majesties are not in residence.

Near the crossroads at Phang Khon district (the road to Ubon) is **Nam Oon** dam and reservoir, where fish frolic in a whirlpool.

An anti-AIDS sign on a Sakhon Nakhon hotel door

▷▷▷ **Sikhoraphum**

Highway 2080. Trains from Surin

On the main road (and railway) from Surin to Si Sa Ket and Ubon, in the south of Isank Sikhoraphum is a comfortable morning's tour from Surin.

The main object, a five-pranged 12th-century Khmer ruin, is a 1km trek from the station. A ride on a *samlor* or motorcycle might save you from dehydration.

The craftsmanship of the carving here is delicate and entrancing. The Thais converted Sikhoraphum into a *wat* around the 16th century and an atmospheric gnarled old tree sits in the compound.

▶▶ **Surin**

Highway 214 in the south of the Isan region. Songthaews connect from Tha Tum

The villages of **Ban Ta Klang** and **Krapoe** provide all the elephants for the famous roundup in Surin town (see panel). The Suay (*Thai Kuy*) tribe catch, rear and train them with a special 'spirit language'.

Accommodation is hard to come by at roundup time. The **Saeng Thong** is a large budget/moderate hotel with cheap rooms on the roof. At the **Phirom Guesthouse** (tel: 044 515140) on Krung Sri Nai Road, budget facilities are more than made up for by Phirom. He runs a tour to 'Site B' refugee camp, giving a glimpse of life outside the tourist sites: at the weekends Thais barter Khmer handicrafts here for food and essentials.

The southern border with Cambodia was until very recently a battleground. While there are some Khmer temples, more interesting is the approach to the border. Passing the eerily deserted refugee camp, ask for the *nam tok* (waterfall) and you can walk down the track to a tremendous panorama of Cambodia's flat, dense forest.

Elephants at the Surin roundup

Normally placid Surin town comes to life in November's roundup, when two teams of elephants, urged on in a tug-of-war by their drivers, take over the football field. The best time to visit Surin is in late afternoon when the elephants return to their stables. Do not approach an elephant without its mahout present. The Suay consider it sacrilege to kill an elephant for his ivory but a few chips off the end of tusks are taken and intricately carved.

209

▶ ▶ ▷ Ubon Ratchathani

Highways 212 23 & 24, bordering Laos and Cambodia. Buses from Nakhon Phanom and Bangkok (northern terminal); trains from Bangkok; domestic flights

The end of the road east, Ubon is a crossroads of Thai, Lao and Khmer influence and is one of the largest provinces in the northeast.

Many old *wats* in town such as **Wat Thong Si Muang** become festive in late July. Locals parade exquisitely carved giant beeswax candles symbolising the onset of *Phansaa,* Buddhist Lent, and which burn for the duration.

Ubon is on the scenic Mool River. Midstream is **Hat Wat Tai island** with a rickety wooden bridge and Isan food. For a night of traditional Isan music go to the **Pathumrat** hotel in town, which is both authentic and entertaining. Way out of town to the southwest is the famous *farang* **Wat Pa Nanachat**, where most of the monks are from the West, and the abbot is a Canadian.

On the long trip east to Pha Taem stop over at the rapids by **Sapheu** and **Tha Na**. These may soon be inundated in a hydroelectricity project, so you will have to hurry.

The incredible ruined temple of Khao Phra Viharn has just opened on the Thai–Cambodian border, having been closed for years as a result of fighting. In Thailand until 1963, it is now in Cambodia although access is from the Thai side only. Approximately 800–1000 years old, it makes all other Khmer ruins look poor by comparison. Built on a limestone escarpment, it is approached by a straight pathway made of hand-hewn blocks, over 1km from bottom to top. There are three huge gatehouses on the way up. A special train service runs form Bangkok to Khao Phra Viharn. Admission charge (hefty for *farangs*).

Clifftop view at Pha Taem, Ubon Ratchathani

▶▶▶ **Utumphon Phisai**

Highway 2028. Trains from Surin

The district of Si Saket, on the highway and railway line to Surin, is the site of two Khmer ruins. **Prasat Hin Wat Sa Kamphaeng Yai** is on a high hill 2km from Utumphon Phisai; the entrance is well signposted. It was originally constructed by Suryavaraman I (*c.* AD1042). Renovation by the Fine Arts Department is almost complete. Its younger sister, **Sa Kamphaeng Noi**, is less impressive but worth a stopover on the trip back into Si Saket town, 14km from Utumphon Phisai.

▶ ▶ ▶ **Yasothon**

Highway 23, east of Roi Et. Buses from Ubon Ratchathani and Khorat

'Yaso' is famous for its rocket festival. The province is not one of Thailand's natural beauties, being mostly flat, its former forests decimated. **That Kong Khao Noi** stands out for its ancient *chedi*, the site of a matricide over a 'little lump of rice' (*kong khao noi*). A Ban Chiang culture site, Tat Thong, is on Highway 23 to Ubon.

The Bang Fai *ceremony*

The rocket festival When May comes, the northeast is scorchingly dry and the rains are eagerly anticipated. Around the 10th, Yaso folk try to tempt Phya Thaen, a rain deity, in the *Bang Fai* ceremony. The rockets are quite powerful; wealthy and corporate sponsors build decorated rocket floats which bear a local belle on top, dancers leading the way; and locals are liberally daubed with mud. The place is packed, and the two local budget hotels, **Yot Nakhon** and **Udomphon**, fill up. Phya Thaen public park was built with income from the festival. Out of season it is a pleasant green space.

Heading north on the main road to Mukdahan is **Phu Tham Phra**, a mountain cave system and weird rock formations, still difficult to reach. **Tham Kheng**, completely shut off from the elements, is favoured by wandering meditators. Yaso handicrafts are exemplified by the *morn khit*, or embroidered cushion, such as those made in the village of **Sri Than** in Patiw district (Highway 202 east). The triangular cushion has become a Thai symbol, the design passed on by an elderly nun. The big ones are ideal for use on a couch.

SOUTHERN THAILAND

0   50   100 km
0   25   50   75 miles

Prachuap Khiri Khan
Huai Yang Waterfall
Thap Sakae
BUR
Bang Saphan
Bang Saphan Noi
Tha Sae
Pathiu
Chumphon
Ka Pho
Kra Buri
Isthmus
of Kra
Pak Nam Chumphon
Mo Phon Herb Garden
Sawi
La-un
Thung Tako
Ko Tao
Ranong
Lang Suan
Gulf
Ko Chang
Ko Phayam
Suan Mok Buddhist Retreat
Ko Phaluai
Ko Phangan
of
Ko Kam Yai
Kapoe
Laem Son N P
Chaiya
Ko Samui
Ko Surin
Ao Ban Dan
Don Sak
Thailand
Khuraburi
Chieo Lan Dam
Khanom
Ko Phra Thong
Yong
Suratthani
Sichon
Takuapa
Tungtong Birds N P
Ban Na San
Ban Pak Long
Ko Similan
Phanom
Khao Sok N P
Khao Luang N P
Tha Sala
Ko Payang
Phang Nga
Thap Put
Phra Saeng
1835m
Nakhon Si Thammarat
Thai Muang
Ao Luk
Thung Yai
Chawang
Laem Talumpuk
Ko Phuket
Thalang
Krabi
Thung Song
Phuket
Ko Yao Yai
Hua Sai
Ko Phi Phi
Wang Wiset
Siban Phot
Thale Noi Bird Sanctuary
Ranot
Ko Lanta
Trang
Sikao
Khao Chong N P
Thale Luang
Phatthalung
1350m
Boripath Waterfall
Lamchan Waterbird Park
Khuan Nian
Thale Sap Songkhla
Kho Khut Waterbird Park
Ko Liang
Palian
Hat Yai
Songkhla
Pak Bara Harbour
Langu
Ton Nga Chang Waterfall
Laem Tachi
Pattani
Panare
Andaman
Thale Ban N P
Ko Ta Ru Tao
Sa Dao
Wat Chiang Hai
Khok Po
Sai Buri
Satun
Yala
Narathiwat
Sea
Ko Rawi
Ko Adang
Raman
Bannang Sata
Tak Bai
Than To Waterfall
Banglang Dam
Chanae
Sungai Kolok
Hot Water Springs
Betong
MAL

Arguably the most popular of Thailand's four regions, the south gently woos its visitors with a predominantly seaboard atmosphere. Sun-worshippers, swimmers, divers and boat-lovers need look no further.

The coasts The Indian Andaman Sea washes the shores of the western provinces of Ranong, Phang Nga, Phuket, Krabi, Trang and Satun. Pacific provinces are Chumphon, Suratthani, Nakhon Si Thammarat, Songkhla, Pattani and Narathiwat.
Classic tropical islands float off both shores, and a few, such as Samui and Phi Phi, welcome the Western traveller with open arms.
This is a region inhabited by humans since early times.

The Buddhist kingdom of Srivijaya blossomed here, while yet more ancient negrito tribes such as the Sakai still survive.

Inland there are many national parks – and some are real gems. The further away from civilisation you get, the wilder it becomes – mountains and waterfalls abound, along with whatever wildlife can stand up to the constant incursions of development.

The borderlands These are the provinces of Satun, Yala, Songkhla and Narathiwat. The Federation of Malaysia is Thailand's most friendly land neighbour and Westerners can come and go with little formality. However, smugglers, Muslim separatists and logging disputes keep security tight.

Islam has made some headway in the Malay-speaking extreme south, but it is not of the most fervent kind.

Economic activity Rubber is the south's number-one cash crop. Other popular crops are cashew nuts and durians. Offshore, Thai fleets are rather too efficient for their own good, now being sent further into Burmese and Vietnamese waters.

Meanwhile tin mining, once the mainstay of Phuket and Phang Nga, has declined somewhat mainly as a result of market forces. Tourism is the rising star. Everyone wants a piece of the action but official policy tends towards plush development.

Bungalows, which started Phuket on its road to world fame, are now a rare sight there. This stand-offish attitude to budget travellers is unfortunate for the small operators but the small-scale, laid-back ethos is still easy to find off the beaten track. Nowadays it just means having to look slightly harder!

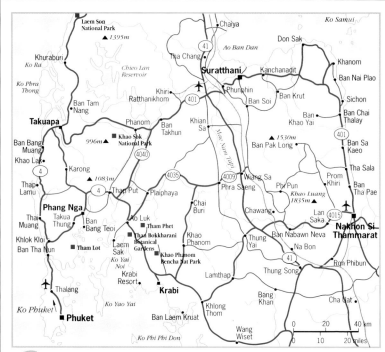

Drives Two circular tours

A tour from Phuket

Allow four to five days for the round trip. It is possible to miss out Suratthani, but the roads are treacherous and stopovers are a bit too far apart. Highway 4040 linking Phanom and Phang Nga town is recommended for a vehicle that can cope with dust, mud and potholes. Highway 4118 is for dry weather only. In either case the tour can take a mere two days from Phuket, with an overnight stay in either Khao Lak or Khao Sok.

Start at Phuket. Phuket to Takuapa is an unhurried drive of 130km up Highway 4. Accommodation can be had on the first night at Khao Lak bungalow (see Phang Nga, pages 238–9).
Plenty of waterfalls and beaches line this road. An early start will make it possible to reach **Khao Sok National Park.** Look out for **Art's Jungle House.**

From Takuapa take Highway 401 towards Suratthani.
The road here is spectacular as it climbs up into the watershed of the Tapi river. Passing the turn-off for Art's, the scenery is stunning almost all the way into **Suratthani**, where the next night can be spent in a hotel. A trip to **Ko Samui** could be taken from Suratthani as there is a car ferry.

Carry on out of Suratthani, still on Highway 401.
The road goes past the attractive beaches of **Khanom** district down into **Nakhon Si Thammarat**, where the next night can be spent.

An early start is recommended for the next day; the destination can be Phang Nga or Phuket. Take Highway 4015 west on the main road out of Nakhon Si Thammarat.
The scenery around **Khao Luang National Park** is stupendous and there are many diversions.

The aim now is Highway 41, west at Jan Dee across the railway line. North up the fast if rather bleak 41, looking out for a left at Wiang Sa, Highway 4009, becoming 4035. Wind through the rubber plantations to Ao Luk.

Accommodation can be found here, advisable if night has already fallen. The smooth main Highway 4 goes through the lovely karst mountains to **Phang Nga** and eventually crosses the Sarasin bridge to return to Phuket.

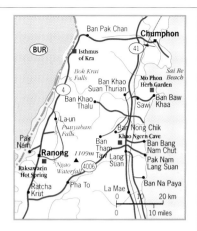

A day trip starting and ending in Chumphon

This can be accomplished in a day, but a more relaxed pace can be maintained with a night in Ranong, staying somewhere such as the Jansom Thara.

Start in Chumphon. The first half of the route runs west along Highway 4 (the Phetkasem Highway). Signs for the Jansom Thara stand out well, but 30km out of town, the left turn at tiny Ratcha Krut is rather harder to spot.
Recross the mountains while avoiding herds of cows on Highway 4006 (tarmac but substandard surface) .

This part of the trip offers marvellous sea views as the mountain chain is crossed at Kraburi. Waterfalls can be seen from the road, and the approach road to Ranong is impressive. (This area is thinly populated, and it would be a good idea to get well equipped in Ranong for the journey ahead.)

A left turn at the junction with Highway 41, is easy to spot, and from here it is a quick journey alongside the paddy fields back into Chumphon.

Nai Harn beach, Phuket

One of Buddhadasa's innovations was to disencumber his 'Garden of Liberation' of the architecture and statuary traditionally associated with a Thai *wat*. His disciples instead put up boldly experimental structures, the most famous of which is the 'spiritual theatre', an art gallery. Other such buildings dot large areas of peaceful forest.

The name, 'Chumphon' (from *Chum-num Phorn*, 'gathering to receive blessing'), reveals the province's strategic role at the head of the of Kra Isthmus.

▶ ▷ ▷ Betong

Highway 410. Buses from Yala town

This town on the Malaysian border, some 133km from Yala, has been developed on a par with the average provincial capital. The big market sells cheap Malaysian goods brought in on the major highway. There has been violence in this area – Muslim separatists are active here, and there has been border disturbance.

At the end of a 20km dirt road from Betong are hot springs, *bor nam rorn*, in a village of the same name. Betong is otherwise famous for the biggest pillar box in Thailand, nearly 4m tall, and the annual invasion of swallows from September to April. They darken the sky, crowd telephone wires and rain their droppings down, fortunately only at night!

▶ ▶ ▷ Chaiya

Off Highway 41. Trains from Suratthani

Chaiya district of Suratthani province is famous for two temples: the **Phra That**, one of the oldest in the south, a classic survival from the Indo-Javanese Srivijayan empire, and **Suan Mokapalaram**, or Suan Mok.

Suan Mok Buddhadasa Bhikkhu, the founder of Suan Mok (the Garden of Liberation), initiated a reform movement in the *sangha* which is still working itself out. It is one of the several temples in Thailand which has attracted a significant number of Western devotees and accepts lay-people on 10-day retreats.

Meditation through concentration on breathing and a vow of silence are on the programme which follows the strict regimen of the monks. Visitors of either sex are welcome to stay in dormitories and sample the simple life. Offerings of cash or food are readily accepted.

Wat Suan Mok is on the left off main Highway 41 going north from Suratthani – its imposing entrance arch cannot be missed. Buses run direct here from Suratthani.

Phra That This atmospheric temple lies north along the right-hand turning to Phum Riang. It dates from the Dvaravati period (AD500–700), and a life-sized Buddha image remains. The main *chedi*, in a pool surrounded by clusters of images, was erected by the Srivijayans (AD700–1000), whose bronzes of the Bodhisattva Avalokitesvara are in evidence.

The many red sandstone images are of Ayutthaya vintage. The Burmese overran the temple in the reign of Rama II, but it was fully restored in the reign of Rama V. There is a small museum opposite the entrance (open Wednesday to Sunday), where Srivijayan artefacts predominate.

▷ ▷ ▷ Chumphon

Highway 4. Buses from Suratthani and Bangkok (southern terminal); trains from Bangkok

Most travellers know Chumphon only as a midnight supper stopover on the way to or from Phuket. It came to the public eye when Typhoon Gaye tore through it in 1989. Almost completely recovered now, the province

...as quiet beaches and islands, all waiting to be discovered.

Thai and Burmese fought here, and in World War II, volunteers repelled a Japanese amphibious assault.

Sights Pharadornphap Beach is near Pak Nam Chumphon, some 13km out of Chumphon town. At adjacent **Sai Re** is a ship encased in concrete, a monument to Admiral Krom Luang Chumphon. Students of herbal medicine may be interested in the admiral's Thai herbal garden. He is most remembered though for re-creating the Royal Thai Navy as a modern fighting force.

Another such shrine graces the beach of **Arunothai** in Thung-Tako sub-district. Like Sai Re, it is a jumping-off point for long-tailed boat tours of the offshore islands.

Corals around here took a heavy beating from Typhoon Gay, such as those off the islands of Ko Raet (named for its rhinoceros-like form), Ko Lak Raet, Ko Thalu, Ko Jorakhe, Ko Mattra and Ko Lawa. The last three also have pleasant beaches.

Pathiu district to the north has long beaches at **Phanung Tuk**, 8km out of town, **Ao Bor Mao** and nearby **Laem Thaen**. This last beach is ideal for camping. Meanwhile there are some famous caves in southerly **Lang Suan**. **Khao Ngern** cave near town is home to a group of monkeys. A further 18km to the south is **Khao Kriap** with a large sunlit cavern.

Beware! Long, narrow Ko Maphrao, like the more famous island of Ko Phi Phi Le, has a swallow colony prized for its nests. Tourists are scared off the long white beach with a shotgun. Ko Ngaam Yai and Ko Ngaam Noi also have swallows' nests, and landing to sunbathe or snorkel could also be dangerous here.

Wat Phra That, Chaiya

Bird's Nest Collecting

■ **Birds' nests have been eaten in China for at least 1,500 years, and their export by the collectors of the Malay peninsula and southern Thailand was well-established by the early 18th century. Nowadays the largest market is Hong Kong, which consumes 100 tons of them, worth US$25 million, every year. A perfect white nest can fetch as much as US$1,200. .....■**

What nest? The nest of the swiftlet *Collocalia fuciphaga* is edible, prized by the Chinese as a powerful pick-me-up tonic, and typically ingested at the banquets of the rich in the form of bird's nest soup. The nests themselves are tiny translucent cups about the size of a small egg. They are made by the male white-nest or black-nest swiftlet from glutinous threads of its own saliva, which it weaves into a cup that dries to become thin and translucent like fine porcelain.

Chinese feed bird's nest soup, cooked with chicken broth or coconut milk, to their children in the belief that it will improve their complexion, promote growth and generally act as a tonic.

> << Bird's nest soup is said to taste rather like noodles by those who have tried it. >>

Recent research has indeed shown that the nests do contain a water-soluble glyco-protein that may promote cell division in the immune system. Some have even speculated that it may help combat the immuno-deficiency in AIDS.

Collecting the nests This is skilled and dangerous work, high up on the ceilings of caves which abound on the Thai coast and its offshore islands. The intrepid collector shins barefoot up rickety trellises of bamboo scaffolding, ropes and bridges, tapping as he goes to make sure the bamboo is sound. He lights his way in the black caves with a torch of bark soaked in resin held between his teeth, and he uses a special three-pronged tool called a *rada* to harvest the nests.

To use bare hands to pick a nest would be considered stealing from the gods and would anger them. If a man happens to forget his *rada,* he will descend at once, taking it as a sign from the gods that it would be dangerous for him to climb that day. The season is from February to May. The collectors work from sunrise without food or water until sunset, when the cave is filled with flocks of bats and roosting swiftlets. Sometimes nest-gatherers have to swim underwater to reach a submerged cavern, or squeeze through tiny blowhole passages to reach the cave ceiling.

The caves themselves are often spectacular cathedrals of stalagmites and stalactites, covered in thick carpetings of guano, and seething with golden cockroaches.

> << Gangster-style killings have occurred as rival gangs fight over scraps of nests left behind after the season. >>

Big business Bird's nest collecting is a lucrative business and is tightly controlled. The Finance Ministry grants five-year concessions to competing private groups, the taxes from which can yield over US$600,000 in one year. The nests are so precious that the islands are virtually off-limits, protected by armed guards during the season to deter robbers who might harm the

baby swiftlets – which would affect the next year's supply of nests. They are also paid to protect the birds from natural predators such as snakes, cockroaches and eagles. In spite of all this protection, regular attempts are made to bribe guards and attack the islands. In Thong Thum district in 1987, one gang of poachers began to encroach on other gang networks. The gang leader and his wife were sprayed with machine-gun fire at their home. Local residents had noted his rapidly increasing wealth, which he spent on gold necklaces and pick-up trucks.

Conservation Meanwhile, nest collecting has taken its toll on the swiftlets whose nests are often over-harvested. Many former nest sites on open cliffs have been abandoned because they were too accessible to gatherers. Another even more serious threat to their survival is the destruction of the inland rainforests where the swiftlets feed.

Ladders against the cliffside where swiftlets nest in Ko Phi Phi Le

The budget Cathay Hotel is a short walk from the station and its old steam engines. It has a welcoming guesthouse aspect right down to the crowded noticeboard.

▶▶▶ **Hat Yai**

Highway 4. Buses from Songkhla and Bangkok (southern terminal); trains from Suratthani and Bangkok; domestic flights

Hat Yai grew on border trade, rubber and, latterly, sex. Hat Yai's 'night industry' generates a higher than average level of associated diseases. There are plenty of all-night cafés and lounges. The town itself is drab, a forced stopover for destinations further south. Hat Yai is an important railway junction; trains were instrumental in the town's growth.

Sightseeing A scenic ride out of town is **Tone Nga Chang Falls**. The 'elephant tusks' of its name are formed at one of the higher stages where the fall splits into two. The road does not go anwhere else but the waterfall is in a wildlife preservation area.

A little way out of town, off Phetkasem Road, **Wat Hat Yai Nai** is remarkable for its very large reclining image of Buddha in white stucco. A curious contraption near by has seven plaster-cast monks bolted to a revolving platform, a novel way of making merit.

The Chinese presence here is evident in Channiwet Road, where **snake farms** make a strange concoction by slashing open a live snake and squeezing the blood out. It is often mixed with whisky and honey, which almost mask the taste.

Local farmers have established Hat Yai as a centre for Southern Thai **bullfighting**. Khlong Wa stadium by the bus station alternates with others in the area in staging the frenetic bull-against-bull contests. Entry is around 120 baht for three rounds of bulls, and the atmosphere is alive with manic betting and sizzling food.

Also on the edge of town but in a completely different direction is the **Thai Cultural Village** which stages dancing shows. The little theatre is set in rolling parkland which also has a small zoo.

People who are attracted to the bustle will enjoy Hat Yai's **markets** and nightlife which are both distinctive. It is here that all goods from Malaysia are unloaded. Smugglers once thought that if they made it to Hat Yai they were safe, but a recent police campaign has been giving them second thoughts.

Shopping at Hat Yai

▶ ▶ ▶ Ko Lanta

Access by boat from Krabi town; or from Ban Hua Hin (a songthaew ride from Krabi)

The little known Lanta islands, off the southwest coast of Krabi Province, have the status of a distinct district. The district takes in a total of 52 islands, of which only a few are inhabited. The islands are mostly forested mountains (highest elevation 492m), with not much in the way of flat land.

There are three main islands: Lanta Yai and Lanta Noi are almost one, being separated by a narrow 200m channel. Boats travel from Ban Hua Hin to Ban Khlong Mak on Lanta Noi; and from this island to Ban Sala Dan on Lanta Yai. Access to the western beaches for the tourist landlubber is best from Chao Fa pier in Krabi town, a few metres north of the Phi Phi pier. This regular supply boat takes 3–4 hours. A turning south from Highway 4 leads to Nam Thor pier, starting point for a much shorter ride.

Tourist development is discreet and low-profile and the beaches are long and idyllic. The longer beaches are on the west coast.

A favourite with yachties, the northern anchorage has bungalow accommodation. The natives mostly live from the sea and their villages dot the coast, most densely at this northern end.

221

An islander at sea

A travelling schedule that may appeal to the independent traveller involves a trip from Phuket to Phi Phi, at least a night or so in one of the island's many reasonable accommodations, followed by a boat ride into Krabi town. This boat leaves Phi Phi for Krabi at 09.00hrs, 13.00hrs and, in the high season, 15.00hrs.

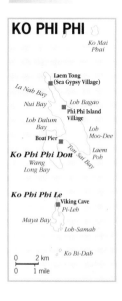

KO PHI PHI

Ko Mai Phai

Laem Tong (Sea Gypsy Village)

La Nah Bay

Nui Bay

Lob Bagao

Phi Phi Island Village

Lob Dalum Bay

Lob Moo-Dee

Boat Pier

Ton Sai Bay

Laem Poh

Ko Phi Phi Don

Wang Long Bay

Ko Phi Phi Le

Viking Cave

Pi-Leh

Maya Bay

Lob-Samah

Ko Bi-Dah

0   2 km
0   1 mile

▶ ▶ ▦ Ko Phi Phi
Boats from Phuket and Krabi town

This pair of islands, blessed with natural beauty, is now perhaps one of the absurdest examples anywhere of a Marine National Park. Some observers have already written it off, as thousands of tourists swarm all over it, the vast majority being day-trippers from Phuket, threatening the fragile ecosystem. The main island, Phi Phi Don, is quite built up, and strenuous efforts are made to keep it clean.

Yet the attraction is easy to understand; nothing short of an earthquake would destroy the stunning natural formation of the back-to-back Loh Dalam and Ton Sai beaches, only 50m apart. Their clear waters are particularly inviting to swimmers, and are enhanced by the optical effect of the shallow sea floor, which gives a beautiful turquoise colour.

Getting there The island communities' needs are served with a regular boat service from Krabi which takes two hours. The islands are almost equidistant from Phuket, and many companies there offer the day tour from around 700 baht upwards, depending on the luxury of the boat used. Top-of-the-line cruisers with every amenity ply the route daily. All the tours include lunch in one of the resort restaurants by Ton Sai Bay on Phi Phi Don.

Boat paintings in the 'Viking Cave' at Phi Phi Le

Phi Phi Don Accommodation on Phi Phi Don is now very comfortable with well-equipped bungalows thick on the ground. To the west of Ton Sai bay lies a Sea People's village. The original inhabitants of this paradise are mostly Muslims.

A general view of the island can be had from several mountain viewpoints to the east of Ton Sai. One path leads down to the beach of Loh Bagao, now site of the expensive **Phi Phi Island Village.**

Laem Tong, where the 'Sea Gypsies', who live in island villages (see page 243) rub shoulders with wealthy guests of the recently built resort, is much further along and accessible only by boat. A very worthwhile glass-bottomed boat tour leaves from here, as at Ton Sai – an opportunity not to be missed by non-swimmers.

Phi Phi Le Neighbouring Phi Phi Le has many fine corals such as those at Maya Bay and Pi-Leh. Boat tours invariably stop at Phi Phi Le's 'Viking Cave', where mysterious paintings of boats adorn the walls near the entrance; the cave is also home to a swallow colony whose nests are harvested for the famous birds' nest soup (see pages 218–19). The smell of swallow droppings is quite overpowering!

Fishermen are well served around Phi Phi Le. All shapes and sizes of fish await the intrepid angler. A group can charter a long-tailed boat for this purpose at between 600 and 800 baht for six to eight hours.

The greenery of Phi Phi Le

Ko Samui used to be famous for mind-expanding drug omelettes but after several notorious incidents that were too much even for the liberal and tolerant Thais, the local police were forced to act.

KO SAMUI

Ko Som
Laem Na
Pbra Lan
Choeng Mo
Ao Bang Po
Mae Nam
Beach
Bo Phut
Beach
Laem
Yai
Ban
Bang Po
Ban
Mae Nam
Ko Faan
Ban Bo
Phut
Ko
Mat Lang
Na Thon
Ban
Chaweng
Hin Lat
Waterfall
Samui Highlands
Ao Chon
Kram
Chaweng Beach
▲ 635m
Don Sak
Car Ferry
Coral Cove
Thong Yang
Ban Saket
Ban Lamai
Na Muang
Waterfall
Lamai Cultural
Hall
Ban
Thaling Ngam
Ban Suan
Thurian
Ao
Phangka
Wat Sumret
Ban Hua Thanon
Ban Bang
Kao
Laem Set
Ao Thong
Krut
0   5 km
Ko Katen
0   3 miles

▶ ▶ ▶   Ko Samui Archipelago

Off the east coast. Buses from Suratthani connect with ferries to Ko Samui; catamaran from Bangkok; domestic flights

A first stop for many visitors, Ko Samui has a laid-back atmosphere even for Thailand. As with most other currently booming destinations it was the much maligned backpackers who discovered it first.

Express boats to and from Suratthani moor up at the Na Thon jetty in the northwest. In the 1991–2 season Royal Jet Ferries launched an air-cushion catamaran service between Ko Samui and Bangkok, boasting journey times of only five hours.

Although the airport is now busy with three daily flights, Ko Samui is still a paradise for young people who want to enjoy themselves relatively cheaply. Rents have been

Ko Samui

Sunset over the Ko Samui archipelago

creeping up, but bargains are still there to be had away from the popular Chaweng and Lamai beaches. Expect to pay anything from 150–200 baht upwards.

The island's natural beauty remains much as it was and not unduly spoiled by the development here, which has been low-rise, though not on a modest scale. Beach frolics by day are combined with Thailand's trendiest nightlife of disco and bar. It proves that a *farang* tourist area need not be crawling with prostitution, although Ko Samui has inevitably attracted its fair share.

Around the island The concrete road circling the island is only 50km long and you can travel around the whole island in a day. As in Phuket, scooters are ideal, being slow and safe. Newer models have power to take on the bigger hills. Rent a scooter at Chaweng and follow the road south to Lamai, taking in the tremendous panorama as the road twists round past Coral Cove.

In **Lamai** you might check out the bizarrely designed 'Mix' club. Lamai's landmark is the unmistakably phallic **Hin Ta** or Grandfather Rock and its female companion **Hin Yai**. The long beach is fairly clean, when the number of visitors is considered, although it certainly isn't as clean as it used to be.

Out of Lamai to the south the road forks. To the left it cuts across the island's south, past **Na Muang**, a spectacular waterfall. The right fork veers around the tidal coast of **Ao Thong Krut.** Boats here service the small **Ko Katen**. Further on is a long dirt road turn-off for the small, sweet and quiet **Phangka Bay**. There are modest facilities here on locally owned land.

225

Ko Samui has more to it than beaches; before the tourist boom, islanders' income came exclusively from coconuts, and the tall palms are still the dominant vegetation.

SOUTHERN THAILAND

The archipelago that makes up Ang Thong Marine National Park can be toured from Ko Samui, but it is impossible to stay without official permission. Most tours take in the fascinating Ko Mae Ko with its 'crater lake'.

North out of Phangka the road takes in wonderful views of distant shimmering sea before you get to the Don Sak car-ferry terminal turn-off. Inland from here are two of Ko Samui's other waterfalls, **Hu Nam** and **Wae Khwai Tok**. The track up to them is quite difficult.

Na Thon is the district seat and as such has a market, post office, banks and other essential services. The road out north yields a fantastic view (if you ignore the municipal tip in the foreground).

Ko Phangan, the other main island in the archipelago, is visible from all along Ko Samui's northern shore. Of the three main beaches along this shore, it is **Bo Phut** that has become the most popular. On the others, Mae Nam and Bang Rak, tourist facilities are still in the process of hasty construction.

Very prominent is the long causeway linking Bang Rak and Ko Fan where, in the temple of Hin Ngu, the so-called Big Buddha looks out over the sweeping bay.

Next on the circuit are roads leading to Ko Samui's airport; flights from here to Bangkok take only an hour and a half.

Turning south the route reaches the top end of **Chaweng**. At 3km it is the longest beach on the island and developers have made the larger projects a feast of traditional teak architecture. Because of its sheer size Chaweng has been able to absorb the feverish rush for the tourist dollar so far – as is usually the case, a balance must be struck between creature comforts and an unspoiled atmosphere.

Ko Phangan Boats from Ko Samui and Suratthani land at Thong Sala on the island's southern coast. Phangan is now taking Ko Samui's overspill and although the beaches are just as good, the level of infrastructure here makes Ko Samui seem urban. Roads are unmetalled but a dirt bike is still useful.

Bungalows line the beaches, being concentrated on the double-backed Hat Rin, home to a lively travellers' society. Boats ply the beaches.

Waterfall fans may take in **Than Sadet**, where kingly visitors have carved their initials in the stones. The journey upstream is still as hard as it was in their day

Ko Tao ('Turtle Island') is only 7km long and the nearest land is well over the horizon. It can be reached from either Chumphon or Phangan. The former is a gruelling five-hour ride, costs 200 baht, and is available only in the high season.

The latter trip, from Thong Sala pier, takes three hours for around 150 baht. When exploring Thailand, remember that remoteness and inaccessibility are usually related to degree of unspoilt beauty. **Sai Ri** and **Mae Hat** are the main beaches lining the west coast. Jungle trails beckon.

A short boat ride from Mae Hat leads to the natural marvel of **Ko Nang Yuan,** where three beaches have joined together. It is even possible to stay overnight here. As on Ko Tao, little bungalows are available, and are still very reasonable.

Express boats set out from the Na Thon jetty, on the northwest coast of Ko Samui

■ **Sometimes life in Thailand seems like one festival or traditional ceremony after another. Some are rites of passage for the events in the lives of individuals, such as birth, puberty, ordination, marriage and death. Those linked with traditional farming rituals are concerned with the annual cycle of seasons and there are others that commemorate historical anniversaries. .....■**

Most festivals are fixed by the lunar calendar, so the dates vary from year to year. The Buddhist holiday of **Magha Puja** is celebrated in February, and the **Chinese New Year** usually falls within this month too. Festivities for the latter usually last three days. Gifts are exchanged, food is offered to ancestors via the ancestral tablets. Altars are set with the tablets and images of benevolent deities, and candles and joss sticks are lit. Chinese shops close for several days.

Songkran This is one of the great festivals – the old Thai New Year which falls in mid-April. It is a time when everyone goes in for water splashing, April being the hottest month in the year. The *Songkran* water splashing festival was originally an occasion to pay genteel homage to one's elders by pouring scented water over their hands and making offerings to the ashes of ancestors.
Songkran begins sedately with Buddhist merit-making ceremonies and offerings to elders and monks. Then it explodes into water-splashing, beauty contests and tippling of Mekhong rice whisky. Everyone gets splashed, even foreigners – all in good fun.

Loi Krathong This most unforgettable celebration is in November, after rice planting has been completed, when toy boats made of moulded leaves carrying a lighted candle and incense stick are floated along rivers and canals, swollen with rain and sometimes flooded at this time of year, to

honour the water spirits. Everyone goes to the river bank in the evening to see the flickering lights on the water, and fireworks are let off. *Loi* means 'to float', and *krathong* means 'leaf cup'. The use of polystyrene for floats was recently banned because of the river pollution it caused.

The sky rocket festival *Bun bang fai*, a festival of the northeast, usually takes place in May or June. With its crude sexual pantomimes, it is performed to celebrate the generative forces of nature and the coming of the rains.

Rites of passage One recurring feature of personal Thai ceremonies is the tying of white thread around the wrists. It has been described as a kind of 'spiritual telegraph' between the participants. At weddings the thread joins the heads of the marrying couple, while at funerals the thread is carried round the crematorium three times.
In their early 20s many Thai men spend a short period as Buddhist monks, which is regarded as a rite of passage into adulthood. Before the formal ordination there is a lay ceremony called *sukhwan nak*. The man's head and eyebrows are shaved (to show freedom from vanity and sexuality) and the ordination candidate or *nak* (meaning 'dragon') is dressed in white robes, garlanded with flowers and banknotes.
The friends and relatives of the *nak* gather in a circle around him while a song recalling the pain and suffering of his mother in giving birth and

stressing his filial obligations is sung – sometimes for up to four hours. Around him, holding a ring of white thread, sit the *nak's* relatives and friends. They pass three sets of lighted candles around in a clockwise direction to protect him while he is in the vulnerable position of being neither a layman nor a monk. The following day the ordination ceremony takes place. Inside the *wat* the new monk kneels before his father, who presents him with the saffron robe of the monkhood before approaching a quorum of monks and asking to be admitted to the *sangha*.

Songkran water-splashing festival starts at a sedate pace and then takes off into mayhem...

► ▮▮▮   **Ko Similan and Ko Surin**

Access by boat from Takua Pa or by tour from Phuket

These two archipelagos, far over the horizon to the west, form a national park famous for its underwater diving opportunities. There are pleasant beaches which are used by snorkellers, swimmers and picnickers. Though spear-fishing is carried out, it is prohibited by the national park authorities.

The Similans are so called because there are nine islands (Malay *sembilan*, nine) of which number 8, Ko Similan, is the largest. They are low-lying and forested, uninhabited before the park wardens brought in regular supplies of fresh water. The park station is on Ko Similan, where there is a campsite with bungalows and a restaurant.

Islanders have come here to fish for a long time. Recent times saw the appalling practice of dynamite fishing when a whole coral reef would be blasted, dead and stunned fish then rising to the surface. Tourists, both daytrippers and yacht sailors, have scared off the dynamite fishermen, but have brought in their turn litter, which they leave on the beaches.

An average tour from Phuket would cost around 1,500 baht. Alternatively, a boat can be chartered from Tap Lamu in Takua Pa. The Similans are being increasingly used as stepping stones to other remote islands. Dive boats run regularly to Ko Surin, Ko Bon (an honorary 'tenth' Similan) and Ko Tachai.

Ko Mien, island number 4, has beautifully set bungalows run by the Royal Forestry Department. **Ko Ba Ngu**, number 9, has tents for hire at normal park rates. If you want to book, which is advisable, the national park office responsible is at Moo 1, Lamgan, Thai Muang (Phang Nga) (tel: (076) 411914). Weekdays are best.

Ko Surin Ban Hin Lat in Khuraburi district, almost on the border with Ranong Province, is the jumping-off point for a five-hour voyage to Surin Marine National Park. (The islands are actually part of Ranong Province.) Again, most people go to dive. The main islands have places to stay and great lobster fishing.

Deep-sea divers (at a cost of around 2,500 baht per day) can see such strange creatures as the star feather and the gross puffer fish off the Similans.

Ko Ta Ru Tao islands

Long-tails from Tam Ma Rang service Pulau Langkawi, a larger Malaysian island to Ta Ru Tao's south. The service runs Satun–Langkawi–Kuala Perlis, a small town connected by bus to the rest of Malaysia. You must make sure that papers are in order – Thai immigration will stamp them as you go out in Satun town; a Malaysian official will stamp them in Kuala Perlis.

Ko Adang, part of the Ta Ru Tao archipelago

▶ ▶ ▶ Ko Ta Ru Tao

Off Satun Province. Boats from Pak Bara

The Ta Ru Tao archipelago is made up of 50-odd islands, from the largest, Ko Ta Ru Tao, down through Ko Rawi, Ko Adang and the smaller islands of Ko Lipo, Ko Hin Ngam, Ko Khai and Ko Rang Nok. Ko Ta Ru Tao is only about 5km from the Malaysian island of Pulau Langkawi. These islands are not geared to tourists; facilities are basic and transport is unpredictable.

Thickly forested with a peak of 704m, Ko Ta Ru Tao must count as one of the most unspoiled of the country's marine national parks; this one was created in 1974. For overnight stays or camping it is possible to reserve a park space from Bangkok (tel: (02) 579 4842/579 0529).

Ta Ru Tao, a penal colony during World War II, now has an exhibition centre and aquarium. The region's famous powdery white sand can be found at Ao Son (Ta Lo Lii Ngai) on the western coast, a beautifully curving bay with clear and shallow waters, which has been established as a sea turtle conservation centre. Walkers can get a good view from the top of Khao Topu.

Ko Khai is a small island with white beaches and a rich community of coral and fish. Turtles come ashore to lay their eggs. **Ko Hin Ngam**, off Ko Adang, has lines of smooth, even, sleek rocks rounded by the sea, whereas next-door **Ko Rawi** has beaches. The area is populated by 'Sea Gypsies', who build their houses on stilts; tiny **Ko Lipe** hosts a community of 600. Unfortunately, a great many trees have been felled here.

Diving is popular among visitors to the archipelago. On the bigger islands there are caves and waterfalls to visit. Long-tail boats service the park office from Pak Bara harbour, Langu district, a long day's drive from Hat Yai or Trang (98km south of Trang). The flimsy long-tail boats get tossed about on the open sea, so the time to go is in the more clement months of November to April.

Overhanging cliff, Krabi

232

Nopparat Thora beach, Krabi

According to a legend which is still told by locals, food used to appear by magic at the mouth of Phra Nang Cave, which looks out on to a gently curving lagoon.

▶▶ **Krabi**

Highway 4, south of Suratthani. Buses from Phuket and Phang Nga

Krabi town is a fishing harbour, giving access to over 100 offshore islands. Ferries arrive here from Ko Phi Phi, entering a mangrove-lined bay before mooring at the centrally located jetty on the broad Krabi river. A gaggle of touts greets passengers as they disembark from the boat.

Krabi town It is a mere minute's walk to the picturesque Uttarakit Road, parallel to the river and the town's main street. Guesthouses and hotels of all standards have sprung up here. Krabi ('Fighting Sword') town has not much going for it besides its views and bike rental shops. The night market which opens after sundown looks over the river.

Krabi Province is quite another thing. Besides the famous Ko Lanta and Ko Phi Phi (see pp 221–3), other interesting islands among Krabi's total of 130 include the pretty **Ko Mai Phai**, 'Bamboo Island', accessible from Ko Phi Phi Don. The local squid fishermen are greatly bemused by the increasing numbers of day trippers from the larger island.

The **Por-Da archipelago** (Ko Dam Hok and Ko Dam Khwaan) is very well worth visiting. It is only 8km off Ao Nang, south of Krabi town, from where boats to the islands can be chartered.

Mainland beaches in Krabi are quite fascinating. **Laem Phra Nang** is cut off by mountains, so the strange arrangement here of three beaches and cliffs can only be reached by boat – 45 minutes from Krabi town or a mere 10 minutes from neighbouring Ao Nang.

Sights Sa Phra Nang (Princess Pool) is a geological oddity – a saltwater lake high among the cliffs. The strenuous walk up to it leads through a series of roofless caves. **Ao Nang**, a long and rapidly developing beach, is only a short *songthaew* ride out of town.

The inland karst (natural underground cavities) along the road makes bizarre scenery. **Nopparat Thora** beach just west of Ao Nang has little Ko An straddling a river mouth. Dense casuarinas and coconut trees provide shade on this beach, which is also the headquarters of the marine national park that includes Ko Phi Phi.

Palaeontologists may wish to stop off at the *Susan Hoi* or 'Shell Cemetery', one of only two or three such sites in the world. Tertiary-period fossilised shells compressed into slabs jut into the sea like a causeway. Many *songthaews* going to Ao Nang pass the site.

Other points of interest within easy reach of Krabi town include **Huay To** waterfall in Phanom Benja, a mere 20km due north. The falls are in ten stages, each stage with a large natural pond. Another road leading north off the main highway leads to **Wat Tham Seua**, a meditation monastery with grim paintings as reminders of mortality.

Ao Luk is a small town on the road to Phang Nga, also with the strange inland karst. Regular buses to Phang Nga and Phuket stop there.

The nearby port of Laem Sak connects to **Ko Mak Noi** (actually in Phang Nga province), an island surrounded by beach. Only five minutes from Laem Sak is the **Chong Talat archipelago**, Ko Pai and Ko Klui, graced with the usual – but still beautiful – corals, beaches, caves and mountains.

Ao Luk, in the north of Krabi province, has many caves. Tham Lot and Tham Hua Kalok (Skull Cave) are two neighbouring caves, which you can reach by chartering a boat from Bo Tho for 150–250 baht. Hua Kalok is well lit by the sun and features paintings 2,000 – 3,000 years old.

233

Boats moored near Krabi Town

A warning: the rainy season in the province of Nakon Si Thammarat lasts longer than elsewhere and can be ferocious.

Local crafts are the delicate Yan Lipao basketry and shadow puppets. At 'Suchat's House' they are cut from the hide.

► ▰▰▰ **Kra Buri**

Highway 4, north of Ranong

The last district before Chumphon in the north of the southern region is Kra Buri, head of the Isthmus of Kra, which at its narrowest is only about 25km wide at 545km on Highway 4.

Unsurprisingly in this mountainous territory there are plenty of waterfalls; **Punyaban, Bokkrai** and **Chum Saeng** are three which you can visit as you travel northwards from Ranong town. Punyaban, as the most accessible, has the most visitors. **Tham Phra Khayang**, a cave in Kra Buri district, 12km north of Kra Buri town, is sacred to locals who believe that 'iron flows' here, taking the form of stalactites and stalagmites.

Wat Mahathat, in Nakhon Si Thammarat

► ▰▰▰ **Nakhon Si Thammarat**

Highway 401, east coast. Buses from Krabi, Suratthani and Bangkok (southern terminal); trains from Bangkok

'Nakhon Si', as the province is known to southerners, is a paradox: the biggest and most populated southern province, while at the same time relatively unexplored. Communications are excellent: the town of Nakhon Si Thammarat is a rail terminus and has air and bus connections. A thriving Srvijaya centre back in the 13th century, it spread its Buddhist teaching to Sukhothai, seat of the first Thai kingdom. More recently, in World War II, local lads repulsed an amphibious Japanese assault; they are commemorated in bronze.

Wat Mahathat, interior (above) and exterior (below)

The town's religious focus is ancient **Wat Mahathat**. Its large *chedi* is topped with gold and contains relics, venerated in the third lunar month. There is a museum in the complex. The city wall dates from the Ayutthaya period. There is also a large National Museum. Shadow plays are performed during temple festivals.

Admirers of these and other attractions, which include a lively Thai nightlife, have a wide choice of all categories of hotel, the cheaper ones nearly all Chinese. Highway 401 connects Nakhon Si with Surat, and near the border with Suratthani province (a right turn along Highway 4014; the Khanom bus) are attractive beaches, popular with locals and becoming increasingly discovered by foreigners.

The beaches of **Khanom**, **Nai Phlao** and **Nai Dan** sport many moderate–expensive places to stay, with the budget **Watanyoo Villa** on Nai Dan. Nearer town is Hat Sa Bua, and halfway up is the boulder-strewn Hat Hin Ngam. Inland nature lovers will not be disappointed by the scenery around **Khao Luang National Park**, skirted by Highways 4015 and 4016. There are many stunning waterfalls in the lush green wilderness, best appreciated on a car tour.

Bullfighting (bull versus bull) is popular here as in Hat Yai – the best fighters have small testicles or, even better, only one!

SOUTHERN THAILAND

Narathiwat Beach, reached by a *samlor* or taxi from the market, nestles in the shade of casuarinas, with food stalls dotted about. It is an ideal camping spot; 5km of broad white sands end in a bar at the mouth of Klong Bang Nara, site of a fishing village. Plans are afoot to build a swimming pool to the north of the promontory.

Fishing boats at Narathiwat

▶ ▶ ■   **Narathiwat**

Highway 42; a border province with Malaysia. Buses from Yala, Sungai Kolok and Bangkok (southern terminal) This border province has a wealth of natural resources with forest, beaches and different customs at the end of a marathon 1,149km from Bangkok. Gold is mined on a small scale. As Malaysia approaches concentrations of Muslims become denser, but this is Islam with a Thai flavour.

Narathiwat town is not of great interest, with traces of earlier development erased. However, atmospheric wooden houses abound and vintage Mercedes Benz taxis ply the streets.
Ba Joh waterfall is on the Pattani–Narathiwat Road. A left out of town on Pattani Highway 42 becomes a dusty (or muddy) laterite road eventually reaching the fall, which flows off a very high cliff with force. One of the biggest waterfalls in the south, it comes within the Budo mountains and Budo National Park. The park office is in Ba Joh district and near the waterfall. Budo National Park is a shelter for endangered rhinos, gibbons and tapir, but there is no news yet of accommodation schemes. Other waterfalls in the region are **Ya Mu Raeney** and **Wang Thong**.
Phra Puttha Taksin Ming Mongkhol is a huge image on Khao Kong mountain in the town district, 6km along Highway 42 to Baa Joh. The 24m figure is decorated with golden mosaic. The same 'Buddhist park' contains a hollow bell-*chedi*, the top of which contains a 'relic'.
Khao Tan Yong Mas, on the opposite bank of the river from town, has beautiful views and is a popular picnic spot for locals. Near by is the inaccessible Taksin Rachaniwet Palace. Further south of town is the medium-sized **Chatwarin waterfall**, reached by turning left at Sungai Padi district hospital. A dry season track winds through thick forest to the fall, passing To Deng village. A distance of 44km makes it a full day trip.
Two *wats* deserve a mention: **Wat Cherng Khao** in Baa Joh district has the body of a monk preserved in a glass coffin and reportedly not decomposing. **Luang Phor Daeng** is an object of great local veneration. **Wat Chol Thara Sing Hey**, near the border, has murals, eclectic southern Thai-Chinese architecture, Hindu statuary, Song dynasty ceramics and a reclining Buddha. However, it is not these features that distinguish it, but its history: this ancient foundation was invoked as the last Siamese territorial stand, when Narathiwat stood out against the British who threatened to incorporate the region in their Malayan possessions..

Tak Bai district This border location can be an interesting visit in itself. Taba village at the end of the road has reasonable views over the large mouth of the Golok river, which forms the national boundary. Fishing boats come and go and it is an easy matter to get the necessary papers stamped and nip out of Thailand and into Malaysia on one of these.
The atmosphere is frenetic, the market prominent. Vehicles must go through a modern passport check and

ross over on a car ferry; Malaysian passport officials
wait on the other side.

► Pattani

*Highway 42, east coast, south of Songkhla. Buses from
Narathiwat, boats from Songkhla*

This old province of the south has a tradition of rebellion
against Siamese authority, and today it is the focus for
Muslim separatist politics. The **central mosque** just
outside town on the road to Yala is the largest in
Thailand and of great importance to the south's many
Muslims. It is a recent construction, opened in 1963.
Visitors are welcome from 09.00 to 15.30hrs.
Seven km out on the road to Narathiwat is the old **Kreua
Se** mosque, dating from the reign of Naresuan in the
16th century. The Chinese shrine of Mother Lim Kor Nio
near by is said to have put a curse on the mosque to
prevent it being completed. She has a major festival in
the third lunar month when her effigy is paraded and
devotees walk on hot coals, as in Phuket.
Wat Chang Hai is to be found 36km from town on the
Khok Po–Yala road (Highway 409). At 300 years old, it is
distinguished for its huge golden *chedi* visible from far
away. Despite being so near Malaysia, the *wat* is wholly
Thai in style.
North of Pattani town is Bang Nara, a picturesque
village. Here there is a campus of the Prince of Songkhla
University. The **Princess Mother Gardens**, a newly laid
out public park which connects with the campus
grounds, is formed from a mangrove swamp tastefully
planted with flowers.

Beaches Khae Khae and Panare, 43km out of town, are
Pattani's most famous beaches. In Khae Khae valley,
they follow the mountain's curve. Boulders and rock
formations alternate with wide bays, and the water is
clear for swimming. The laterite road winds for 8km; a
limited food service serves a beach otherwise unspoiled.
A long way down the coast from here towards Sai Buri
is Patatimoh beach and the village of Paseyawor, a large
fishing community that builds decorative *kor-lae* boats.

Sai Khao National Park, a Royal Forest Department
park, with its waterfall, is to be found off the Khok
Po–Yala road. At the highest stage the fall drops 8m
down a cliff on the side of Nang Jan mountain. This is a
popular local spot.

237

A major Malay heritage
product on sale in the
modern-looking town of
Pattani is bright and busy
batik.

*Smiling faces at
Pattani*

In the district of the Sai Khao National Park is a fine royal pavilion originally constructed for Rama VII to view a solar eclipse.

Limestone islands off Phang Nga

Ko Tapu

▶ ▶ ▶ Phang Nga

Highway 4, west coast, north of Phuket. Buses from Phuket and Krabi

Phang Nga province has two distinct coastlines: the mangrove-fringed bay formed by Ko Phuket, and the

long, straight, beach-lined Andaman coast, north of Phuket. Limestone rock formations rise out of the sea at Phang Nga Bay, to dramatic effect. Inflatable-canoe tours are very popular, and rubber dinghies can also be used to enter the island caves which are like weird 'rooms' of water, but canoes are better for silently approaching any wildlife. Of course, the discriminating diver has long known about the Similan Islands some 40km to the west, part of Phang Nga province (see page 230). Boat tours from Phuket are something of a hackneyed tourist trip but one of the cheapest. Coaches whisk you to a long-tail boat jetty from where you snake out of mangrove channels to the open sea. **Khao Phing Kan**, not very far out, is a leaning megalith which with its nail-like companion **Ko Tapu** was the setting for the James Bond film, *The Man with the Golden Gun*. The boats then head back to **Ko Panyi**, a village on stilts attached to a tall rock. It is as well to be aware of local customs and sensitivities; the Muslim village does not tolerate alcohol. Photograph the attractive little green mosque but show due respect. After a generous repast the tour re-embarks for the return to base. The coach may take a route round shops and temples in Phuket on the way back.

Phang Nga town like Phuket, grew up around the tin-mining industry. The small town, set in a spectacular backdrop of mountains containing an assortment of caves, is even smaller than Krabi and has little nightlife.
Suwan Khuha cave, to the west of town, contains images of Buddha and is important to the Thais.
Phang Nga port, 8km to the south, serves the important islands – the largest, **Ko Yao Yai** and **Ko Yao Noi**, are two hours away. There are beaches and even a pearl farm on Ko Yao Yai, but little in the way of accommodation.

The western coast of Phang Nga Province could not be more topologically different from the indentations of Phang Nga Bay. Starting at Khao Pilai off Phuket, the long, straight sands run for a score of kilometres into Thai Muang district. This is the territory where the endangered sea turtle lays its eggs from November to February; the eggs are eaten by some people.

There are plenty of stopovers as you carry on up through **Khao Lampi-Hat Thai Muang National Park**. **Khao Lampi**, opposite the beach side of the road, is a pretty waterfall where a swim in the pool below is possible. **Bang Sak** is a typically inviting large beach, not quite empty, and there are drinks for sale. There is also Tap Tawan beach and Coral Cape; signposted waterfalls are a way off the road.

North of here is **Khao Lak National Park**. There are many bungalows and resorts in this park, about 35km short of bus-stopover Takua Pa. The **Khao Lak Resort** is a typical example, with budget–moderate tariffs. Clean rooms overlook the ocean with fantastic sunsets, and there is yet another quiet and swimmable beach. Go north up to Khuraburi and you may be tempted by **Hat Phra Thong** where the Lost Horizons Co have exclusive, if moderate–expensive, houses which can be reserved on tel: (02) 279-1915 (Bangkok).

Other western Phang Nga attractions: Highway 401: Ban Bangklang Spa. Highway 4032: Lam Ru Fall, Laeng Hin Fall, Ban Plai Phu Spa.

239

A village on stilts: Ko Panyi, which can be seen on boat tours from Phuket

To avoid embarrassment, note that 'Phuket' is pronounced *poo-ke(t)*, with an almost silent 't'.

► ■ Phatthalung

Highway 4, east of Trang on the east coast. Buses from nakhon Si Thammarat, Hat Yai, Songkhla, Trang and Phuket; trains from Bangkok

On the route of the main Trang–Songkhla artery, this inland province has its own peculiar attractions, such as a beach on the huge lake, not far out of Phatthalung town. Dense casuarinas give welcome shade at Hat Saen Sukhrim (Thale Sap Lam Pa), which has a charming view of little islands in the lake.

Also near town are **Khuha Sawan** caverns, where light floods in through the spacious northern entrance, and huge Buddha images can be seen inside. **Thale Noi Bird Sanctuary**, 32km northeast of Phatthalung town, is a large watery swamp that connects with the lake through a canal. It is an ideal waterfowl habitat, and large birds such as cranes and storks can be spotted.

The nine-stage **Khao Khram Falls**, halfway to Trang, have pools large enough for swimming, and **Khao Pu Khao Ya National Park** spreads over a wild landscape to the northwest. Near the park office in Sri Banphot district are **Matja Pla Won caves**, with stalactites hanging like a delicate curtain near a large fish pool. Another famous waterfall among the many in the park is **Rien Thong**, otherwise known as 'Roi Chan' or 'Hundred Stages'. Stage 13 is the most beautiful, with views over Thale Noi and the mountains, Pu and Ta.

► ► ► Phuket

South of Phang Nga on the west coast. Buses from Bangkok (southern terminal; journey time 13 hours) and neighbouring towns; domestic flights

Thailand's largest island is crammed with things to see. The upper west coast has some beautifula beaches. **Nai Thon Beach** is usually missed by the hordes – probably because it has awkward access. From here north up to Sarasin Bridge, which connects Phuket with the mainland, is all Nai Yang National Park. With its beautiful casuarinas, **Nai Yang Beach** has managed to acquire

The Buddha images of Khuha Sawan caverns

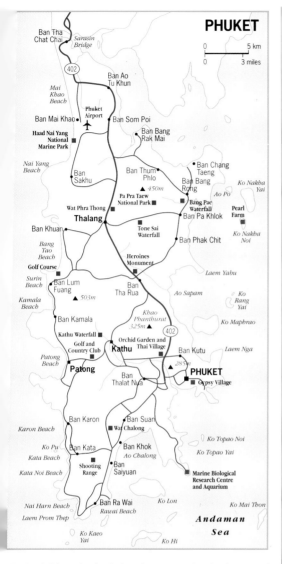

PHUKET

0   5 km

0   3 miles

*Paragliding at Phuket's
Patong Beach*

limited (if exclusive) development. At the long and straight **Mai Khao (White Trees) Beach**, conservationists have made real efforts to save diminishing turtle populations whose females come to lay their eggs in November to February. Past the exclusive resort of Pansea is long **Bang Tao Beach.**

Going south from Bang Tao, access to the privately owned **Laem Sing Beach** is down a path off the road from Surin Beach to Kamala Beach For such perfection however, there is a charge in the high season.

Most package tours are catered for on the complexes of Kata and Karon Beaches and Patong Beach. Diving and game-fishing are popular here. **Patong Beach** is where the trend towards mass tourism has gone the furthest, with the proliferation of high-rise hotels and blocks of flats, but it may yet be some time before even Patong is as crowded as Nice (with which Phuket has been twinned). Recently opened is a Pattaya-style transvestite show.

Kamala Beach is what Patong must have been like before the feverish speculation started. **Surin Beach** to the north has a 'front' of small bars, restaurants and souvenir shops. **Karon and Kata**, to the south of Patong, have witnessed rapid large-scale development – in the case of the smaller Kata, with claustrophobic results.

Open-air 'bar-beers' similar to those at Patong have mushroomed. The **Club 44** discothèque in Karon is one of the oldest establishments – you can tell by its cheap shed-like appearance – but it has a welcoming atmosphere, drawing both gays and heterosexuals until well after midnight.

242

Invaded by tourists: Patong Beach

The small **Kata Noi and Nai Harn Beaches** to the south have each hosted one lavish resort (**Kata Thani** and the **Phuket Yacht Club** respectively) which tend to dominate otherwise peaceful beaches. The Yacht Club has turned a public road through its land into an underground car park! It leads to the lushly wooded and quiet Ao Saen beach.

Few visitors leave without a view of Prom Thep Cape, the island's southernmost extremity. Between it and Nai Harn is the diminutive and charming **Ya Nui Beach**, popular with the locals. Snorkelling is a cheap pleasure and although corals on the coast have been degraded there are still some dazzling fish.

Many Thai tourists prefer **Rawai Beach** on the eastern side of the cape, with its restaurants overlooking the

vater. Boats go from here to nearby islands.
he main road north from Rawai into Phuket town
passes **Chalong Bay**, a fine yacht anchorage, and
hereby a firm base on the international yachting circuit.
The King's Cup Regatta in November is becoming ever
more popular and yacht charters are available for the
wealthy.

Phuket Town The town takes its name from the Malay
bukit meaning 'hill'. It became the provincial capital
relatively recently; prior to that Thalang, further to the
north up Highway 42, was pre-eminent.
The island has rich agricultural land and deposits of tin
ore. Mining and smelting have been continuously carried
out by Europeans and Chinese, and much of the town's
architecture dates from the last century. The terraces of
Krabi and Thalang Roads in particular are very quaint.
The modern town is centred on the market roundabout
where blue buses leave for the beaches. The grassy hill
called Khao Rang dominates the town; a metalled road
goes to the summit where the view takes in offshore
islands and much of the flat eastern plain. Another good
trip is to the **Marine Biological Research Centre**, at the
end of Laem Phanwa (Phanwa Cape), 9km south of
town, where you can see a whale's skeleton and many
varieties of the colourful reef fish.

Other sights The island's central landmark is the
unmistakable **Heroines Monument**, at the road junction
for the upper west coast beaches. The two militant
ladies in stone are Thao Thep Krasatri and Thao Sri
Sunthorn, who saved Thalang from the Burmese in
1785. Next door, and well worth a visit, is the **National
Museum of Thalang** (*open*: Wednesday to Saturday,
09.30–16.30hrs). The displays are skilfully thought out
and visually appealing.
The route north to Thalang passes the rather gaudy **Wat
Phra Nang Sang** with its massive image of Guan Im,
the female Bodhisattva. Near by is the buried Buddha
image of **Wat Phra Thong** which not even a Burmese
army could dig up. It was discovered by a buffalo boy
who tethered his buffalo to the image's head.
Back at the museum the road east leads to **Pa Pra Taew
National Park** with Phuket's two waterfalls, Tone Sai
and Bang Pae. Yet further on is Ao Por, the port for trips
to the pearl-farming Naga Noi island.

The village of Ko Ban Yee near Phuket town is one of many built on stilts in and around the mangrove swamps. There is another at Rawai Beach. The *Chao Le* or Sea Gypsies, who inhabit these villages, have their own Malay-related language, *Moken*. The Sea Gypsies, originally from Malaysia, are fishing folk who once led a nomadic existence. They still practise an animistic religion.

243

Mangrove swamps at Phuket

Traditional Products

■ **The quality of Thai rice has been internationally known since the 1930s. Apart from rice, the other traditional exports for which Thailand is famous are rubber, tin, teak and gems. Each of these has traditional export markets in different parts of the world. ....■**

Rice The distinctive quality of Thai rice is still recognised across the world. People will buy cheaper rice, from other countries, but would prefer the more expensive Thai rice if they could afford it.

The first Rice Experimental Station was set up, with the encouragement of the King, in 1916. Over 4,000 domestic varieties of rice were studied, of which the *Pin Kaew* variety won first prize at the World Grain Exhibition in Canada in 1933.

244

Rubber The southern provinces of Thailand were traditionally dominated by the production of rubber and tin. Rubber trees are cultivated principally by Thai, Thai-Malay and Chinese smallholders, and the industry was mainly developed after World War I. Production is for export, primarily, and has boomed since World War II, especially in sales to the US market. Annual production has reached 130,000 metric tonnes a year.

A tree planted today can begin to be tapped for rubber within about six years. The raw sheets can then be sold, or smoked in a smoke house which costs the buyer more; the buyer is invariably a Chinese merchant.

Today the development of synthetic rubber has challenged natural rubber production, and the planters face problems, although new, higher-yielding methods of cultivation since the 1960s have helped rubber to be more profitable.

Tin Tin-mining goes back to ancient times. By the post-war period, most mines had come into the hands of British, Australian and local Chinese mine-owners. The tin used to be exported, but now the canning industry for tuna and other food products has created a domestic demand. Entitlement to all mineral rights is vested in the King, allowing the government to control tin-mining.

Teak This is also an important export product, shared with neighbouring countries, particularly Burma. Thai and Burmese teak are considered to have the highest quality in the world market.

Teak plantations were first set up in Thailand in the middle of the 19th century, and there has been an

Tapping for rubber

annual planting programme since 1942. Teak trees intended for timber export are usually replanted every 70 years, so this is a long-term business.

A new method of vegetative propagation of teak trees using tissue culture techniques has been tried. This means that one single bud from a mature élite teak tree can be mass-propagated to produce millions of plantlets of the same genetic make-up.

Teak is a quality hardwood used for speciality carving and durable finish wherever wood is used as a material. The demand is such that the recent logging ban, imposed for ecological reasons, has sent Thai exporters into neighbouring countries for concessions. Thai teak is particularly valued for shipbuilding purposes.

The trees grow in the northern part of Thailand, and the timber is brought down by waterways. The teak forests belong to the state, and short-term leases are given. Some European companies have concessions.

Both unset gems and finished jewellery are popular buys in the Bangkok markets.

Jade, rubies and sapphires are the most popular stones, traditionally produced in Thailand but also found in neighbouring countries. Thailand is very much a centre of the gem trade in Asia.

The mines for these gems are often small, employing fewer than 40 people, sometimes only five. In some areas they have to be dug out from more than 15m below the ground. The gemstones can then be heated to a high temperature to improve their brilliancy and colouring for market purposes.

Nowadays locally produced gems are supplemented by imports from Laos, Sri Lanka and Australia. There are distinct districts in both Bangkok and Chantha Buri specialising in the gem trade. The trading tables, where the gem dealers sit tête-à-tête with their customers can be seen directly inside the shop windows – sunlight being essential in order to examine the stones' cut brilliance and blemishes.

245

> **<<** Two years before a teak tree needs to be felled, its trunk is girdled by a ring cut through to the heartwood. This kills and seasons the wood slowly, and makes it sufficiently dry to float. Felling takes place during the rainy season, and elephants drag the logs down to the nearest stream. It takes about three years for a log to reach Bangkok from the forest. **>>**

Gems In Bangkok you will see hundreds of shops selling gems and ornaments, another Thai speciality.

> **<<** Rubber, tin and gems remain important export commodities for Thailand, worth about 14,1.5 and 8 billion baht a year respectively. Almost half of the rubber goes nowadays to meet the materials needs of Japan's industries, with Singapore, China and the USA providing other important rubber markets. Japan is the biggest customer for tin, and Holland is also a major buyer. Japan, Hong Kong and the United States are the principal markets for Thai gems. **>>**

▶ Ranong

Highway 4 east of Chumphon, on the Burmese border.
Buses from Chumphon, Suratthani and Phuket

Highway 4 is the main road running through the narrow province of Ranong. (*Ranong* means 'Rains a Lot', and this is evidenced by the province's lush rainforest.) Thousands of tourists pass through but most only admire its scenery from a coach window on the journey southwards to Phuket, Phang Nga and Krabi. They can also catch glimpses of neighbouring Burma (Myanmar) and its offshore islands.

The general public can 'take the waters' in **Raksa Warin Forest Garden**, 2km to the east of Ranong town. This is actually in the compound of a temple, Wat Tapotharam, and the municipality has provided all the requisite amenities.

The three hot springs: Phor, Mae and Luk (Father Mother and Child) are rich in dissolved mineral salts as they bubble up through the local limestone. A road leads away from here to Som Paen beach some 7km distant.

Those looking for the last word in luxury may find it in the Jansom Thara Hotel, 1km east out of Ranong town. Here are featured jacuzzis which are filled with natural spring water pre-heated to 65°C.

A local boy drying fish at Ranong

For nature-lovers Coming up by Highway 4 from Phang Nga the first main attraction reached is **Khlong Nakha Wildlife Sanctuary.** Dress for forest walking is essential – stout shoes and covered shins may save a deal of pain. In recompense are the wonders of a real rainforest which is unlike anything that Europe has to offer. There is a fine waterfall here waiting to be discovered by intrepid walkers: the lovely **Khao Phra Narai** falls near Kapoe district.

Further north towards Ranong town is the huge (over 300sq km) **Laem Son National Park.** The road leading to it at Km 657 crosses a vast expanse of mangroves to reach the national park headquarters at Bang Ben. This beautiful and little-visited beach has access to a number of islands, Ko Chang Khao ('Bat Island'), Ko Kam Nui and Ko Kam Yai among others. Around Ko Chang are some fascinating corals.

There are bungalows on Bang Ben and they must be booked in advance; contact the Forestry Department in Bangkok (tel: (02) 579 0529 and 579 4842)

Coastal trips Ngao waterfall is 12km short of Ranong town and can be seen from a long way off, lying inside a bend of the road. The *tha reua* or landing at Ranong is actually a few kilometres out of town. There is a great fishery here, accompanied by the unmistakable aroma of raw fish. A popular island to visit from here is **Ko Phayam** with its beaches, cashew nut plantations, pearl farm and *Chao Le* (Sea Gypsy) village. The trip takes two hours.

Another boat crosses over to the coast of Burma (Myanmar) for 200 baht. 'Prior immigration formality must first be gone through', you are told. This could well take a while for Westerners, as it would probably entail a change of government. However, it is possible just to take a look without actually landing; the journey takes about half an hour.

However, there is the Thai island of Ko Phi to visit by way of consolation. That the Burmese can cross over into Thailand is evidenced by males sporting Burmese dress around the port area; in addition various signs and notices in the town are written in Burmese script.

Victoria Point is Burma's most southern extremity and Thais cross over to shop for ivory and gems. Near the village of Pak Nam, opposite Victoria Point and to the northwest of Ranong town, is Charndamri Beach, where it is possible to watch the sunset over the point.

North of Ranong, heading towards Chumphon, the road becomes increasingly idiosyncratic twisting up and down improbable hills as it passes the district of La-un where the hulk of a Japanese warship can be seen in the river at low tide.

Ranong became a province in its own right when it was officially separated from Chumphon in 1862.

247

A hot mineral water spring

Songkhla has a large
expatriate community,
employed by the oil industry
which exploits the southern
gulf.

*Songkhla's copy of
the Copenhagen
mermaid*

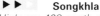

▶ ▶ **Songkhla**
*Highway 408 south of Phatthalung on the east coast.
Buses from Hat Yai and Bangkok (southern terminal)*
A town of ancient heritage, much of which is still largely
visible, Songkhla occupies the tip of a peninsula
guarding the entrance to the vast **Thale Sap Songkhla**,
(**Songkhla Lake**). The lakeside is busy with the town's
port, where huge catches of fish are iced and packed.
On the eastern side of the town is open sea with a
couple of fine beaches. **Hat Samila** lines the wide part
of the peninsula. **Son Orn** ('casuarina point') is a sliver of
land further north which offers only sea, trees, beach
and breeze. There are strategic restaurants along the
road on the port side. Drive up from the town centre,
passing the stone mermaid inspired by the one at
Copenhagen, who sits with her back to the offshore Cat
and Mouse islands, a favourite spot for anglers.
You can get a better view of the whole set-up from the
top of either Khao Noi or Khao Tang Kuan; Khao Noi is
easier as it is possible to drive up.
The beaches are fine for swimming but this area has a
decorous Thai atmosphere, which results in a curious
reluctance to take the plunge.
The most relaxed beach is way down towards Kao Seng,
well away from the port, with strange rock formations
such as 'Mr Raeng's Head', and a Muslim fishing village

which decorates its boats in the colourful *kor lae* style.
Hotels are plentiful. The budget/moderate **Saen Samran**
by the clock tower is clean and comfortable enough.
The **Sunday market** gathers near here around Songkhla
railway station, where groups of old men wait for a train
that will never come: the branch was closed in 1972.

Other sights in town include the **National Museum** (*open*: Wednesday to Sunday, 09.00–16.00hrs), housed in a Chinese mansion that has its own charm, especially the side away from the entrance with huge gnarled old trees. The 17th-century **Te Noi Fort** is hard to find at the top of a little knoll near the fishing port.

Maybe the cheapest ferry in Thailand (as little as 50 satang for foot passengers) connects Son Orn with the lake's top lip, a deep-sea port where the Khao Daeng is a sister fort to Te Noi on the Songkhla side.

Environs

For getting about, renting a motorcycle is easy in Songkhla town. To appreciate the lake properly, rent a vehicle and head west towards Hat Yai. About halfway there, take a prominent turning right which leads past a rather barren public park to the first of the **Tinsulanonda bridges**, linking the island of **Ko Yor**, straddling the mouth of the lake at this point, to the mainland. The view from the bridge is fantastic. Thale Sap Songkhla is not a true lake but a long lagoon that is fresh water and boggy at the northern end, becoming increasingly saline towards the south.

The view over Thale Sap Songkhla from Ko Yor is spectacular, looking over the second Tinsulanonda bridge which links the long thin land separating Songkhla Lake from the sea, with fish corals – bamboo and net structures erected around houses in the ocean – to the leeward side.

Highway 408 north up the coast from Ko Yor to Ranot is a typical Thai country road with villages and *wats* every few kilometres. Of the latter, **Hat Sai Keo** is an isolated meditation island on the Pacific side, a right turn shortly after meeting the main road.

The town of Ranot and the ancient temple Wat Pa Kho are a long way up this road, which is served by a regular bus from Songkhla. Halfway there, and the reasonable aim of a day trip from Songkhla, are Wat Jathing Phra, with a 10th-century *chedi*, and **Khu Khut Waterbird Park**.

A few kilometres off to the right, the lake and swampland are very popular with winter visitors, during which time many birds are on the wing. Truly dedicated ornithologists can hire a cheap boat at the sanctuary office, where there is a small amount of English information.

It is possible to speed over Ko Yor but the island has several attractions such as a weaving industry, strange rocks and the Institute of Southern Thai Studies, part of Songkhla University. The exhibits, some of Srivijayan antiquity, illustrate and illuminate the origins and crafts of Songkhla's people.

249

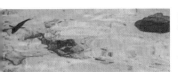

■ **The warm, tropical waters surrounding Thailand's islands are a relatively unspoiled paradise of multi-coloured fishes and intricate coral reefs. ....■**

Coral has a special meaning for many people, summoning up images of clear tropical water, white sand and the idyllic island life. But its allure is part of its undoing: it is collected to be used as a decorative item, it is damaged by the keels and anchors of tourist boats, and it is all too easily broken by careless handling or flailing flippers. A particularly destructive way of fishing – dynamiting – is also hastening this destruction. Coral grows slowly and it cannot possibly replace itself more quickly than it is being destroyed, so its future looks bleak.

Underwater swimming is obviously the best way to experience what the sea has to offer; scuba diving lessons will cost you something like US$100 per day, but snorkelling or just using a mask in shallow water can be very rewarding.

Exotic species can be seen surprisingly easily: parrot fish, with their wing-like blue fins, and dish-bodied butterfly fish built for manoeuvring in tight corners rather than for speed, can both be seen only a little way from the shore.

Coral is fascinating and precious. Like an underwater forest, it harbours many sorts of creatures; like a forest it is a living thing, gradually growing and evolving over the centuries. This treasure can be destroyed very easily by clumsy handling, and in any case a coral splinter is excruciatingly painful – so don't touch. Also beware the waving tentacles of sea anemones which are beautiful but which pack a painful sting. The boldly striped clownfish has developed an immunity to the anemone's poison and so can lurk in the protective tentacles, safe from attack, but ready itself to seek out its prey.

Other creatures have developed close relationships with one another: for example, moray eels (large, predatory, not friendly) have a following of cleaner shrimps, which feed on their skin parasites. Both species benefit.

Seahorses are among the most endearing of fishes, and are well worth seeking out. They are much easier to find than the aptly-named needlefish, which resembles nothing so much as a stick floating upright. At the other end of the size scale is the plankton-

Sea anemone

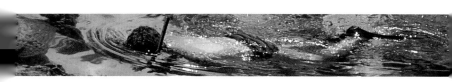

feeding whale shark, the world's largest fish, which is an occasional visitor to these waters. Marlin are much more frequently seen. These elegant beauties are one of the species most sought out by game-fishermen. Dolphins are often seen, and sometimes frolic round boats such as the ones which go to Ko Si Chang on the east coast. This is also a good vantage point from which to look out for flying fish, which sometimes glide a metre above the surface on their elongated fins.

On coastal beaches, you might still see sea turtles, although these huge creatures, which come ashore to lay their eggs, are now at great risk, their nesting areas disturbed and destroyed by tourist facilities. The nests themselves are often plundered for food. Here, pressure from concerned visitors might help to ensure a future for these gentle giants.

The distinctively coloured clown fish

Sungai Kolok

Highway 4056; border town with Malaysia. Buses from Narathiwat and Hat Yai

This important border crossing with Malaysia is 60km from Narathiwat.

Sungai Kolok is a newish town and not of itself remarkable. The market is opposite the railway terminus, and inside the station compound are racks of goods from Malaysia.

There are modern duty-free shops on the Malay side. Pay in the shop and collect the goods from Malay guards on the bridge. If crossing by foot over the old bridge into Thailand, a *tuk tuk* is recommended for the 3–4km journey into town.

Suratthani

Highway 401. Buses from Bangkok (southern terminal), Phuket and Nakhon Si Thammarat; trains from Bangkok

The 'land of the good people' is a huge sprawling province whose major attraction is **Khao Sok National Park** along Highway 401. Dam politics have bedevilled the fate of the forests. One scheme inundated millions of acres. Another, however was thwarted.

For accommodation, besides **Art's Jungle House**, a collection of tree houses charging moderate rates, there are some budget bungalows and national park accommodation. Art's is best booked by calling 279 4967 East of Suratthani town on Highway 401 at Kanchanadit is the 'college' where monkeys are trained to pick coconuts.

▶ Trang

Highway 404, on the southwest coast. Buses from Hat Yai, Phatthalung and Bangkok (southern terminal); trains from Bangkok; domestic flights

Communications with Trang are excellent, with access by air, rail and road.

Out of town past the airport is **Thung Khai Forest Garden** and further along Highway 4 is **Lamchan Waterbird Park**, which is richly endowed with waterfalls.

Offshore islands A train journey to the end of the Trang branch line at Kantang is met by buses to the sea port with its fine views. Ko Kradan is considered the most beautiful of Trang province's many islands and Ko Hai, (actually part of Krabi province) has some accommodation. The boat from Hin Pak Meng takes 40 minutes. Ko Libong to the southeast of Ko Kradan is Trang's biggest island. Royal Forest Department accommodations (total, 10 people) are free.

The mainland opposite has many fine beaches. Hat Yao (Long Beach), Yong Ling and Hat San (Short Beach) are all in Kantang district. Behind them is a hot spring. The southerly Palian district has some fine beaches in Samran and Hat Ta Se off Koh Sukorn.

The road up to Sikao district leads to Hat Chang Lang and Hat Pak Meng, with a waterfall; camping is encouraged. Inland waterfalls, Tone Khlan in Huay Yot and Roichanphanwang near the border, are fairly remote.

Palian district is home to some of the the Sakai tribe, a Negrito people believed to be the aboriginal inhabitants of Indo-China.

Thailand's first Yang Para or rubber tree was planted in Kantang district, Trang province by Phraya Ratsadanupradit, a local hero.

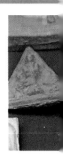

■ **Superstition has woven itself into the fabric of Thai Buddhism, especially in rural areas. For example, Thais take astrology very seriously and Brahmin astrologers are still consulted at the royal court. The Buddhist church in Thailand is divided on these matters although Buddha himself was only concerned with the compatability of a belief with the quest for enlightenment. ....■**

Astrology and lucky charms The last Prime Minister, Chatichai Choonhavan, was led by an astrologer to announce the members of his new cabinet before his coalition partners had decided their nominations for cabinet posts.

Offerings to the spirits

The Chinese are especially fond of lotteries, and tickets are sold on every street corner. In one village an ant hill was worshipped because it housed a ghost who could supposedly tell which lottery numbers were about to win prizes. Some monasteries earn an important part of their income by blessing lucky Buddha amulets. Amulets were issued by the army to officers fighting in the border areas, and even science graduates wear them as protection from unknown dangers.

Spirits In the animist tradition Thais believe that *khwan*, a spirit or genius which resides in the physical body, reflects a person's essential characteristics and is indispensible to a person's wellbeing. If the spirit is scared into leaving that person, misfortune or illness will ensue. The very first post raised in a traditional Thai house is known as the *khwan*

post. Most woods used for building are said to possess female spirits.

There is a more nebulous realm of spirits or *phi*. A newborn baby is said to have a spirit mother. Three days after birth a child is initiated into the human world in a ceremony which involves buying it with a coin from its spirit mother.

The Thais also believe in a kind of spirit companion, called *chetabhut*, which leaves a person during dreams and times of worry. A man who walks alone in the forest, hears footsteps following and turns to find no one there, has heard his *chetabhut*.

<<   Many homes have a spirit house, a cross between bird table and doll's house and always elaborately decorated. Offerings are placed on it every day and joss sticks burn there continuously. >>

A Bangkok spirit house

SOUTHERN THAILAND

Yala's foremost ethnic minority, the negrito Sakai, are assumed to be the peninsula's oldest inhabitants. Formerly scattered around Betong and Bannang Sata districts, the government rounded them up into one village in 1973. Known simply as Mooban Sakai, the village is 80km from Yala town on the road to Betong. The 90 or so inhabitants were given a few hundred acres of rubber to tend, and all took the surname 'Sri Than To', in honour of HRH the Princess Mother.

Wat Khuha-phimuk

▶　　　**Yala**
Highway 410, southernmost border province with Malaysia. Buses from Narathiwat, Pattani, Sungai Kolok and Bangkok (southern terminal); trains from Hat Yai, Sungai Kolok and Bangkok

Yala town itself is grand and spacious, the result of careful planning. There are two public parks. One is around San Jao Phor Lak Muang, the city pillar, which was donated by the present king. Rites in respect of the town's tutelary deity occur here at the end of May. Near by is Suan Khwan Muang, more of a sports ground.

It is difficult to explain the significance of singing doves among Southerners, and Yala folk in particular, but entrants in the annual **Java Dove Singing Contest** held here on the first weekend of March come from as far afield as Indonesia and Brunei.

About 8km north of town by Highway 409 to Hat Yai is Wat Khuha-phimuk, also known as Wat Na Tham. Turn left down Highway 4065 to Yaha district. The reclining image in a cave which is part of the temple is presumed to date from AD857, and is of classic Srivijayan style.

Environs

Fish fanciers might stop off at **Beung Nam Sai** in Raman district, famous for its decorative 'dragon fish'. Widely bred in Southeast Asia, these fish are supposed to bring their owner luck. The village is a further 8km from Raman on the road to Ruso district.

Than To waterfall is one of Yala's star attractions. It is to be found in Mae Wat sub-district, Bannang Sata district, 57km down Highway 410 to Betong, a seven-tiered fall in a forest garden surrounded by mountains. Visitors can bathe and there is easy access for cars. In the immediate vicinity is the Banglang dam over the river Pattani, which generates electricity. Although there are places provided to admire the view, the way up is steep and only recommended for four-wheel drive vehicles.

Ginseng is grown at the Than To self-built community near the waterfall.

TRAVEL FACTS

Arriving and Departing

Visas Nationals of Australia, Canada, Ireland, New Zealand, the United Kingdom and the US can stay in Thailand for 15 days without a visa, but extensions are not given. A confirmed onward travel ticket must be produced.

Those who wish to stay longer must apply before travelling to Thailand for a 30-day transit visa or a 60-day tourist visa, both of which are valid 90 days from the date of issue. Extensions are not normally given but this often depends on individual immigration officers. New Zealanders can stay 90 days without a visa.

Applicants must hold a passport valid for at least six months from the date of application. Completed forms must be accompanied by two passport photographs; postal applications take up to 10 working days, but personal applications are much quicker .

Non-immigrant visas, valid for 90 days, are issued to those who can show they are travelling for business purposes. These can be extended provided evidence of business or education in Thailand can be shown.

> << Visa expiry: there may be a charge of 100 baht per day for every day exceeded, and overstays are recorded on your passport. >>

Visa extensions Thirty-day extensions of transit or tourist visas (500 baht) can be obtained at the discretion of the Immigration Division, Soi Suan Phlu, South Sathorn Road, Bangkok (tel: (02) 286 9176), or any provincial immigration office, eg Phuket. Tax clearance certificates are no longer required. Visiting another country from Thailand and then returning requires an additional visa for each return visit from Thailand.

Arriving by air Bangkok International Airport (also known by its former name Don Muang Airport) is one of the major air destinations in Southeast Asia, with over 35 international airlines and a number of charter companies operating flights to the city.

Money exchange desks (offering the same rates as downtown), a hotel reservation desk, a limousine service desk and cafeteria are open 24-hours; shops and restaurants open from 06.00hrs or 07.00hrs to midnight.

The hotel desk does not require commission (the deposit is deducted from the bill) but only more up-market hotels are offered.

Travel into Bangkok Allow at least 60 minutes for possibly the ugliest journey in Thailand. The painless way to do it is to go straight to the limousine counter and pay about 300 baht for **limousine service.**

Alternatively, the same counter will sell a 100 baht ticket for a Thai Airways **minibus** (24-hour service, departing every 20 minutes) to any central hotel destination.

Unfortunately the special train service which used to run from **Don Muang Railway Station** to the central station for around 100 baht was recently withdrawn.

The **public bus** option is of interest only to confirmed tight budgeters and masochists; the costs are negligible but first experiences of Thailand will probably be of standing for over an hour with people clambering over your luggage. There

are bus-stops under the right-hand footbridge over Vipavadi -Rangsit Road as you leave the airport; and down the slip-road to the right on the

> << Travel to Pattaya:The limousine desk offers a bus service for about 180 baht per person (leaving at 09.00hrs, noon and 19.00hrs) and a sedan service for about 1,500 baht per trip. >>

way out of the airport. Buses 29, 59 and 95, and air-conditioned buses 4 and 10 head downtown.
From the main road it is possible to flag down a **taxi**; agree a fare around 120–150 baht before getting in; official taxis have yellow licence plates and taxi signs on the roof.

Avoiding Bangkok Two long-distance trains per day stop at Don Muang station across the road, offering immediate escape from the capital for those arriving before 09.00hrs. Ayutthaya and Lop Buri make interesting first-night stops; trains to Chiang Mai do not stop here. Additionally, the Northern Bus Terminal is easily reached by taxi or limousine bus and buses run to several places north of Bangkok.

Arriving by rail Travellers from Singapore and Malaysia can enter Thailand by taking the train which runs the length of the Malaysian peninsula (1,927km) and takes over 34 hours, passing through Kuala Lumpur, Butterworth (for Penang) and Suratthani; second-class sleeping berths are comfortable and must be reserved in advance.

> << Malaysia is ahead of Thailand by one hour, so the border closes at 17.00hrs on the Thai side. >>

Arriving by road Possible from Malaysia only, via cheap taxis and minibuses. Malaysia closes the border each day at 18.00hrs.

Departing by air Airport flight enquiries tel: (02) 535 1310. General enquiries tel: (02) 535 1111. Remember to keep 200 baht for airport tax which is payable for all flights on departure.
Allow plenty of time to get to the airport – two hours should be safe; the **airport express train** service ensures a 35-minute trip. Tour agencies and guesthouses in Khao Saa Road offer cheap, hourly **minibuses;** book in advance. Even if you have a departure date on your ticket, it is essential to re-confirm 48 hours before travel.

Bookshops
Generally prices for English-language books in Thailand are high. This shortlist is a selection of shops with English-language and foreign titles.

Bangkok Asia Books, Sukhumvit Road; DK (Duang Kamol) Books, Sukhumvit Road and Surawong Road (both new books). Used books are sold from stalls in Khao San Road. Neilson Hayes, Suriwongse Road, is a superb library for residents; 95 per cent of the books are in English and stock is constantly updated. The fascinating old building (founded 1869) alone is worth a visit.

Chiang Mai DK Book House, 234 Tha Phae Road, (new books; hill-tribe trekking and contoured military survey maps, useful for hiking); Library Service, 21/1 Rathchamankha Soi 2 (used English-language paperbacks); Suriwong Book Centre, 54/1–5 Si Donchai Road (good range of new books on Asia).

Hat Yai DK Books, outside Hat Yai station.
Pattaya Used paperback shop, Soi Post Office, 158/3 South Pattaya.
Phuket Seng Ho, Montree Road, (English newspapers and best sellers).

Camping
Beach camping shouldn't be a problem if you can ask permission politely: *Kor thot, khun rop guan mai, ta rao ja gangs dten ti ni?* However, rough camping is not advised, the risk of robbery – or worse – is too

high. It always helps to establish a rapport with the locals.

Nearly all of Thailand's national parks have campsites. Ready-erected two-person tents cost about 40 to 50 baht per night; a minimal charge is made if you bring your own. Tents are also provided in some up-market bungalow resorts (eg near Chiang Mai).

Be warned that camping is a chilly experience in the hilly regions. In Khao Yai an additional hazard is the wildlife – a wandering elephant has been responsible for trampling a tent and destroying expensive camera equipment (fortunately the occupants were not inside).

Children

Thais love children and many visitors bringing young offspring report how easy it is to meet locals as a result. Climate and health hazards are obvious drawbacks, and sandals are advisable on major beaches where broken glass may by lying around. Some children take to the breakfast fish soup but few will like chillis (ask for *mai sai prik* – without chilli). Western-style **baby food and nappies** are available in Bangkok and other major centres or supermarkets.

The people love looking after babies so there is rarely a problem if a babysitter is needed. Hotel discounts are given for small children.

Climate

Most of the year is hot and humid, with daytime temperatures in the 30–34°C (86–93°F) range, falling to 24°C (75°F) at night. March to May or June is the hottest and stickiest period, as the thermometers rise to 38°C (100°F) and the humidity is high – at least 80 per cent most of the time.

The rainy season is June or July to October, when most of the rain falls around dusk and there is widespread flooding. However, most of the day is fine and generally this is quite a pleasant time to travel; there are fewer tourists. Prices are cut and there are more rooms available, but rule out about three days from a fortnight's holiday.

By far the most popular time to visit is the so-called cool season from November to February when rainfall is low and daytime temperatures are very warm – typically 28–32°C (84–90°F) – but rather less

<< Leeches are a problem in forest areas in the rainy season. Do not pull them off but make them let go with salt or a lighted cigarette. >>

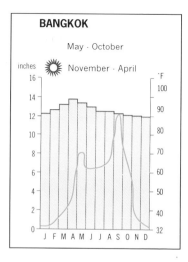

BANGKOK

May · October

November · April

inches   °F
16   100
14   90
12
10   80
8   70
6   60
4   50
2   40
0   32
   J F M A M J J A S O N D

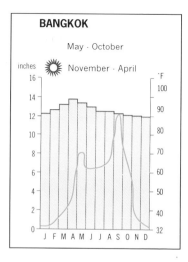

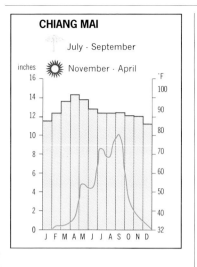

CHIANG MAI

☂ July · September

☀ November · April

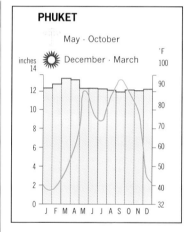

PHUKET

☂ May · October

☀ December · March

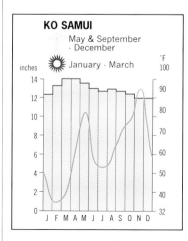

KO SAMUI

☂ May & September · December

☀ January · March

oppressive than at other times of the year. Accordingly this period is the main tourist season.

Regional factors If visiting the hills in the cool season, be prepared for some sharp drops in evening temperature to about 13°C (52°F); wind chill can make it seem a lot cooler, so take a sweater, and maybe a padded sleeping bag too.
Avoid the plains of the Northeast region in the hot season, when temperatures are frequently over 38°C (100°F). Flooding can extend beyond the rainy season, as the subsoil is saturated for some time. Monsoon winds can make the Ko Samui archipelago and the southeastern coast unpleasantly wet and windy in November and December when much of the rest of the country (even the nearby southwest coast) is at its best. Conversely, this coast is dry in the rainy season.

Crime
(See also **Emergency Telephone Numbers** and **Money Matters**.)

Theft The friendliness of the Thai people is one of the country's great assets, but it pays to be streetwise, especially in Bangkok. Take special care of your baggage, particularly in crowded buses where the razor-blade thieves are at work and can remove the contents of a bag or cut through a camera strap without the owner realising it.

Never leave valuables unattended in hotel rooms. Most hotel and guesthouses have safe deposits; be sure to obtain an itemised receipt for all items left. If trekking for a few days, take a credit card as stories abound of visitors receiving their next credit-card bill back at home and finding that someone has gone on a spending spree in their absence. At airports keep an eye on your luggage and never carry parcels for strangers; you might be unwittingly carrying hard drugs. Gross overcharging for services such as taxi fares can be avoided by agreeing on the price beforehand. Beware especially of seemingly friendly strangers offering to take you on a boat trip in Bangkok; this can lead to a huge bill at the end, or even robbery in the middle of the river. The offer of a free can of drink or a bar of chocolate may be harmless enough, but some people have been drugged in this way and wake hours later to find all their belongings have disappeared.

Fakes Thailand is famous for fake goods – designer clothes which are obviously not the real Benetton or Lacoste represent the more innocent end of the scale. So-called Rolex watches look remarkably like the real thing at a fraction of the price. Those trying to crack down on copyright pirating on behalf of American film and record companies often meet with bribery. More serious are fake gems. As it is possible to go *very* wrong buying gems, it is best not to buy unless you really know what you are looking for. Get a receipt and a certificate of quality in case of problems; disregard offers of helpful advice from strangers or promises of refunds at embassies.

Customs Regulations
Items to be declared Video players, televisions, cassette recorders, radios, gold and currency (but not traveller's cheques under US$10,000 /£5,400.

Prohibited imports Firearms, narcotics, pornography and over 2,000 baht in Thai currency. Merchandise is taxable, and it is possible to face a tax bill if several new-looking electronic goods of the same type are brought in. There is no limit on foreign currency brought into Thailand, but large amounts must be declared.

Prohibited exports Thai currency in excess of 500 baht and foreign currency in excess of US$10,000 (£5,400) (or the amount declared on arrival, if higher) cannot be taken out of the country.
Permission to export Buddha and other deity images (even reproduction ones, but not small figurines worn as part of a necklace)

must be obtained from the Bangkok National Museum, (tel: (02) 224 1370) and the Ministry of Commerce; this is seldom granted even for reproduction images, unless it can be shown they are required for worship by practising Buddhists.
The export of other antiques requires permits from the Department of Fine Arts; this involves submitting two photographs of the object (maximum five objects per photograph) and a copy of your passport to the National Museum in Bangkok, Chiang Mai or Songkhla; allow 3 to 5 days for the application to be processed.

Duty-free allowances 200 cigarettes or 250g of cigars or pipe tobacco and one litre of wine or spirits can be brought in. Theoretically only one still camera and five rolls of film can be brought in duty free, but this regulation is seldom enforced.

Driving
Nerves of steel are needed to drive in Bangkok, where factors to contend with include signs written in the Thai language, a complex and congested one-way system and poor lane discipline.
Taxis or public transport in the capital would be a better option. In country areas, public transport is so cheap and plentiful and driving standards so hair-raising that it is probably wise to forget about driving altogether. However, the Chiang Mai, Phuket and Pattaya areas are not too daunting to explore by car.
Long-distance country roads are of quite a good standard, but surfaces are patchy on even major highways. Some minor country roads are still unsurfaced, making them a sticky experience in the rainy season; potholes and ruts are frequent hazards.

Accident rates are high and adequate insurance is essential; most Thais do not carry even third party insurance. In the event of an accident, foreigners seldom have the benefit of any doubt.
Usually the police will settle disputes about liability with the witnesses. Both parties will accompany the police to the nearest station or make

an appointment to settle the dispute about damages.

> << Avoid travelling alone in the more remote areas of the country, particularly after dusk; travellers are sometimes attacked and robbed. >>

In Bangkok, traffic violations are punished with a fine, instantly payable, of varying amounts.

Driving regulations Traffic drives on the left. Visitors driving cars must hold an International Driving Licence. It is possible to get a Thai licence with a letter from your embassy.

Fuel Both leaded and unleaded fuel are available; filling stations are Western style and often give a free

> << Speed limits are 100kph outside cities, 60kph in cities and 80kph on Bangkok expressways. >>

windscreen cleaning service. Other filling stations take the form of red drums with little glass meters above them.
A car must have at least 'soo-per' whereas two-stroke motorcycles are fine on *thammadaa* (ordinary). Specify the amount needed and the petrol runs out of a hose by gravity.

Garages These are well distributed and spares and labour are very cheap; standard Japanese vehicles are easier. Insist on spares *khorng tair,* made in Japan. *Khorng tiam* from a Thai workshop, however, will save at least 50 per cent in prices.

Highway police (emergency number 193) can provide much assistance, both in the case of accidents and breakdowns.

Motorcycle hire Widely available (deposit of passport normally required) and inexpensive by Western standards. It can be a fun way to explore country areas for

those brave enough. A driving licence is not required.
Motorcyclists are very susceptible to Thai driving standards; take care and have adequate insurance. Insist on a crash helmet and protect the skin. Check the vehicle (brakes, tyre wear and lights are among the easiest faults to identify) and clarify who is liable for repairs if it breaks down. The biggest danger is undoubtedly *sip lor,* 10-wheeled trucks. Drivers have punishing schedules which they keep to with the aid of stimulant drugs. Buses make up for frequent stops with wild bursts of speed and reckless overtaking. The roads are full of ancient machines, push carts and herds of cows.
On main roads, signs are in English. Once on to minor roads Thai script has to be contended with so it is useful to have destinations written down in both alphabets.

Electricity
220 volts, 50-cycle AC. For those carrying 110-volt appliances, some hotels supply transformers, but if up-country travel is on the itinerary, bring your own or else forget about hairdryers and shavers; towels and disposable razors are adequate substitutes.

Embassies and Consulates
Loss of passport or tickets should first be reported to the Tourist Police. Next, present this report to your national embassy or consulate who will deal with it and other disasters.

Nearly all countries have representation in Bangkok, making it a good place to obtain visas for travel elsewhere.

Australia 37 Sathon Tai Road, (tel: (02) 287 2680).
Canada 11th Floor, Boonmiter Building, 138 Silom Road, (tel: (02) 234 1561).
Ireland United Flourmill Building, 205, Ratchawongse Road, (tel: (02) 223 0876).
New Zealand 93 Witthayu Road, (tel: (02) 251 8165).
United Kingdom 1031 Ploenchit Road, (tel: (02) 253 0191).
United States 95 Witthau Road, (tel: (02) 252 5040).

Emergency Telephone Numbers
Fire 199.
Police 191
Ambulance (Bangkok) (tel: (02) 252 2171/5).
Emergency dentist (Bangkok) Siam Square Clinic (tel: (02) 252 8921).
English-speaking doctors (Bangkok) JP Dickson and Partners (tel: (02) 252 8056).
Hospitals (Bangkok) Bangkok Nursing Home (tel: (02) 233 2610); Bangkok Christian Hospital (tel: (02) 233 6981); Bangkok Adventist Hospital (tel: (02) 281 1422). (Chiang Mai) McCormick Hospital (tel: (053) 241107); Maharaj Hospital (tel: (053) 221122); Lanna Hospital (tel: (053) 211037). (Phuket) Wachira Hospital (tel: 211114); Mission Hospital (private), Thepkasattree Road (tel: 212386). (Pattaya) Pattaya Memorial Hospital, Pattaya Road (tel: (038) 429422).

Etiquette
(See also pages 26–7.)
Thais do not care for shows of anger or irritation or even raised voices. They respect a *jai yen*, or cool heart. Criticism or blunt confrontation can cause loss of face. Politeness and respect are the rule. Because the head is considered the most honoured part of the body and the feet the most base and despised, it is best to be aware of offending, even unwittingly. For instance, sitting with crossed legs might mean pointing at someone with a foot.

<< If a banknote blows away in the wind never trap it with your foot; this is the ultimate *faux pas* – touching a portrait of the King's head with the lowliest part of your body. **>>**

Kissing and hugging in public is not acceptable.
On visiting a temple, the shoulders should be covered. Do not wear shorts or revealing dresses. Remove shoes when entering the main shrine and when visiting a private house. Nudity and topless sunbathing among tourists is common on many beaches but it is offensive to many Thais. First names are used universally. Thais also have nicknames, which tend to be shorter and easier to remember.
Never criticise the Thai royal family in front of another Thai. Each day at 08.00 and 18.00hrs, the national anthem is broadcast over railway station loudspeakers, during which time you should stand and remain silent.
Smoking is banned in theatres, in railway carriages and in all buses. Never smoke in a *wat*.
Women travellers should try to avoid touching a monk. If this happens he will have to go through a complicated and lengthy penance. Never climb on to Buddha images or show any signs of disrespect to Buddha.

Health
First Aid Although virtually all medical supplies are on sale in pharmacists, it is advisable to have a first-aid box with you equipped with a few basic things:
• sticking plasters
• antiseptic cream
• elasticated bandages
• aspirins or paracetomol
• ointment to soothe insect stings and bites
• rub-in cream for muscular sprains
• talcum powder to ease prickly heat
• cigarette lighter or matches for lighting mosquito coils (the coils themselves are too fragile to carry about)
• mosquito repellent

- tablets for diarrhoea and upset stomachs

Heat Thailand's persistent heat can be quite debilitating; avoid over-exertion on the first few days and steer clear of alcohol in the daytime. Drink plenty of fluids to avoid dehydration. Thirst is not always an accurate guide to the body's needs; do not let urine get too dark. Shower two or three times a day.
A sun hat or parasol will make the midday sun more bearable. Use a high protection sunscreen to avoid sunburn; remember it is possible to get badly burned in the sea too.
The heat often depresses the appetite, so make sure protein intake is adequate; rice is one of the commonest sources.

Malaria This is a serious problem in forest areas and certain islands, particularly in the hilly borderlands and on Ko Samet. There is no risk in cities or in the central plains. Malaria is transmitted by malarial mosquitoes; if visiting a risky area be sure to wear clothes to cover arms and legs. Cover exposed skin with mosquito repellant and sleep under a mosquito net. The danger time is 18.00—02.00hrs. Malarial symptoms are a headache and fever; if you experience these, contact any malarial control centre (found throughout the country) for a 10-minute blood test.
Many visitors take malaria prophylactics, However, these are ineffective against most Thai mosquitoes and the **Malaria Control Centre** (18 Boonrhagjit Road, Chiang Mai) and the Tourism Authority of Thailand do not recommend them. Also, these tablets often have side-effects, including skin problems, corneal damage and temporary hair loss. Ask your GP for advice

Stomach problems To minimise the risk of stomach upset, avoid unpeeled fruit, unwashed raw vegetables and tap water. Bottled water is on sale everywhere and is quite safe; many hotels, guesthouses and restaurants buy this in bulk, so water set down in front of you to drink is usually fine.

Similarly, cylindrical-shaped ice cubes are bought in and should be safe. Ice cream bought from street vendors may have melted and refrozen, which could cause problems.

Vaccinations The only mandatory vaccination is yellow fever if you are coming from an infected area, but it is strongly recommended to inoculate against cholera, hepatitis A, polio, tetanus and typhoid; check with your GP before leaving.

VD and AIDS Sexually transmitted diseases, particularly AIDS, syphilis and gonorrhoea are common. Using a condom (tung yang anamai) otherwise known as a sheath (plork) is the most effective protection and they are on sale in pharmacies throughout Thailand. The English words are usually understood too. Worries about infected hospital needles can be allayed by buying a specially sealed pack of needles marked as being a safety measure against AIDS.

263

> << VD clinics abound in Ploenchit Road in Bangkok. One intramuscular injection cures within 24 hours. >>

Insurance
Don't leave home without it and shop around for the best price and most extensive cover. Take a photocopy of the insurance document with you and leave the original at home with a list of the items taken. Obtain the cover as soon as the flight is reserved to insure against cancellation.
The policy should cover:
- delayed departure and delayed baggage
- all reasonable medical, hospital and emergency dental treatment expenses, and flight home by air ambulance
- personal liability
- cancelling or curtailment in the event of the illness or death of yourself, your travelling companion or a close relative; or in the event of redundancy; or in the event of being called as a witness; or in the

event of your home being damaged by fire, flood or storm or being burgled; the policy should compensate the cost of the holiday

- belongings and money, including sufficient cover for your camera
- items left in a car in daytime or overnight
- any special needs such as motorcycling, water-skiing and rock climbing
- 24-hour emergency telephone number

Points to notice Delays below 12hrs are not normally covered; after a 24-hour delay you may be entitled to a refund for the full cost of your holiday if you cancel.

There may be a ceiling for the amount you can claim for the loss of an item. There is usually a small excess whereby you pay the first *x* amount of the claim.

Cover is not provided for pre-existing illnesses.

Contact lenses and dentures may need special insurance.

When things go wrong Get written evidence and receipts wherever applicable. Delayed departure of 12 hours or more usually qualifies for compensation, provided you have the length and cause of the delay confirmed in writing by the airline. If luggage is damaged in transit, get two repair estimates; if it is lost by the airline get a report form from the airline before leaving the airport, notify the police (if the policy requires it) and keep relevant receipts.

Theft of personal belongings while in Thailand must be reported to the local police within 24 hours; ask for a **certificate of notification** from them. Keep copies of any bills or receipts for any additional costs if medical treatment is required; many insurance companies give an emergency telephone number.

Language

The Thai language is extemely difficult to master, and even armed with a phrase book and dictionary intonation is likely to be a problem. Fortunately, the Thais are helpful in overcoming the language barrier.

Accordingly, it is worth learning a few basic words and phrases; a little will go a long way. English is widely used in tourist areas, including the guesthouses, hotels and some restaurants, and many Thais have a smattering.

Basic phrases

hello	(man) sawat dee krup
	(woman) sawat dee ka
goodbye	laa gorn
thank you	korp koon
sorry/excuse me	kor toh
how much?	tao rai?
too expensive	phaeng pa
where is…?	…yu thii nai?
we want to go to…	…rao yahk bpai
how do I get to?	bpai…yung ngai?
how long does it take?	chai way-lah tao-rai?
that doesn't matter	mai pen rai
what is this called?	nee ree-uk wah a-rai?
yes	chai!
no	mai! chai!
turn right	lee-o kwah
turn left	lee-o sai
straight on	dtrong dtrong
I'm not feeling well	pom (woman: chun) roo-seuk mai koy sa-bai
I understand	pom (chun) kao jai
I don't understand	pom (chun) mai kao jai
do you understand?	kao jai mai?
see you later	pop gan mai

Numbers

1	neung
2	sorng
3	sahm
4	see
5	hah
6	hok
7	jet
8	bpairt
9	gao
10	sip
11	sip-et
12	sip sorng
20	yee-sip
21	yee-sip-et
30	sahm-sip
100	neung roy

200	sorng roy
1,000	neung phan
10,000	neung meuun

Glossary Common geographical element in Thai place names (note double aa, double ii and h are optional, eg thani/thaani (city), ko/koh (island).

baht	unit of Thai currency (100 satang = 1 baht)
ban	house, village
bang	waterside village
bot	the main chapel of a *wat*
chedi	a pagoda, topped by a spire, where holy relics are kept
farang	foreigner
hat, hatsai	beach
hup	valley
khok, don noen	hill
nam tok	waterfall
ko/koh	island
laem	peninsula, cape, promontory
mae, mae nam	
lam nam	river
nakhon, muang, thanii	city
pa, dong	jungle
paknam	river mouth
pha	cliff
phanom	hill
prang	Khmer-style *chedi*
nong	swamp
samlor	bicycle rickshaw taxi
songthaew	pickup van which isused as a minibus
tam	cave
tha	port, harbour
thale sap	lake
thanon	road
tuk tuk	motorised pedicab taxi
wai	Thai greeting (hands placed together as if in prayer)
wang	palace
wat	temple/monastery
wiharn	hall where religious duties are carried out

Pronunciation Thai has five tones: mid; high; low; rising, and falling. The differences seem small to the untrained *farang* ear but it is a crucial part of speech. Mispronounce the Thai for 'snow' and you may find yourself talking about a delicate part of a dog's anatomy!

To make matters harder still, consonant sounds are slightly different: 'k', 'p' and 't' for instance, are mouthed rather than sounded at the end of a word. For example, the city of Phitsanulok is actually pronounced 'Piss-anu-loh'. 'Th and 'ph' are pronounced like simple 't' and 'p' – so Phuket is 'Poo-ke(t)' – and there is even talk of getting the official spelling changed. Other groups of letters to note:

kh	k
k	hard g
p	plosive 'bp'
r	often silent (eg Krathong = 'Katong'))
th	t
t	plosive 'dt'

265

Lost property
Contact the police (see page 262); for lost property at the airport contact the Lost and Found office at the rear of the building, (tel: (02) 535 2173).

Maps
Maps are not part of Thai mentality! For those who need greater detail than the maps, in this book give, or for those who like to compare maps, look for the following: for general planning, the **Bartholomew World Travel Map of Thailand** covers the whole country at a scale of 1:500,000. The Department of Highways puts out a set of four maps of the country which is available from the Tourism Authority of Thailand office in Bangkok or the Highways Department on Si Ayutthaya Road.

Bangkok's labyrinthine street network probaby will never be mapped accurately to include the last tiny back-alley. In the meantime, the **Latest Edition Guide Map of Bangkok** is indispensable in showing bus routes of as much of the city as is needed by most people, and it also locates points of interest, hotels, embassies and places of entertainment.

Phrannok Witthaya publish quality maps of Bangkok (Bangkok Guide) and most provinces. Their map of Krabi is particularly recommended. For Bangkok and Chiang Mai, Nancy Chandler's hand-drawn colour maps are full of comments on where to eat noodles, buy crafts or English-language books, find a doctor and go to early-morning aerobic classes – all in addition to sights and hotels. For drivers, DK Books publish a useful road atlas (**Thailand Highway Map**), showing all highways and many dirt tracks, with place names in Thai, and major ones in English; there are town plans in the back. Free local maps are available from tourist offices and many guesthouses. While the standard of cartography is not high, these maps are often very useful sources of tourist information.

The best map for the northwest is the PN map of Chiang Mai and area, which has a city plan on the front, and a contoured 1:500,000 map on the reverse.

Measurements and Sizes

Although the metric system is widely used, certain Thai measurements are sometimes given, especially when referring to land.

1 *niu*: 2cm; 1 sq *wa*: 4sq m; 1 *rai*: 1,600sq m.

> **<<** The Thai year dating system is 543 years 'ahead' of ours; for example, AD2000 becomes in Thailand 2543. **>>**

Media

Newspapers The *Bangkok Post* and *Nation* are English-language newspapers published in Bangkok but on sale throughout Thailand. Both have foreign coverage although the *Nation* is more parochial whereas the *Post* has many features taken from such publications as the *Independent, The Economist, Rolling Stone* and others.

The most readily available foreign English-language paper is the

CONVERSION CHARTS

FROM	TO	MULTIPLY BY
Inches	Centimetres	2.54
Centimetres	Inches	0.3937
Feet	Metres	0.3048
Metres	Feet	3.2810
Yards	Metres	0.9144
Metres	Yards	1.0940
Miles	Kilometres	1.6090
Kilometres	Miles	0.6214
Acres	Hectares	0.4047
Hectares	Acres	2.4710
Gallons	Litres	4.5460
Litres	Gallons	0.2200
Ounces	Grams	28.35
Grams	Ounces	0.0353
Pounds	Grams	453.6
Grams	Pounds	0.0022
Pounds	Kilograms	0.4536
Kilograms	Pounds	2.205
Tons	Tonnes	1.0160
Tonnes	Tons	0.9842

MEN'S SUITS

UK	36	38	40	42	44	46	48
Rest of Europe	46	48	50	52	54	56	58
US	36	38	40	42	44	46	48

DRESS SIZES

UK	8	10	12	14	16	18
France	36	38	40	42	44	46
Italy	38	40	42	44	46	48
Rest of Europe	34	36	38	40	42	44
US	6	8	10	12	14	16

MEN'S SHIRTS

UK	14	14.5	15	15.5	16	16.5	17
Rest of Europe	36	37	38	39/40	41	42	43
US	14	14.5	15	15.5	16	16.5	17

MEN'S SHOES

UK	7	7.5	8.5	9.5	10.5	11
Rest of Europe	41	42	43	44	45	46
US	8	8.5	9.5	10.5	11.5	12

WOMEN'S SHOES

UK	4.5	5	5.5	6	6.5	7
Rest of Europe	38	38	39	39	40	41
US	6	6.5	7	7.5	8	8.5

Singapore edition of the *International Herald Tribune. Where?* magazine, free from hotel desks and tourist offices in Bangkok, Chiang Mai, Pattaya and Phuket, lists events and restaurant promotions, and is filled with advertisements for shops and nightspots.

Radio There is no problem tuning into rock or Thai pop music. English-language programmes (hourly news bulletins, sport and business) are broadcast on 97FM; 107FM has news at 07.00hrs, 12.30hrs and 19.30hrs, with jazz and pop in between. English-speaking DJs are found on 105FM. Between 21.30 and 23.30hrs Western classical music is played on 101.5FM. BBC World Service and Voice of America wavelengths are complex (depending on the time of day); the TV/radio page of the *Nation* lists these.

Television Cable TV with international channels is available in top-class hotels; it is also possible to get TV news on 105.5FM for Channel 3, 103.5FM for Channel 7, 107FM for Channel 9 and 88FM for Channel 11 (which mostly broadcasts educational programmes and documentaries; news is at 20.00hrs).

Money Matters

Currency The unit of currency is the baht (often abbreviated to B) and this is divided into 100 satang. Rates do not vary much but are better for traveller's cheques than for currency. Coins are 25 satang, 50 satang (both copper), 1 baht (currently three sizes, the older designs do not have Arabic numerals), 5 baht (with copper edge) and 10 baht. Notes have Arabic numerals and are issued in denominations of 10, 20, 50, 100 and 500.

Foreign exchange It is not possible to obtain Thai currency outside Thailand, so on arrival at the airport a visit to the money change desk is necessary. It is open 24 hours and the rates are reasonable.
Most banks will exchange foreign money and traveller's cheques;

exchange dealers in tourist areas offer competitive rates and are open 07.00hrs–20.00hrs or 21.00hrs. The Bangkok Bank is open daily, even on national holidays, 07.00hrs–20.00hrs. If really stuck, big hotels have exchange desks, but rates are poor. The best bet is to take cheques in major foreign currency, in reasonably large denominations as commission is charged on each cheque cashed. Additionally you can change money using a credit card (Access/Mastercard, American Express, Diners Club and Visa are the most commonly used). Be sure to have details of emergency telephone numbers should a card get lost. Keep traveller's cheque counterfoils separate from the cheques themselves. Make a record of which cheques have been cashed, so if some are lost you know which ones to claim for. Collection of new cheques can be arranged through any bank.

Haggling Taxi drivers and vendors of clothes and souvenirs expect you to bargain over the price. While there are no hard and fast rules, offering half of what is asked seems to be common practice, then settling for about two thirds.
Sometimes the first price offered may be ten times over the odds so ask other people, Thais and seasoned travellers, what you would

expect to pay. Don't worry about not getting haggling down to a fine art immediately, the sums involved are often paltry anyway. Above all, keep cool and smile.

It is sometimes possible to negotiate cheap rates for hotel rooms, particularly outside the main tourist season. Restaurant and street-stall food and items in department stores (except for expensive goods such as jewellery) nearly always have fixed prices.

National Holidays

As in some other Asian countries, certain public holidays are calculated according to the lunar calendar and vary from year to year.
Accommodaton can be hard to find, especially in New Year, Songkran in Chiang Mai and when a holiday forms part of a long weekend. Tourist offices some banks and all government offices close during these periods; Bangkok Bank (branches nationwide) and hotel money desks are open, as are most shops.

31 Dec and 1 Jan	New Year
Early to mid-Feb	Chinese New Year
Mid-Feb	*Maga Puja*
6 April	Chakri Day
12–14 April	Thai New Year (*Songkran*)
Early May	Royal Ploughing Ceremony
5 May	Coronation Day
May/June	*Visaka Bucha*
July	*Asalaha Bucha*
12 August	Queen Sirikit's Birthday
Mid–late Oct	*Ok Pansa*
23 Oct	Chulalongkorn Day
5 Dec	King Bhumipol's Birthday
10 Dec	Constitution Day

Festival Days The biggest festivals, with their locations, are given below to provide an idea of where and when accommodation may be hard to find.

7–9 Feb	Flower Festival (Chiang Mai)
April	Pattaya Festival (Pattaya)
21–22 Nov	Elephant Roundup (Surin)
Nov full moon	*Loi Krathong* (Nationwide, especially Sukothai and Ayutthaya)
Nov–Dec	River Kwae Bridge Week (Kanchana Buri)

National Parks

Thailand's 58 national parks are dotted nationwide, and include mountainous, forest and coastal regions, individual waterfalls and archipelagos. Many offer accommodation in the form of tents (about 40 baht for one or two people), dormitory accommodation (typically 20–40 baht per person) and 10-bed bungalows costing 100–300 baht per person or 1,200–1,600 baht per bungalow.

Reservations are advisable for weekends and public holidays, through the Forestry Department, Phahonyothin Road, Bangkok, (tel: (02) 579 0529).

Warm clothing is needed in mountain areas, where temperatures can drop to 5°C and it is advisable to bring a torch. Mapped information for walking is generally poor and it is imperative to keep to the marked paths.

Opening Hours
Banks Monday to Friday, 08.30hrs–15.30hrs; Bangkok Bank (branches nationwide) and foreign exchange counters (in tourist areas) 07.00hrs–20.00hrs daily.

Government offices Monday to Friday, 08.30hrs–12.00hrs, 13.00hrs–16.30hrs.

National Museum branches Mostly Wednesday to Sunday, 08.30hrs–12.00hrs, 13.00hrs–16.30hrs; closed Monday, Tuesday and public holidays.

Tourist offices Daily, 08.30hrs–16.30hrs; closed on public holidays.

Small stores Daily, 12hrs a day.

Large stores Daily, mostly 10.00hrs–18.30hrs or 19.00hrs.

During Chinese New Year in February, many small shops are closed. Large stores stay open but take a holiday afterwards.

Pharmacies
Thai pharmacies are extremely well-stocked for the most part; in fact it is possible to buy many products, such as antibiotics, for which a doctor's prescription would be needed in other countries. Pharmacies are open daily from 08.00hrs–17.00hrs or 18.00hrs in smaller places, or until 21.00hrs in large cities.

There is no all-night emergency service; in case of difficulty, contact a hospital.

Photography
Daylight is very bright so use a 50 or 100 speed film for best results outside.

Thais are very tolerant of having their picture taken, but it is common-sense manners to point your camera first (smiling as you do so!); some hill-tribe folk are more shy, and some may demand a few baht.

Many temples display signs in English prohibiting photography inside the main *wiharn,* and some museums request that exhibits are not photographed. Video cameras are banned entirely from the grounds of the Grand Palace in Bangkok. Print and slide film is widely available and reasonably priced.

<< Pack silica gel with cameras or another drying agent in order to counter the effects of humidity. >>

Places of Worship
For non-Buddhists these are fairly thin on the ground, with the notable exception of the significant Muslim element in Southern Thailand (with the largest mosques in Pattani and Yala).

Roman Catholicism is followed in some towns with a substantial Vietnamese or Laotian population, particularly in Si Chiangmai in Northeastern Thailand (not to be confused with Chiang Mai in the Northwest). There is a Roman Catholic cathedral in Chantha Buri. In Bangkok, the following welcome outsiders:

Hindu Wat Khek, Pan Road, off Silom Road.

Jewish Jewish Association of Thailand, 121/3 Soi 22, Sukhumvit Road (tel: 258 2195).

Muslim Darool Aman Mosque, Phetchaburi Road (near Rajtewi Intersection); Haroon Mosque, Charoen Krung (New) Road (near post office).

Protestant Calvary Baptist Church, 88 Soi 2, Sukhumvit Road, (tel: 251 8278); Christ Church (Anglican/Episcopal), Convent Road, (tel: 234 3634); International Church, 67 Soi 19, Sukhumvit Road, (tel: 253 2205).

Roman Catholic Assumption Cathedral, 23 Oriental Lane, Charoen Krung (New) Road (tel: 234 8556); Holy Redeemer Church, 123/19 Soi Ruam Rudee (behind US embassy) (tel: 253 0353).

Seventh Day Adventist Bangkok Chinese Church, 1325 Rama IV Road (tel: 215 4529); Bangkok Ekamai Church, 57 Soi Charoenchai, Ekamai Road (tel: 391 3593).

Police

The brown-uniformed policeman is a common enough sight; many speak a little English and they often approach lost-looking *farang* (maybe just to practise their English).
Police boxes (small police stations) are placed at frequent intervals along main roads. For Bangkok, Chiang Mai, Pattaya and Phuket a special Tourist Police service assists visitors (see **Emergency Telephone Numbers**).
Contact the police in the event of road accidents, theft, lost property, disputes or car breakdowns; they will also help with giving guidance (occasionally as escort) in remote or dangerous areas.

Post Offices

Postal services in Thailand are efficient and domestic rates are cheap. Approximate times for airmail to arrive are 5–7 days for Europe, and 7–10 days for Australia, Canada, New Zealand and the US.
Large parcels (maximum weight 15kg) should be sent surface mail; this takes 10–12 weeks. Main post offices sell boxes in different sizes and bubble-wrap; some of the largest offices (including Bangkok and Chiang Mai) offer a parcel-wrapping service.
Bangkok Central Post Office is at Charoen Krung (New) Road. It is open Monday to Friday 08.00hrs –16.30hrs; weekends and holidays, 09.00hrs–13.00hrs. Telephone and telegram services are open 24hours.
Post offices outside Bangkok are open Monday to Friday, 08.30hrs –16.30hrs, major ones are open 09.00hrs–13.00hrs on Saturdays.
Nearly all post offices offer a *poste restante* service (1 baht per item), by which mail can be sent to a given post office until the addressee claims it; such mail should be labelled 'Poste Restante' and the surname of the addressee should be underlined.
Additionally many hotels and guesthouses are happy to keep mail for guests; in Bangkok particularly many guesthouses have screens with letters for guests attached to them (often with six-month old postmarks!).
Main post offices, large hotels and some street bureaux have fax facilities. Stamps are sold at some hotels and at many newsagents. Aerogrammes (fixed price anywhere in the world) and postcards are a few baht cheaper to send than airmail letters.

Public Transport

See also pages 114–15.
Thailand is well-served with with a dense network of inexpensive public and semi-public transport. Some is quite luxurious, much is crowded and uncomfortable; some forms of travel will leave you aching, hot or cold, while others will entertain with scenery, *en route* snacks and sheer downright eccentricity; all of it part of the experience.
The language barrier can be frustrating (attempts at pronouncing place names often encounter blank looks), but generally bus and *songthaew* drivers and conductors are helpful about making sure that foreigners alight at their intended destinations.
Embarassingly, in crowded buses Thais (sometimes elderly ones) may give up their seat for you.

Internal flights If time is short, consider these as a method of seeing more; it only takes an hour from Bangkok to Phuket or Chiang Mai (against a full day or night by bus or train).
Thai Airways International flies to Chiang Mai, Chiang Rai, Lampang, Mae Hong Son, Mae Sot, Nan, Phitsanulok, Phrae and Tak in the North Region; Khon Kaen, Loei, Nakhon Ratchasima, Sakon Nakon, Ubon Ratchathani and Udon Thani in the Northeast, and Hat Yai, Ko Samui, Nakhon Si Thammarat, Narathiwat, Pattani, Phuket, Suratthani and Trang in the South. Reserve seats well in advance if flying from Bangkok, through Thai Airways (tel: (02) 513 0121).
Each of these towns has a Thai Air office, where advance bookings can be made.

Rail While the rail network does not serve every corner of Thailand and services are less frequent than buses, for views from the window and for general comfort, the train wins easily over the bus as a means of travel.

There are three classes, covering the range from first class air-conditioned two-berth compartments, to second class air-conditioned reclining seats, to third class padded bench seats (wooden slat variety on ordinary trains may need improvised padding).

Generally, unbooked third class is adequate for short journeys, while the other two classes may give a bit more room; first class is about twice as expensive as second, and four and a half times more than third. Sleeping berths on overnight journeys must be reserved in advance (even the berthless carriages get packed on the Bangkok–Chiang Mai and Bangkok–Singapore lines).

The sleeping berths on second class are excellent (berths are arranged so that you sleep in the same direction as the rails, and not across them). On longer journeys, there is a restaurant service, with the menu and food brought to your seat.

For long journeys out of Bangkok it is usually necessary to book several days in advance as trains are often very full, especially on the Bangkok–Chiang Mai and Malaysia routes. Reservations can be made through travel agents or booking counters at most major stations. For Bangkok (Hualomphong) station, tel: (02) 223 7020.

Holders of international passports can purchase 20-day passes giving freedom of second and third class rail travel throughout Thailand; the cost is 1,500 baht for a Blue Pass; the Red Pass includes extra charges (including for Express Train, air-conditioning and sleeping berths) and costs 3,000 baht.

Buses Thailand's excellent bus network fans out from Bangkok, connecting with virtually every town. Services are cheap and frequent; air-conditioned buses are more expensive but less crowded. Tickets are on sale at bus stations or on the bus and can be bought just before travelling, or sometimes in advance. On long routes the bus stops for toilets and refreshments, and vendors often come on board offering snacks and drinks.

Few buses show where they are going in Roman script, but *farangs* always get plenty of assistance. The major **bus stations** for Bangkok are *Taladmochit*, Paholyothin Road (for journeys north and northeast), *Ekamai*, Sukhumvit Road (east) and *Sai tai*, Nakhon Chaisri Road (straight on from the Pin Klao bridge) (south).

Private bus operators abound and are a popular budget method of long-distance travel; numerous agencies, particularly in Khao San Road in Bangkok, advertise these.

Driving standards on buses are not that good and the fact that private companies often race against each other doesn't help. One lasting memory of Thailand will be looking in the driver's mirror and spotting his reflected glance – five seconds on the road alternating with five looking at the video suspended above the garland of everlasting flowers that decorates the window.

Private overnight buses organised for foreign visitors can be a grim experience as the driver turns out the reading lights just as the journey

271

begins ('power failure') and a Thai voice blares out for most of the night, entertaining the driver but no one else.

There have been hair-raising tales of thefts on one or two of these buses where the passengers were given doped cokes as they boarded and woke to find everything gone. Government-operated buses on shorter inter-city routes generally run between 06.00hrs–18.00hrs daily. Long-distance VIP and 999 buses are pricier than ordinary ones but are quite comfortable, with reclining seats and reasonable leg-room.

Minibuses Known as *songthaews*, (literally 'two rows'). these are covered trucks or vans with two long, hard benches at the back. They fill up to capacity with passengers squashed together, hanging on to the back and standing on the footplate. You seldom see anything apart from other passengers' limbs and shopping baskets but the *songthaew* is often the only way of reaching your destination.

Fares are fixed, strictly no haggling, and very cheap. The destination is not advertised , but usually the driver and conductor are shouting it out and will usher you aboard.

Taxis Plentiful in supply, but most have no meters so it means bargaining over the fare before travelling. The very new (and thin on the ground) metered taxis in Bangkok can be up to half as cheap for long journeys with average to light traffic jams. Air-conditioned taxis are usually 10 baht or so more than ordinary ones.

> << As taxi drivers seldom speak fluent English, ask your hotel to write your destination in Thai and suggest the fare. >>

Tuk tuks The less luxurious version of the taxi; also known as pedicab or motorised *samlors*, these are covered, open-sided two-passenger chariots built around a scooter and unmistakable for their 'tuk tuk' noise. They are not particularly safe, but

cheaper than taxis for short distances and you have to try a ride as part of the Thailand experience. Bargain hard before travelling ; short trips are generally in the 20–40 baht range, although there is talk of making fares standardised.

Bicycle samlors The unmotorised version of the *tuk tuk* is seen in many provincial towns. Again, agree the fare in advance; 5–20 baht is the rule.

Long-tailed boats Beside the service along the Bangkok canals west of Thonburi there has recently started a service from Wat Saket to Bangkapi along Klong Saen Saep. Be prepared for a ride in an open sewer, although the trip takes just half an hour as against two hours by road. Get off at *Ekamai* and get a 72 bus down Soi Ekamai for the Eastern Bus Station. Reach the Southern Bus Station by long-tail from Tha Chang.

Sport
See also pages 110–13.
Scuba diving and swimming With so many idyllic beaches to choose from it is no surprise that Thailand has come to the fore as a major destination for sand and sea holidays. Scuba-diving boat trips are widely available in places such as Ko Samui, Chumpon Province, Pattaya, Krabi Province and Phuket. The spectacular array of marine life makes the experience unforgettable. Numerous places hire out snorkels,

> << Corals grow in profusion but are endangered because of the numbers of tourists who break off souvenir chunks. Do not follow suit – the coral never looks as pretty back home after it has dried out. >>

masks (often not large enough for the largest *farang* heads) and flippers, but you can save yourself quite a few baht by bringing your own equipment.

Golf Fees are 90–300 baht; caddies, usually women, charge 50–150 baht;

club hire is 150–300 baht. There are several courses in and around Bangkok, including the popular **Navatanee Golf Course** (tel: (02) 374 6127), designed for the 1975 World Cup Tournament, and the **Railway Training Centre Course** (tel: (02) 271 0130). Courses are also found at Hua Hin, Lanna near Chiang Mai, Phuket, Sattahip near Pattaya and Tong Yai in Songkhla.

<< A booklet free from the Tourist Authority of Thailand gives details of over 20 golf courses, with reservation information. >>

Spectator Sport Thailand's national sport is *Muay Thai* (Thai Boxing). Also popular are kite fighting, sword fighting and *tagraw* (see pages 110–113).
Less exotic but also popular are soccer and horse-racing. Racing takes place every Sunday from 12.15hrs and alternates between the Royal Bangkok Sports Club, Henri Dunant Road, and the Royal Bangkok Turf Club, Phitsanulok Road.

Telephones
Local calls can be made from any telephone and cost 1 baht for 3 minutes; only small 1 baht coins are accepted; long-distance domestic calls can be made from blue telephone boxes, hotels and post offices, or through the operator (dial 101) on older telephones.
While it is generally straightforward

to make long-distance calls from Bangkok, smaller places up-country may require a visit to the local post office, where you may have to queue.
Credit-card pay phones do not exist in Thailand; green phonecards (100 baht) can be used in green call boxes.

International calls can be made from some hotels and guesthouses, from major post offices and from private telephone offices.
Hotels with International Direct Dialling telephones often charge 20 per cent or more for the service.
The international dialling code is 001, followed by the number of the country. Country codes are as follows:

Australia	61
Canada	1
Ireland	353
New Zealand	64
United Kingdom	44
United States	1

Omit the 0 prefix for the city code after dialling the country code. Alternatively go via the operator (dial 13 in order to get an English-speaking operator service).

Local codes Bangkok 02, Chiang Mai, 053, Pattaya 038, Phuket 076.
If you need to get directory assistance, dial 13.

Fax facilities are mainly restricted to larger hotels and private bureaux (in large cities).

Time

At 12 noon in Thailand it is 15.00hrs in Sydney, Australia; 17.00hrs in New Zealand; 05.00hrs in the UK and Ireland (06.00hrs, BST); 21.00hrs the previous day in Los Angeles and midnight in New York.

Tipping

Taxi drivers are never tipped, and tipping is very rarely done in restaurants, although 10 per cent is usually appreciated if there is no service charge. For hairdressers and masseurs 20 baht is appropriate and 10 baht for porters.

Toilets

The classier hotels have conventional WCs, but if you are intending to stay in guesthouses you will doubtless encounter Thai-style toilets, which involve squatting over a floor-level basin. Initially it seems a feat of both careful balancing and aiming, but as no part of the body is in contact with the basin (in theory) it is quite hygenic.

A hose with spray attachment may be provided for cleaning your nether portions afterwards; the water pressure can be ferocious and mildly alarming first time around. For those who prefer to use toilet paper (which is commonly available) bins are usually provided as the discarded pieces often block the pipes.

Public toilets are rare but most restaurants do not object to non-customers using this facility. Simply ask for the *horng nahm*.

Tourist Offices

The Tourism Authority of Thailand (TAT) has offices across Thailand; on the whole, these are a fairly useful source of local information and free hand-outs, although even here there is often a frustrating language barrier. TATs do not provide a booking service.

TATs in Thailand

Bangkok	(Head Office) 4 Ratchadamnoen Nok Avenue, Bangkok, 10100; (tel: (02) 282 1143).
Chiang Mai	105/1 Chiang Mai–Lamphun Road, Chiang Mai 50000; (tel: (053) 248604).
Chiang Rai	Singklai Road, Chiang Rai 57000; (tel: (053) 717433).
Cha-am	500/51 Phetkasem Road, Amphoe Cha-am, Phetcha Buri 76120; (tel: (032) 471502).
Hat Yai	1/1 Soi 2 Niphat Uthit 3 Road, Hat Yai, Songkhla 90110; (tel: (074) 243747).
Kanchana Buri	Saeng Chuto Road, Kanchana Buri 71000; (tel: (034) 511200).
Khon Kaen	2nd Floor Salaphachakhom, Soonratchakarn Road, Khon Kaen; (tel: (043) 244498).
Nakhon Ratchasima	2102–2104 Mittraphap Road, Nakhon Ratchasima 30000; (tel: (044) 243427).
Nakhon Si Thammarat	1180 Bovorn Bazaar, Ratchadamnoen Road, Nakhon Si Thammarat 80000; (tel: (075) 356356).
Pattaya	382/1 Chaihat Road, South Pattaya 20260; (tel: (038) 428750).
Phitsanulok	209/7–8 Surasi Trade Center, Boromtrailokanat Road, Phitsanulok 65000; (tel: (055) 252742).
Phuket	73–5 Phuket Road, Phuket 83000; (tel: (076) 212213).
Suratthani	5 Talat Mai Road, Ban Don, Suratthani 84000; (tel: (077) 282828).
Ubon Ratchathani	264/1 Khuan Thani Road, Ubon Ratchathani 34000; (tel: (045) 243770).

TATs Overseas

Australia	Royal Exchange Building, 56 Pitt Street, Sydney 2000; (tel: (02) 247 7549).

| **UK** | 49 Albemarle Street, London W1X 3FE; (tel: (071) 499 7679). |
| **US** | 5 World Trade Center, Suite No 3443, New York, NY 10048; (tel: (212) 432 0433); 3440 Wilshire Boulevard, Suite 1100, Los Angeles, CA 90010; (tel: (213) 382 2353); 303 East Wacker Drive, Suite 400, Chicago, IL 60601; (tel: (312) 819 3990). |

There are also offices in France, Germany, Hong Kong, Italy, Japan, Malaysia and Singapore, but not in Canada, Ireland or New Zealand.

Walking and Hiking

If you want to see Thailand on foot, the obvious way is to take an organised trek.

There are trails in national parks, two described in this book, but the nationwide spread of purpose-made walks is rather thin and the central plain is too monotonous for worthwhile hiking anyway.

The dangers of getting lost in remote areas are very real, and foreign visitors have been attacked in borderlands. Those who plan to do some hiking should take some light boots with ankle support, plenty of water and spare food; be prepared for mosquitoes, leeches and heat exhaustion.

Treks to Hill Tribe Villages Treks are big business in the north; street bureaux, hotels and guesthouses offer packages lasting between two and seven days, where you stay in tribal village homes, and trek in the hills on foot, by elephant and by bamboo raft. At best this can offer exhilarating views and a glimpse into subsistence cultures. However, a poorly run trek, passing zoo-like commercialised villages and going through unvarying scenery can be an expensive disappointment.

Hints

- Recommendation from other travellers is the best way to choose a trek. Check exactly what is included (food, first-aid, transport, itinerary) and what the trek is like.
- Don't necessarily restrict yourself to treks from Chiang Mai; less frequented places (Mae Hong Son, Chiang Rai, Pai, Mae Sot and Nan among them) may be better.
- Try to meet the other members of your party before you go. Four to eight is a good group size.
- Leave valuables behind (except your credit cards); take only a little cash (but itemise anything you leave in a guesthouse).
- Walking can be tough going in the hills, elephant rides are uncomfortable and rafts often capsize.
- Travel light; take a backpack, sleeping bag, sweater, washkit, towel and swimsuit, and rainwear between June and October.
- Ask before taking photos of tribespeople.
- Carry mosquito repellent and take clothes to cover your arms and legs; tobacco and water combined makes a good leech repellent.

275

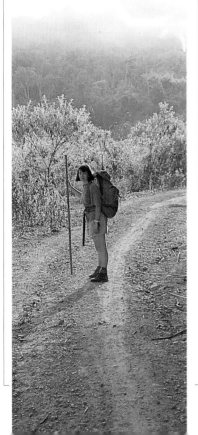

DIRECTORY

Accommodation
Thailand offers a huge range of accommodation.

Luxury
Top hotels are every bit as luxurious as their Western counterparts, and prices are nearly as high. In major cities and tourist areas the up-market hotel scene has boomed in recent years. Nearly all the better hotels are modern, typically with marble foyers like airport lounges and comfortable (though not memorably interesting) air-conditioned rooms with bathrooms *en suite*. Many have swimming pools, restaurants, laundry service, currency exchange, international telephone and tour desk, and some have business centres. Bangkok's Oriental and the Hotel Sofitel Central in Hua Hin are among the few quality old-style hotels.

At weekends many rich Thais stay in and party at 'resort hotels' — bungalow developments in quiet country areas. Many such establishments pride themselves on their gardening skills: waist-high orchids border immaculate lawns dotted with old-style buffalo carts (every resort must have at least one of these!). These places can be wonderfully relaxing, and good for meeting Thais.

Budget
At the budget end of the scale two can stay for under 100 baht per night. Don't expect clean sheets (usually an under-sheet only is provided), and it is wise to take a sheet, pillowcase, bath plug, toilet paper, soap and towels. As a rule, showers dispense cold water only, except in the far north. Most places are noisy – crowing roosters, traffic, music and howling dogs keep all but the deepest sleeper awake; earplugs are invaluable.

Cheap accommodation divides into hotels, often bland concrete blocks – many double as brothels – and guesthouses. Many of the most basic hotels are depressing; the advantages are private bathrooms (a cold shower and toilet) and a bed (as opposed to a mattress on the floor).

Guesthouses
These vary much more in style; many are private Thai homes adapted for the purpose, while some in country areas are thatched bamboo bungalows. Nearly all offer meals, with an English menu. Beds are hard; you may sleep on a thin mattress on the floor. Guesthouses are excellent for meeting other travellers (Thais rarely stay in such places), and often have local tourist information; many offer tours and treks (in Chiang Mai trekking is a hard-sell business; guests who don't want to go on a trek are often told to leave). There is rarely a problem finding accommodation except at certain holiday periods. *Tuk tuk* and *samlor* drivers get commissions from guesthouses when they bring you to them and will ask virtually any luggage-bearing *farang* if they need somewhere to stay. Even in non-tourist towns there is usually a cheap hotel (not necessarily with an English sign). Although room rates are fixed in high season, it is possible to get generous discounts on higher-priced accommodation off-season. As a rough guide, price bands denote prices for a standard double room:

Budget Up to 300B. Hotels and guesthouses marked * fall into the super-cheap category, with rooms for two for 100B or less.
Moderate 300—800B.
Expensive Over 800B.

Eating out
This is an essential part of the national lifestyle. Accordingly, food is served on virtually every street corner and prices are very low. The Thais are fastidious about food preparation and generally you don't have to be concerned about your stomach.

Run-of-the-mill restaurants tend not to dress themselves up; plastic tables are the norm and with a lot of places you will find yourself sitting outside. Look for the places which the locals frequent; some will have an English menu, but it is wise to carry a phrasebook. If you get stuck, simply point to a dish someone else is eating and which you happen to fancy. Menus are often very long, typically based on stir-fry rice concoctions (rice with chicken and ginger, sweet and sour pork with rice, fried morning glory with rice), seafood, soups and noodles. Sometimes you pay a little more for surroundings; floating restaurants are popular in many waterside towns. Western food is offered in many tourist areas; prices are substantially higher than Thai food and the quality will sometimes only tempt the very homesick traveller! But there are numerous places where you can eat as well as back home; many of these are included in these listings. Up-market eating establishments are plentiful in the main tourist centres; in smaller, less frequented towns the best restaurants are often to be found in the top hotels.

Except in big centres, try to eat reasonably early; many establishments close by 21.00hrs.

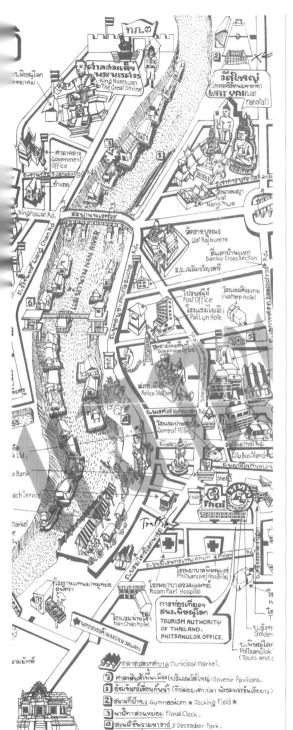

ทภ.๓

ศาลสมเด็จ
พระนเรศวร
King Naresuan
The Great Shrine

วัดใหญ่
(วัดพระศรีรัตนมหาธาตุ)
WAT YAI (Wat Mahatat)

ว.พิษณุโลก
พิทยาคม

ศาลาลาง
Government
Office

การนครอง
อำเภอ

Singhawat Rd.

สะพานนเรศวร

แม่น้ำน่าน NAN RIVER

วัดนางพญา
Wat Nang Phya

ถ.พุทธบูชา Phutta Bucha Rd.

วัดราชบูรณะ
Wat Rajburana

สี่แยกบ้านแขก
Bankee Cross Section

ร.ร. เฉลิมขวัญสตรี

ไปรษณีย์
Post Office

โรงแรมศิวเทพ
Sivathep Hotel

โรงแรมไพลิน
Pai Lyn Hole

ที่ทำการโทรศัพท์
Telephone Office

สถานีตำรวจ
Police Station

ถ.นเรศวร Naresuan Rd.

โรงแรมรัตนาปาร์ค
Sombat Hotel

ที่โรงแรม

Sailuethai Rd.

City Bus Stand

ถ.เอกาทศรฐ Ekatossaroth Rd.

ถ.อยุธยา Ayothaya Rd.

Shell

Esso

Thai

Trolli

ถ.ราชดำเนิน

โรงพยาบาลเทพ Khun A Phiter

โรงพยาบาลพิษณุเวช
Phitsanuvej Hospital

โรงพยาบาลรวมแพทย์
Ruam Paet Hospital

โรงแรมน่านเจ้า
Nan Chao Hotel

นครสวรรค์/NAKORN SAWAN

การท่องเที่ยว
สนง.พิษณุโลก
TOURISM AUTHORITY
OF THAILAND.
PHITSANULOK OFFICE.

Golden

บ.พิษณุโลก
Phitsanulok
(Tours and

ยามยักษ์

วัดจุฬามณี Wat Chula Manee

ตลาดเทศบาล Municipal Market.

⑥ ศาลาสันเต้านั่มเมือง (บริเวณวัดใหญ่) Sovenir Pavilions.

① อนุสรณ์สะพานข้ามน้ำ (ที่ลอยเต้า,ปลา พัชชุมแพงจันเรือยาง) Jocking Field ★

② สนามกีฬา จ. Gymnasium ★

③ นาฬิกาส่วนหย่อม Floral Clock .

④ สวน๕ธันวาความหาราช 5 December Park .

⑤ ตลาดนัดเช้าตรู่ Early Morning Vegetable Market (๔.00 a.m.

DIRECTORY

BANGKOK

Accommodation

Expensive

Airport Hotel 333 Choet Watthakat Road (tel:(02) 566 1020–1; 566 2060–9). Only decent hotel in airport area; short stays available.

Ambassador Hotel Soi 11 Sukhumvit Road (tel: (02) 254 0444). Good entertainment complex and food centre.

Dusit Thani Hotel Rama IV Road (tel: (02) 233 1130). One of the more expensive.

Imperial Hotel Wireless Road (tel: (02) 254 0023). Extensive grounds in embassy district.

Indra Regent Ratchaprarop Road (tel:(02) 251 1111).

Montien Hotel 54 Surawong Road (tel: (02) 234 8060).Also puts on plays.

The Oriental 48 Oriental Avenue, Bangkok (tel: (02) 236-0400/39). Attraction in itself, the old wing carefully preserved.

Regent 155 Ratchadamri Road Bangkok (tel: (02) 251 6127). Elegant dining room.

Shangri-La Hotel 89 Soi Wat Suan Phlu, Charoen Krung Road (tel: (02) 236 7777). Riverside views.

Siam Intercontinental Hotel 967 Rama I Road (tel: (02) 235 0355).Spread out at ground level.

Viengtai Hotel 42 Tanee Road (tel: (02) 282 5788). Banglamphu's luxury offering.

Moderate

Federal Hotel 27 Soi 11 Sukhumvit Road (tel: (02) 253 0175/6). Clean, efficient and safe, pool; old ex-pat stamping ground.

Grace Hotel,12 Nana North (Soi 3) Sukhumvit Road (tel: (02) 252 9170–3).

Honey Hotel 31 Soi 19 Sukhumvit Road (tel: (02) 253 30646–9). All the mod cons, relatively expensive.

Lost Horizons House Phaholyothin Road 2 (tel: (02) 79 4967). Bed-and-breakfast, classical old Thai house.

Malaysia Hotel 54 Soi Ngam Duphli (tel: (02) 286 3582/7263). Hot water, swimming pool.

Mermaid's Rest Guesthouse 6/1 Soi 8 Sukhumvit Road, Bangkok, 10110 (tel: (02) 253 3648). Swimming pool, quiet garden, good restaurant.

Miami Hotel Soi 13 Sukhumvit Road (tel: (02) 252 5140; 252 4759; 252 5036).

Old; good pool.

New World Guest House and Apartment 2 Samsen Road Soi 2 (tel: (02) 281 5596). Sparse air-conditioned rooms, long-term option.

Reno Hotel Soi Kasem San 1, Rama I (tel: (02) 215 0026/7). Open 24 hours, pleasant swimming pool.

Rex Hotel 762/1 Soi 32 Sukhumvit Road (tel: (02) 259 0106). Comfortable.

Royal Hotel 2 Ratchadamnoen Road (tel: (02) 222 9111–20). Famous old hotel, entrance on Sanam Luang.

Star Hotel 31/1 Soi Kasem San 1, Rama I Road (tel: (02) 215 0020/1). Old, clean, near Siam Square, OK.

SV Guesthouse 19/35/36 Soi 19 Sukhumvit Road (tel: (02) 253 060; 253 1747). Small, no extras, clean.

Budget

* 59 Guesthouse 59 Tanao Road (Trok Boworn Rangsi) (tel: (02) 281 9031)). Basic, moderately comfortable wooden house, shared bathroom.

* Apple Guesthouse 10/1 Phra Athit Road (tel: (02)281 6838). Basic but relaxed atmosphere.

* Bonny Guest House 13 Khao San Road (tel: (02) 281 9877). Clean and quiet.

* Central Guesthouse 10 Trok Boworn Rangsi (tel: (02) 282 0667). Cheap shared bathrooms, clean.

CH Guest House 216 Khao San Road (tel: (02) 282 2023). Opens late, lively mix.

Green Guesthouse 27 Soi Chanasongkhram, Phra Athit Road (tel: (02) 282-8994).

Hello Guesthouse 63–5 Khao San Road (tel: (02) 281 8579). Has a fair restaurant.

New Siam Guesthouse 21 Soi Chanasongkram, Phra Athit Road, Banglamphu (tel: (02) 282 4554). Recently opened, quiet and clean. Handy location for the river-bus.

Peachy Guesthouse 10 Phra Athit Road (tel: (02) 281 6471). Organised much more like a hotel. Convenient for the Express Boat pier at Tha Phra Athit.

Rose Garden Guesthouse 62 Soi Chanasongkhram (tel: (02) 282 4724). Fine situation of tall shophouse with quiet courtyards outside.

Windy Guesthouse 6/116 Soi Plokjit, Rama IV Road (tel: (02) 251 3176). Cool, clean, cheap, wonderful view of city.

Restaurants

Expensive

Bourbon Street 29/4-6 Washington Square, Soi 22, Sukhumvit Road (tel: (02) 259 0328/9). Jambalaya, crawfish pie and other

Southern American specialities.

Himali Cha Cha (Indian) 1229/11 Charoen Krung Road (between Surawong and Silom roads) (tel: (02) 235 1569) Very good Indian food, book in the evening.

Sorn Daeng Democracy Monument (tel: (02) 224 3088). Old-established Thai establishment.

Whole Earth Vegetarian Restaurant Lang Suan Road (off Rama I Road) (tel: (02) 252 5574). Clean but rather pricey.

Moderate

Ambassador Food Centre Ambassador Hotel (tel: (02) 254 0444) Self-service cornucopia of regional and foreign foods, with all the Thai favourites. Pay by coupon.

Mrs Balbir's (Indian) 155/18 Sukhumvit Soi 11 (tel: (02) 253 2281/255 4236). Good range, good décor, good prices.

Bussaracum, 425 Soi Pipat 2, Silom (tel: (02) 234 2600); 35 Soi Pipat 2, off Convent Road, Silom (tel: (02) 235 8915). Top marks for content and presentation; traditional Thai food with traditional musical backing.

Budget

Vegetarian Restaurant Trok Boworn Rangsi, Tanao Road, Banglamphu (no tel). Very tasty; excellent value.

CENTRAL THAILAND

AYUTTHAYA
Accommodation
Budget
B J Guesthouse off Naresuan Road (tel: 251512). One of few guesthouses in the area.

KANCHANA BURI
Accommodation
Moderate
Erawan Resort 140 Moo 4 Tha Kadan Srisawat (tel: (034) 513568). Handy for Erawan waterfalls.
Kasem Island Resort (south of JEATH museum), Kanchana Buri (tel: (034) 511603). Pretty, island site; thatched-hut resort; tours. Rather noisy during weekends.
River Kwae Cabin (Tham Krasae railway station), Amphon Sai Yok (tel: (02) 421 4869). Bungalows set on scenic river curve below historic railway viaduct.
Sam's Place Song Khwai Road (tel: (034) 513971). Quaint river-raft ambience, clean.

Budget
Bamboo Guesthouse 3–5 Soi Vietnam, Tha Makham, Kanchana Buri (tel: (034) 512532). Quiet, river views; near the Kwae Bridge.
*Jolly Frog Backpackers 28 Maenamkwea Road, Chaina (Sub) Road, Kanchana Buri, (tel: (034) 514579). Set on the river.
*PS Guesthouse 3 Rong Heeb Oil Road, Kanchana Buri (tel: (034) 513039). Out of the main noise zone; charming sitting room area above river; tours.
*River Guesthouse 42 Rong Heeb Oil Road, Kanchana Buri (tel: (034) 512491). Rafthouses built on the Kwae; tours.

KHAO YAI
Accommodation
Expensive
Juldis Khao Yai Resort 54 Moo 4, Thanarat Road, Thumbol Moo-Sri Pakchong (tel for reservations: (02) 255 5070 ext 7112981). One

of several up-market resort hotels outside Khao Yai; rural location.

KO SAMET
Accommodation
Budget/Moderate
Naga Bungalow Ao Hin Khok. Pleasant layout; amenities include a lending library.
Sea Breeze Bungalow, Ao Phai. Self-contained units available.

LOP BURI
Accommodation
Budget
Asia Lop Buri Sorasak Road, Lop Buri (tel:(036) 411892). Standard but very clean; located opposite palace gate.
*Nett 17/1–2 Ratchadamnoen Road, Lop Buri (tel: (036) 411738). Behind the Asia; has slightly smaller rooms.
*Travellers' Drop-in Centre 34 Wichayen Road, Soi 3 Muang, Lop Buri (no tel). Run by an English teacher; guests are encouraged to join in with English lessons! Very informal and relaxing atmosphere.

PHETCHA BURI
Accommodation
Budget
Khao Wang 36 Tambol Klong Krasang (tel: (032) 425167). Good value, simple and straightforward accommodation.
Phetkasem 14 Tambol Rai Som (tel: (032) 425581).Clean and basic: also good value.

SI RACHA (Ko Si Chang)
Moderate/Budget
Thiw Phai Guesthouse Tha Thewawong (tel: (038) 216084/5) Big price range, helpful owner, late-night café.
Benz Bungalow Moo 3 Tha Thewawong (tel: (038) 216091). Sea view from private bungalows.

TRAT
Accommodation
Moderate/Budget
Thai Roong Roj 296 Viwattana (tel: 511141). Clean; has air-conditioned rooms.

CHIANG MAI
Accommodation
Expensive

Chiang Inn 100 Changklan Road, Chiang Mai (tel: (053) 270070). Comfortable hotel near night market.

Chiang Mai Orchid 100–102 Huay Kaew Road, Chiang Mai (tel: (053) 222099). Celebrated, exclusive and priced accordingly.

Chiang Mai Plaza 92 Sri Donchai Road, Chiang Mai (tel: (053) 270036). Roomy, well-sited; swimming pool, good restaurant; shopping mall.

Dusit Inn 112 Changklan Road, Chiang Mai (tel: (053) 251033). Stylish, light interior; swimming pool, restaurants.

Once Upon a Time (Kan La Khrang Neung) (see **Restaurants**).

Rincome Huay Kaew Road, Chiang Mai (tel: (053) 221044). Fine luxury hotel, antiques and tasteful decor.

Rim Ping Garden 411 Charoen Prathet Road, Chiang Mai (tel: (053) 281060). On the river; landscaped garden setting, pavilion-style.

River View Lodge 25 Charoen Prathet Road Soi 2, Chiang Mai (tel: (053) 271109). Family run, simple rooms.

Moderate

Erawan Resort 149/10 Chiang Khian Road, Amphoe Mae Rim, on Highway 1096 (tel: (053) 272120). Popular hill resort with pretty grounds.

Galare Guesthouse 7 Chareon Prathet Road, Chiang Mai (tel: (053) 273885). On the river; excellent value and central location.

Gap's House 3 Ratchadamnoen Road Soi 4, Chiang Mai (tel: (053) 278140). 'Antique house' in a garden haven; traditional teak-built rooms.

Lai Thai Guesthouse 111/4–5 Kotchasarn Road, Chiang Mai (tel: (053) 251725). Cheerful if plain; main-road site.

Kansadal Resort (on Highway 1096), Km 18, Maerim Samerng Road (tel: (053) 252853). Hillside bungalows overlooking waterfall.

Mae Ping 153 Sri Donchai Road, Chiang Mai (tel: (053) 270160). Tower block near night bazaar. Has tour desk and many other services; attractively designed.

Mae Sa Valley PO Box 5 Mae Rim, Chiang Mai 50/80 (on Highway 1096) (tel: (053) 297980). Charming bungalows in a hillside resort.

Suan Doi House 38/3 Soi Charntrasup, Huay Kaew Road (opp. Rincome Hotel), Chiang Mai (tel: (053) 221869). Amid quiet, intimate gardens.

Top North Guesthouse 15 Moon Muang Road Soi 2, Chiang Mai (tel: (053) 213900). Plain, quiet; pool.

Top North Hotel 41 Tha Phae Road, Chiang Mai (tel: (053) 210531). Fair comfort at a modest price.

Moderate/Budget

Riverfront Resort (Tha-Nam), 43/3 Mua 2 T.Pardad, Changklan Road, Chiang Mai (tel: (053) 275125). Antiques, river terrace; quiet location, south of centre.

Thailand Guest House 38/1 Moon Muang Road Soi 2 (no tel). Clean, friendly.

Budget

*Je t'Aime Guesthouse 247–9 Charoenrat Road, Chiang Mai (tel: (053) 241912). White houses surround a lawn shaded by palms and longan trees.

*La Maloon Guesthouse 1 Jaban Road, Tambon Pha Singh, Chiang Mai (tel:(053) 271001). Old-style house at centre of city moat.

Pha Thai Guesthouse 48/1 Rachapakinai Road, Chiang Mai (tel: (053) 278013). Clean, quiet and friendly.

*Saitum Guesthouse 21 Moonmuang Road, Chiang Mai (tel: (053) 248545). Basic backpackers' bungalows, convenient site. No hard-sell treks!

Restaurants
Expensive

Jasmine Dusit Inn Hotel, 112 Changklan Road, Chiang Mai (tel: (053) 251033). Leading Chinese restaurant with good *dim sum*.

Le Coq d'Or 68/1 Koh Klang Road, Nong Hoi, Chiang Mai (tel: (053) 282024). Fine continental cuisine; just south of town.

Le Grillade Chiang Inn Hotel, 100 Changklan Road, Chiang Mai (tel: (053) 270070). Top French cuisine, top service.

Le Pavillon Orchid Hotel, 100–102 Huey Kaew Road, Chiang Mai (tel: (053) 222099). The quality and prices one expects from the city's classiest hotel.

Moderate

Ban Suan 51/3 San Kamphaeng Road, Chiang Mai (tel: (053) 242116). Authentic Thai food; in a teak house just out of town.

Diamond Hotel 33/10 Charoen Phratat Road, Chiang Mai (tel: (053) 234155). Kantoke dinners in an antique hall.

Galae 65 Suthep Road, Chiang Mai (tel: (053) 222235). Nicely set by a lake at the foot of Doi Suthep.

The Gallery 25–29 Charoenrat Road, Chiang Mai (tel: (053) 248601). Well-prepared Thai food; riverside venue.

Old Chiang Mai Cultural Centre 185/3 Wualai Road, Chiang Mai (tel: (053) 235097). Leading kantoke dinner venue, popular with tour parties.

Once Upon A Time (Kan La Khrang Neung), 385/2 Charoen Prathet Road, near Mengrai Bridge, Chiang Mai (tel: (053) 274932). Beautifully restored old houses, period décor, kantoke dinners.

Riverfront (Tha Nam), 43/3 Mua 2 T Pardad, Changklan Road (tel: (053) 275125). Quiet riverside location; traditional Thai orchestra.

Whole Earth 88 Si Donchai Road, Chiang Mai (tel: (053) 282463). Lanna style house; Thai vegetarian, Indian and Pakistani meals.

Budget

Aroon Rai 45 Kotchasarn Road, Chiang Mai (tel: (053) 276947). Plain but good; North Thai cuisine.

AUM Vegetarian Restaurant Moon Muang Road (near Ratchadamnoen Road at Tha Phae Gate), Chiang Mai

(no tel). Run by an Indian sect; threadbare décor, but appetising food.

JJ Bakery and Coffee Shop Montri Hotel, 2–6 Ratchadamnoen Road, Chiang Mai (tel: (053) 211069). Bright, fast-service, wholly Westernised.

Takrite 13–19 Samran 1 Road, Chiang Mai (tel: (053) 278333). Celebrated Thai food; a favourite with locals.

CHIANG RAI
Accommodation
Expensive

Dusit Island 1129 Kraisorasit Road, Chiang Rai (tel: (053) 715777). Island site; great views, top prices.

Wangcome 869/90 Pemawiphata Road, Chiang Rai (tel: (053) 711800). A safe bet, in the town centre. Modern, comfortable rooms.

Wiang Inn 893 Phahonyothin Road, Chiang Rai (tel: (053) 711543). Smart modern block; spacious and popular.

Moderate

Saenphu 389 Baphaprakam, Chiang Rai (tel: (053) 717300). Good value modern comfort.

Budget

*Ben Guesthouse** 351/10 Sankhongnoi Road Soi 4, Chiang Rai (tel: (053) 716775). Modern Lanna-style; hot showers; 1km out.

Boonbundan Guesthouse 1005/13 Jedyod Road, Chiang Rai (tel: (053) 717040). Spotless, modern, quiet yet central.

Chiang Saen Guesthouse Chiang Saen–Sop Ruak Road (no tel). Odd but comfortable 'wigwam' huts, clean bathrooms.

***Mae Hong Son Guesthouse** 126 Singhakai Road, Chiang Rai.(no tel). Characterful but very basic.

Mae Kok Villa 445 Singhakhai Road (tel: (053) 711786). Cheap and well-equipped bungalows.

Siam Guesthouse Chiang Saen–Sop Ruak Road (tel: (053) 711077). Motorcycle hire service

Tourist Inn 1000/4–6 Jedyod Road, Chiang Rai

(tel: (053) 714682). Offers Thai massage, free cycles.

Restaurants
Moderate

La Cantina 528/20–21 Banpaprakan Road, Chiang Rai (tel: (054) 716808). Authentic Italian food.

Phrae Barbeque 869/135 Thaiwiwat Road (near Wangcome Hotel), Chiang Rai (tel: (054) 714519). Japanese, Thai, Chinese and European food.

Budget

Chiang Rai Deli 528/16 Banpaprakarn Road, Chiang Rai. Excellent bakery selling fresh-baked, filled rolls.

LAMPANG
Accommodation
Expensive

Thipchang 54/22 Takrao Noi Road, Lampang (tel: (054) 226501). 131-room tower block in city centre.

Moderate

Asia Lampang 229 Boonyawat Road, Lampang (tel: (054) 217844). Competent if unspectacular.

Budget

***No 4 Guesthouse** 54 Pamai Road, Vieng Nuea, Lampang. Old-style house with polished teak floors. One of an excellent chain in the north.

Restaurants
Budget

Riverside 328 Thipchang Road, Lampang (tel: (054) 221861). Fair menu, live country music; on the river.

MAE HONG SON
Accommodation
Expensive

Holiday Inn 114/5–7 Khunlumprapas Road, Mae Hong Son (tel: (053) 611390). Comfortable, imposing block just outside town. International cuisine.

Mae Hong Son Resort 24 Ban Huay Daer, Mae Hong Son (tel: (053) 611504). Secluded resort 6km from town. Shuttle to airport.

Tara Mae Hong Son Hotel 149, Moo 8, Tambon Pang Moo, Mae Hong Son 58000

DIRECTORY

(tel: (053) 611 473 611272/ 611483). Opened Jan 1991. Located in a teak forest.

Budget
*Cave Lodge Tham Lot, Soppong (outside Mae Hong Son; no tel). Finely sited by Tham Lot cave; organised day treks.
*Holiday House 23 Pradit Jongkam Road, Mae Hong Son (no tel). Plain; nicely sited by Jongkharn Lake.
Jean's House 6 Pracha Uthit Road, Mae Hong Son (tel: (053) 611308). Informal, airy; the owner is an artist.
Maelana Guesthouse Maelana village, off a T-junction halfway along the Mae Hong Son–Pai road (no tel). Very basic, a must for the adventurous.
*Jungle Guesthouse Soppong (no tel). Pretty, if basic, huts above a stream.
*Pai River Lodge Guesthouse Pai (no tel). Huts ranged around a riverside lawn.
*PS Riverside Guesthouse Pai (tel: (053) 699159). Ask for a hut fronting the river; the other huts are unremarkable.
Sang Tong Huts Phachachon U-Tish Road, Mae Hong Son (no tel). On the edge of town; the prettiest of a cluster of guesthouses, with good views.
*Wilderness Lodge west of Soppong, 2km off main road, at Ban Nam Khong (no tel). Ultra simple paradise for the adventurer; run by same owners as Cave Lodge.

Restaurants
Moderate
Fern 87 Khunlumprapas Road, Mae Hong Son (tel: (053) 611374). Mellow, cane decor, soft-lit; very reasonable prices. Thai.

Budget
Inthira 170/1 Moo 2, Wiang Mai Road, Mae Sariang (tel: (053) 681441). Popular, cheap; above-average food.
Thai Yai 12 Rungsiyanon Road, Pai (tel: (053) 699093). *Farang*-oriented café; good wholemeal bread.

MAE SAI
Accommodation
Expensive
Golden Triangle Resort 222 Golden Triangle, Chiang Saen (tel: (6653) 714801). Scenically poised high-rise block at the meeting point of three countries.

Budget
*Ban Tam-mi-la 8/1–8/4 Sai Klang Road, Ban Wat Kaeo Wieng, Chiang Khong (tel: (053) 791234). Thatched bungalows in tiny garden by the Mekong River.
*Mae Sai Guesthouse 688 Wiengpangkam, Mae Sai (tel: (053) 732021). Wonderful river site looking into Burma.
*Northern Guesthouse 402 Tumphajom Road, Mae Sai (tel: (053) 731537). Pleasant riverside bungalows.
Ruenthai Rim Nan Guesthouse Sai Klang Road Soi 1, Chiang Khong (tel: (053) 791023). Perched above the Mekong River; carved wood veranda.

MAE SOT
Accommodation
Expensive
Mae Sot Hills 100 Asia Highway, Mae Sot (tel: (055) 532601). Just out of town; pool; travel centre adjacent.

Budget
*No 4 Guesthouse 736 Indharakiri Road, Mae Sot (no tel). Clean teak house 1km from town centre.
Porn Thep 25/4 Soi Srivieng, Prasartviti Road, Mae Sot (tel: (055) 532590). Fair budget–moderate hotel near market.
Siam 185 Prasartviti Road, Mae Sot (tel: (055) 531176). Functional concrete block; fan and air-con.
Umphang Hut Umphang (tel: (055) 513316 or 513320). Situated in village centre; four-bed rooms and bungalows; hot showers.

NAN
Accommodation
Moderate
Dhevaraj 466 Sumondhevaraj Road, Nan (tel: (054) 710094). The best in town; central.

Budget
*Nan Guesthouse 57/16 Mahaphom Road, Nan (tel: (054) 771148). Basic but friendly; good local information.
*Youth Hostel 3/1 Robmung Road, Nan (tel: (054) 710322). Plain, friendly. Trekking.

Restaurants
Budget
Tiptop 99/6–7 Mahawong Road, Nan. Swiss-owned; pizzas and other Western fare.

PHITSANULOK
Accommodation
Expensive
Phailin 38 Baromatrailokanart Road, Phitsanulok (tel: (055) 252411). Roomy suites and the best views in town.
Rajapruk 99/9 Pra-ongdarm Road, Phitsanulok (tel: (055) 258788 or 258477). Fair comfort, fair value. A few steps away from the centre.

Moderate
Thep Nakorn 43/1 Sri
hamtripidok Road,
Phitsanulok (tel: (055)
44070). Good value,
standard hotel.

Budget
No 4 Guesthouse 11/12
Akathodsarot Road,
Phitsanulok (no tel).
Friendly family house; Thai
massage, free bicycles.
Ratchaphruk Guesthouse
Pra-ongdarm Road,
Phitsanulok (tel: (055)
258477). Fan and air-con;
tolerably quiet.
*Youth Hostel 38 Sanam
Bin Road, Phitsanulok;
15–20 minutes' walk from
centre (tel: (055) 242060).
Antique beds and creaky
charm; no evening meals.

PHRAE
Accommodation
Expensive
Maeyom Palace
Yantarakijkosol Road, Phrae
(tel: (054) 522906). Pleasant
six-storey block opposite
bus station.

Budget
*No 4 Guesthouse 22 Soi 1,
Yantarakijkosol Road, Phrae
(no tel). Small, cool house;
friendly; local information.
Quiet back road near bus
station.

SI SATCHANALAI
Accommodation
Expensive
Wang Yom 78/2 Moo 6 Si
Satchanalai (tel: (055)
611179). Peaceful gardens
with rustic bungalows;
simple facilities. By old city.

Restaurants
Moderate
Wang Yom 78/2 Moo Sri
Satchanalai, Sri Satchanalai
(tel: (055) 61179).
Standard menu, but a lovely
garden setting.

SUKOTHAI
Accommodation
Expensive
Phailin 10 Moo 1
Jarodvithithong Road,
Sukothai (tel: (055) 613310).
Hexagonal courtyard
around a pool; handy for
the old city.

Moderate
Rajtanee 229
Jarodvithithong Road,
Sukothai (tel (055) 611031).
Convenient, well located;
dining room, coffee shop.

Budget
*No 4B Guesthouse 170
Thanee Road, Sukothai (tel:
(055) 611315). Prettiest of
three No 4 Guesthouses in
town; teak house by river.
River View 92
Nikhonkasem Road,
Sukothai (tel: (055) 611656).
Good river views; fan and
air–conditioning.
*Somprasong Guesthouse
32 Pravetnakoly Road,
Sukothai (tel: (055) 611709).
Modern block by river; free
bicycles.

Restaurants
Moderate
Dream Café Chaba
Suwatmaykin, 86/1
Singhawat Road, Sukothai
(tel: (055) 611682). Antique-
laden fantasy interior.
Western and Thai food.

NORTHEAST
THAILAND

LOEI
Accommodation
Expensive/Moderate
King Hotel 11/9-12 Chumsai
Road (tel: (042) 811701,
811783) Best in town;
Chinese hotel.

Budget
*Nong Ball Guesthouse
Chai Khong Rd, Chiang Kong
district (no tel). Good
restaurant..

MUKDAHAN
Accommodation
Budget
*Hua Nam Hotel 20 Samut
Sakdarak Road (tel: (042)
611137) Clean, shared
bathroom.

NAKHON RATCHASIMA
(Khorat)
Accommodation
Moderate
Anajak Hotel 62/1
Chomsurangyart Road (tel:
(044)243825) Very good
service.

Budget
*Muang Thong Hotel 46
Chomphon Road (tel: (044)
242090). Cheapest in town,
picturesque old building.
Fa Sang Hotel 1124
Mukkhamontri Road (near
railway station) (tel: (044)
242143). Next cheapest; air-
conditioned rooms.

NONG KHAI
Accommodation
Budget
Sawasdi Guesthouse
Mechai Road (no tel). Cheap
Russian air-conditioning.
Pool Sub Hotel 843 Mechai
Road (tel: (042) 411031).
Oldest hotel in town,
average Chinese fare.
*TXK Guesthouse.
Sangkhom district, on the
river bank (no tel). Tranquil
setting, rural facilities.

SURIN
Accommodation
Budget
Saeng Thong Hotel 155–61
Thanasan Road (tel: (044)
511302). Big, anonymous.
*Phirom Guesthouse Krung
Sri Nai Road (tel: (044)
51540). Friendly owner;
tours (see page 209).

SOUTHERN
THAILAND

CHUMPHON
Accommodation
Expensive/Moderate
Jansom Chumphon
188/56–66 Saladaeng Road
(tel: (077) 502502). Excellent
service; comfortable.

Moderate
Chumphon Cabana Thung
Wua Laen Beach, Saphil (tel:
(077) 501990; reservations
(02) 224 1884). Deserted
beach, boat tours, diving.

Budget
Si Tai Fa Hotel 73–4
Saladaeng Road (tel: (077)
511063). Clean, view of
green gardens; restaurant.

HAT YAI
Accommodation
Moderate/Expensive
Kosit Hotel 199 Niphta
Uthit 2 Road (tel: (074)

283

DIRECTORY

244711). Clean, well located, quiet.

Budget
Cathay Hotel Niphat Uthit Road (near railway station; no tel). Guesthouse atmosphere.

HUA HIN
Accommodation
Expensive
Sofitel Central 1 Damnoen Kasem Road (tel: (034) 512021–30) Old railway hotel now in restored splendour.

KO PHI PHI (Krabi)
Accommodation
Expensive /Moderate
Phi Phi Island Cabana Ao Ton Sai (tel: (075) 612132). Good (if pricey) restaurant, lively.

KO SAMUI
Accommodation
Budget
Pearl Bay Bungalow Pangkha Bay. Comfortable huts, quiet, out of the way.

KRABI
Accommodation
Moderate
Phra Nang Place near Krabi (tel: (075) 612172). Bungalows by an idyllic beach and palms amid stunning limestone cliffs; 45 minutes by boat from Krabi. **Thai Hotel** 7 Issara Road (tel: (075) 611122). Clean and comfortable; tour services available.

Budget
Thai Wiwat Hotel 40/1–2 Moo 2, Ao Leuk District. Convenient place for a stopover.

PHANG NGA
Accommodation
Moderate/Budget
Khao Lak Resort Khao Lak National Park (Takua Pa). Clean; great sunsets.

PHUKET
Accommodation
Expensive
Pearl Hotel Montree Road 2 (tel: (076) 11901/3, 211044). Typical luxury hotel, offering memorable

traditional massage.
Metropole 1 Montree Road (tel: (076) 215050/9). Large, luxury hotel.
Phuket Yacht Club 23/3 Viset Road (tel: (076) 381156-63). Comes alive in December (racing season), wonderful views.

Moderate
Phuket Fishing Lodge 59/2 Moo 9 Chalong Bay (tel: (076) 381 223). Every room has a waterfront view (yacht anchorage); good food. **Jungle Beach Resort** Ao Sane Beach (near Nai Harn) (tel: (076) 381 108, 214 291). Shady, quiet beach-side paradise, with every amenity. **Phuket Garden Hotel** Bangkok Road, Phuket town (tel: (076) 216 6900/8). Reasonable rates for itsluxuries. **Rawai Plaza and Bungalow** Rawai beach (tel: (076) 381346/7). Nice people, touristy, good communications. **Thaworn Hotel** Rasada Road (tel:(076) 211333/5). Lots of facilities. **Kata Guest House** Kata Beach (tel: (076) 381627). Good view; simple, basic rooms.

Budget
***On On Hotel** Phang Nga Road (tel: (076) 211154). Pleasant travellers' hotel.

Restaurants
Moderate
Mae Porn 50-52 Phang-Nga Road, Phuket town (tel: (076) 212106). Curries and *farang* favourites. **Muslim Restaurant** 1/3 Thepkasattree Road, Thaewnam Intersection (tel: (076) 223930). Tasty *khao mok kai* with yellow rice, liver curry. **Salaloi Restaurant** 52/2 Rawai Beach (tel: (076) 381297/381370). Seafood by the sea.

RANONG
Accommodation
Expensive
Jansom Thara Hotel 2/10 Phetkasem Road (tel: (077) 811511, 821511). All luxuries

and facilities, not forgetting the mineral-water jacuzzis, of course.

SONGKHLA
Accommodation
Expensive
Samila Hotel 1/11 Ratchadamnoen Road (tel: (074) 311310). Best hotel in town, with a beautiful location.

Moderate
City Hotel Saiburi Road. Clean, new, friendly. **Charn Hotel,** 469 Saiburi Road (tel: (074) 311903). Clean but shabby.

Budget
Saen Samran Hotel 2 Ramwithi Road (tel: (074) 311090). Small but spotless rooms, TV.

SURATTHANI
Accommodation
Moderate
Art's Jungle House Khao Sok National Park (Bangkok reservations: tel: (02) 279-4967). Tree houses by a pretty stream.

TRANG
Accommodation
Moderate
Thumkin Hotel Thumkin Square, Trang (tel: (075) 211011). Best in town, very Thai style.

Budget
***Sri Trang Hotel** 24 Lang Sathani Road (near railway station) (tel (075) 218122). Some air-conditioned rooms, basic.

Index

INDEX

INDEX/ACKNOWLEDGEMENTS

Acknowledgements

The Automobile Association would like to thank the following photographers, libraries and associations for their assistance in the preparation of this book. RICK STRANGE took all the photographs in this book (© AA Photolibrary) except those listed below: BANGKOK POST 60b Dr Pridi Panomyong and family, 62a US Troopers, 62b POW 63a US pilot, 65b Field Marshal Sari Thamarat, 66/7a Students, 67b Uprising, 68b Royal barges, 69b General Prem, 70a Chatichai Choonhaven, 70b General Chavalit, 71a General Suchinda Krapayoon. TIM LOCKE 133b Death Railway, 253c Spirit House, 256a Movie poster, 271a Train. NATURE PHOTOGRAPHERS 250 Sea Anemone (S C Blisserot), 251 Clown Fish (S C Blisserot). TOURISM AUTHORITY OF THAILAND 17a Royal barges, 18 Thai wedding, 50a Crown Princess 51 King visiting his people, 83 Wat Ratchanadda, 93 Royal barge, 94a Bung Fai festival, 110a Thai kick-boxing, 121a Making dolls, 195a Spiral pottery, 197a Silk worm, 202a Phu Pha Terp, 203a Silver Lake Park, 209a Elephants, 210a Mae Khong river, 211a Bung Fai festival, 213a Navalat beach, 215a Nai Ham, 221 Chao Le tribe, 224, 225a Ko Samui, 226a Na Thon, 228, 229 Songkran, 229b Water festival, 230a Ko Ta Ru Tao, 231a/b Ko Adang, 248 Mermaid